Law Made Simple

Advance Health Care Directives
Simplified

Advance Health Care Directives
Simplified

by Daniel Sitarz
Attorney-at-Law

Nova Publishing Company
Small Business and Consumer Legal Books and Software
Carbondale, Illinois

ISBN 978-1-892949-23-3
Book w/CD-Rom   price: $24.95

Cataloging-in-Publication

Sitarz, Dan, 1948-
Advance health care directives simplified / by Daniel Sitarz. -- 1st ed. --
        Carbondale, Ill. : Nova Pub. Co., 2007.
        p. ; cm. + 1 CD-ROM.
        (Law made simple)
        ISBN-13: 978-1-892949-23-3
        ISBN-10: 1-892949-23-7
        Includes index.
        1. Advance directives (Medical care)--United States. 2. Advance
        directives (Medical care)--United States--Forms. 3. Informed
        consent (Medical law)--United States. 4. Medical care--Law and
        legislation--United States. I. Title.
            R726.2 .S58 2007   362.1--dc22 0710

Nova Publishing Company is dedicated to providing up-to-date and accurate legal information to the public. All Nova publications are periodically revised to contain the latest available legal information.

1st Edition; 1st Printing /October 2007

This publication is designed to provide accurate and authoritative information in regard to the subject matter covered. It is sold with the understanding that the publisher and author are not engaged in rendering legal, accounting, or other professional services. If legal advice or other expert assistance is required, the services of a competent professional person should be sought.
—*From a Declaration of Principles jointly adopted by a Committee of the American Bar Association and a Committee of Publishers*

DISCLAIMER

Because of possible unanticipated changes in governing statutes and case law relating to the application of any information contained in this book, the author, publisher, and any and all persons or entities involved in any way in the preparation, publication, sale, or distribution of this book disclaim all responsibility for the legal effects or consequences of any document prepared or action taken in reliance upon information contained in this book. No representations, either express or implied, are made or given regarding the legal consequences of the use of any information contained in this book. Purchasers and persons intending to use this book for the preparation of any legal documents are advised to check specifically on the current applicable laws in any jurisdiction in which they intend the documents to be effective.

Nova Publishing Company
Small Business and Consumer Legal Books and Software
1103 West College St.
Carbondale, IL 62901
Tech Support: (800) 748-1175
Editorial: (618)457-3521

Distributed by:
National Book Network
4501 Forbes Blvd., Suite 200
Lanham, MD 20706
Orders: (800) 462-6420 or
www.novapublishing.com

Nova Publishing Company Green Business Policies

Nova Publishing Company is committed to preserving ancient forests and natural resources. Our company's policy is to print all of our books on recycled paper, with no less than 30% post-consumer waste de-inked in a chlorine-free process. In addition, all Nova books are printed using soy-based inks. As a result, for the printing of this book, we have saved:

21.8 trees • 6,300 gallons of water • 3,690 kilowatt hours of electricity • 54 pounds of pollution

Nova Publishing Company is a member of Green Press Initiative, a nonprofit program dedicated to supporting publishers in their efforts to reduce their use of fiber obtained from endangered forests. For more information, go to www.greenpressinitiative.org. In addition, Nova uses all compact fluorescent lighting; recycles all office paper products, aluminum and plastic beverage containers, and printer cartridges; uses 100% post-consumer fiber, process-chlorine-free, acid-free paper for 95% of in-house paper use; and, when possible, uses electronic equipment that is EPA Energy Star-certified. Finally, all carbon emissions from office energy use are offset by the purchase of wind-energy credits that are used to subsidize the building of wind turbines on the Rosebud Sioux Reservation in South Dakota (see www.nativeenergy.com/coop/).

Table of Contents

LIST OF FORMS (in book and on CD) All Forms on CD are in PDF and text format unless noted.

    Revocation of Advance Health Care Directive
    Witness Affidavit of Oral Revocation of Advance Health Care Directive
    Additional Information for Advance Health Care Directive
    Living Will
    Revocation of Living Will
    Health Care Power of Attorney and Designation of Health Care Agent and Proxy
    Revocation of Health Care Power of Attorney
    Unlimited Durable Power of Attorney for Financial Affairs (Effective on Disability)
    Unlimited Durable Power of Attorney for Financial Affairs (Effective Immediately)
    Revocation of Unlimited Durable Power of Attorney for Financial Affairs
    Designation of Primary Physician
    Organ Donation Form
    State-Specific Statutory Advance Health Care Directives are provided for all 50 states and
        Washington D.C. These forms are provided on the CD as PDF fillable forms only.

CHAPTER 1
How To Use This Book

In each chapter of this book you will find an introductory section that will give you an overview of the types of situations in which the forms in that chapter will generally be used. Following that overview, there will be a brief explanation of the specific uses for each form. Finally, for each form, there is a listing of the information that must be compiled to complete the form. The preferable manner for using these forms is to use the enclosed Forms-on-CD. Instructions for using the Forms-on-CD are included later in this chapter. However, it is perfectly acceptable to prepare these forms directly from the book by making a copy of the form, filling in the information that is necessary, and then retyping the form in its entirety on clean white letter-sized paper.

Before you prepare any of the forms for use, you should carefully read the introductory information and instructions in the chapter where the particular form is contained. Try to be as detailed and specific as possible as you fill in these forms. The more precise the description, the less likelihood that later disputes may develop over what was actually intended by the language chosen. The careful preparation and use of the legal forms in this book should provide you with the proper documents for most advance health care situations. If in doubt as to whether a particular form will work in a specific application, please consult a competent lawyer.

Installation Instructions for the Forms-on-CD

Quick-Start Installation for PCs
1. Insert the enclosed CD in your computer.
2. The installation program will start automatically. Follow the onscreen dialogue and make your appropriate choices.
3. If the CD installation does not start automatically, click on START, then RUN, then BROWSE, and select your CD drive, and then select the file "Install.exe." Finally, click OK to run the installation program.
4. During the installation program, you will be prompted as to whether or not you wish to install the Adobe Acrobat Reader® program. If you do not already have the Adobe Acrobat Reader® program installed on your hard drive, you will need to select the full installation that will install this program to your computer.

Installation Instructions for MACs®
1. Insert the enclosed CD in your computer.
2. Copy the folder "Forms for Macs" to your hard drive. All of the PDF and text-only forms are included in this folder.

3. If you do not already have the Adobe Acrobat Reader® program installed on your hard drive, you will need to download the version of this software that is appropriate for you particular MAC operating system from www.adobe.com. Note: The latest versions of the MAC operating system (OS-X) has PDF capabilities built into it.

Instructions for Using Forms-on-CD

All of the forms which are included in this book have been provided on the Forms-on-CD for your use if you have access to a computer. If you have completed the Forms-on-CD installation program, all of the forms will have been copied to your computer's hard drive. By default, these files are installed in the C:\Advance Directives\Forms folder which is created by the installation program. (Note for MAC users: see instructions above). Opening the Forms folder will provide you with access to folders for each of the topics corresponding to chapters in the book. Within each chapter, the forms are provided in two separate formats:

Text forms which may opened, prepared, and printed from within your own word processing program (such as Microsoft Word®, or WordPerfect®). The text forms all have the file extension: .txt. These forms are located in the TEXT FORMS folders supplied for each chapter's forms. You may wish to use the forms in this format if you will be making changes to text of the forms. To access these forms, please see below.

PDF forms which may be filled in on your computer screen and printed out on any printer. This particular format provides the most widely-used cross-platform format for accessing computer files. Files in this format may be opened as images on your computer and printed out on any printer. The files in Adobe PDF format all have the file extension: .pdf. Although this format provides the easiest method for completing the forms, the forms in this format can not be altered (other than to fill in the information required on the blanks provided). To access the PDF forms, please see below. If you wish to alter the language in any of the forms, you will need to access the forms in their text-only versions. To access these text-only forms, please also see below.

To Access Adobe PDF Forms

1. You must have already installed the Adobe Acrobat Reader® program to your computer's hard drive. This program is installed automatically by the installation program. (MAC users will need to install this program via www.adobe.com).

2. On your computer's desktop, you will find a shortcut icon labeled "Acrobat Reader®" Using your mouse, left double click on this icon. This will open the Acrobat Reader® program. When the Acrobat Reader® program is opened for the first time, you will need to accept the Licensing Agreement from Adobe in order to use this program. Click "Accept" when given the option to accept or decline the Agreement.

3. Once the Acrobat Reader® program is open on your computer, click on FILE (in the upper left-hand corner of the upper taskbar). Then click on OPEN in the drop down menu. Depending on which version

of Windows or other operating system you are using, a box will open which will allow you to access files on your computer's hard drive. The files for Advance Directives are located on your computer's "C" drive, under the folder "**Advance Directives**." In this folder, you will find a subfolder "**Forms**." (Note: if you installed the forms folder on a different drive, access the forms on that particular drive).

4. If you desire to work with one of the forms, you should then left double-click your mouse on the sub-folder: "**Forms**." This will open two folders: one for text forms and one for PDF forms. Left double click your mouse on the PDF forms folder and a list of the PDF forms for that topic should appear. Left double click your mouse on the form of your choice. This will open the appropriate form within the Adobe Acrobat Reader® program.

To Fill in Forms in the Adobe Acrobat Reader® Program

1. Once you have opened the appropriate form in the Acrobat Reader® program, filling in the form is a simple process. A 'hand tool' icon will be your cursor in the Acrobat Reader® program. Move the 'hand tool' cursor to the first blank space that will need to be completed on the form. A vertical line or "I-beam" should appear at the beginning of the first space on a form that you will need to fill in. You may then begin to type the necessary information in the space provided. When you have filled in the first blank space, hit the **TAB** key on your keyboard. This will move the 'hand' cursor to the next space which must be filled in. Please note that some of the spaces in the forms must be completed by hand, specifically the signature, witness, and notary blanks.

2. Move through the form, completing each required space, and hitting **TAB** to move to the next space to be filled in. For information on the information required for each blank on the forms, please read the instructions in this book. When you have completed all of the fill-ins, you may print out the form on your computer's printer. (Please note: hitting **TAB** after the last fill-in will return you to the first page of the form.)

3. IMPORTANT NOTE: Unfortunately, the Adobe Acrobat Reader® program does NOT allow you to save the filled-in form to your computer's hard drive. You can only save the form in a printed version. For this reason, you should wait to complete the forms until you have all of the information necessary to complete the chosen form in one session. You may, of course, leave the Acrobat program open on your computer and leave a partially-completed form open in the program. However, if you close the file or if you close the Acrobat Reader® program, the filled-in information will be lost.

To Access and Complete the Text Forms

For your convenience, all of the forms in this book are also provided as text-only forms which may be altered and saved. To open and use any of the text forms:

1. First, open your preferred word processing program. Then click on **FILE** (in the upper left-hand corner of the upper taskbar). Then click on **OPEN** in the drop down menu. Depending on which version of Windows or other operating system you are using, a box will open which will allow you to access files on your computer's hard drive. The files for Advance Directives are located on

your computer's "C" drive, under the folder "**Advance Directives**." In this folder, you will find a sub-folder: "Forms."

2. If you desire to work with one of the forms, you should then left double-click your mouse on the sub-folder: "Forms." A list of form topics (corresponding to the chapters in the book) will appear and you should then left double-click your mouse on the topic of your choice. This will open two folders: one for text forms and one for PDF forms. Left double click your mouse on the text forms folder and a list of the text forms for that topic should appear. Left double click your mouse on the form of your choice. This will open the appropriate form within your word processing program.

3. You may now fill in the necessary information while the text-only file is open in your word processing program. You may need to adjust margins and/or line endings of the form to fit your particular word processing program. Note that there is an asterisk (*) in every location in these forms where information will need to be included. Replace each asterisk with the necessary information. When the form is complete, you may print out the completed form and you may save the completed form. If you wish to save the completed form, you should rename the form so that your hard drive will retain an unaltered version of the form.

Technical Support

Nova Publishing will provide technical support for installing the provided software. Please also note that Nova Publishing Company cannot provide legal advice regarding the effect or use of the forms on this software. For questions about installing the Forms-on-CD, you may call Nova Technical Support at 1-800-748-1175.

In addition, Nova cannot provide technical support for the use of the Adobe Acrobat Reader®. For any questions relating to Adobe Acrobat Reader®, please access Adobe Technical Support at www.adobe.com/support/main.html or you may search for assistance in the HELP area of Adobe Acrobat Reader® (located in approximately the center of the top line of the program's desktop).

CHAPTER 2

Understanding Advance Health Care Directives

What is an Advance Health Care Directive?

An Advance Health Care Directive is a legal document that may be used in any state that allows you to provide written directions relating to your future health care should you become incapacitated and unable to speak for yourself. Advance Health Care Directives give you a direct voice in medical decisions in situations when you cannot make those decisions yourself. Your Advance Health Care Directive will not be used as long as you are able to express your own decisions. You can always accept or refuse medical treatment and you always have the legal right to revoke your Advance Health Care Directive at any time. Instructions regarding revocations are discussed later in these instructions. The Federal Patient Self-Determination Act encourages all people to make their own decisions about the type of medical care they wish to receive. This act also requires all health care agencies (hospitals, long-term care facilities, and home health agencies) receiving Medicare and Medicaid reimbursement to recognize a living will and health care power of attorney as advance directives. Under this Act, all health care agencies must ask you if you have advance directives and must give you materials with information about your rights under state law.

Advance Health Care Directives are not only for senior citizens. Serious life-threatening accidents or disease can strike anyone and leave them unable to communicate their desires. In fact, the rise of the use of Advance Health Care Directives can be attributed in part, to legal cases involving medical care to young people, particularly Karen Ann Quinlan and Nancy Cruzan, and most recently, Terry Schiavo. Anyone over the age of 18 who is mentally competent should complete an Advance Health Care Directive. Be aware, however, that Advance Health Care Directives are intended for non-emergency medical treatment. Most often, there is no time for health care providers to consult and analyze the provisions of an Advance Health Care Directive in an emergency situation.

The Advance Health Care Directives that are contained in this book contain four separate sections, each dealing with different aspects of potential situations that may arise during a possible period of incapacitation:

- Living Will
- Selection of Health Care Agent (generally, by Health Care Power of Attorney)
- Designation of Primary Physician
- Organ Donation

In addition, this book also provides a fifth legal form that may be useful in many health care situations if you are unable to handle your own financial affairs: a Durable Power of Attorney for Financial Affairs. Later in this book, you will be provided with detailed explanations of each of these legal forms. A brief explanation of each of these forms follows:

Living Will: A *living will* is a document that can be used to state your desire that extraordinary life support means not be used to artificially prolong your life in the event that you are stricken with a terminal disease or injury. Its use has been recognized in all states in recent years. The purpose of a living will is to provide doctors and other health care workers with clear directions regarding how you would like your medical care handled toward the end of your life. A living will makes it possible for you to specify, in advance, exactly what your preferences are regarding the use of life-sustaining medical procedures if you are ever in a terminal medical condition or in a vegetative state, and are unable to give such directions yourself. The Appendix provides information regarding the recognition of living wills in each state. For detailed information on preparing a living will, please see Chapter 3.

Health Care Power of Attorney: This relatively new legal document has been developed to allow a person to appoint another person to make health care decisions on one's behalf, in the event that he or she becomes incapacitated or incompetent. Generally, a *health care power of attorney* will only take effect upon a person becoming unable to manage his or her own affairs, and only after this incapacitation has been certified by an attending physician. The person appointed will then have the authority to view your medical records, consult with your doctors and make any required decisions regarding your health care. This document may be carefully tailored to fit your needs and concerns and can be used in conjunction with a living will. It can be a valuable tool for dealing with difficult healthcare situations. For instructions and forms for preparing a health care power of attorney, please refer to Chapter 4.

Designation of Primary Physician: Through the use of this document, you will be able to designate your choice for your primary physician in the event you are unable to communicate your wishes after an accident or during an illness. Although your family may know your personal doctor, it may still be a good idea to put this choice in writing so that there is no question regarding who your choice for a doctor may be. Instructions for preparing this form are in Chapter 5.

Organ Donation: You may also wish that your vital organs or, indeed, your entire body be used after your death for various medical purposes. Every year, many lives are saved and much medical research is enhanced by organ donations. All states allow for you to personally declare your desires regarding the use of your body and/or organs after death. The details of providing for this important consideration are included in Chapter 6.

Durable Power of Attorney for Financial Affairs: Situations may arise when you are unable to handle your own financial affairs due to an incapacitating illness or accident. For those situations, a durable power of attorney for financial affairs has been developed to allow you to give authority to another person to take care of your financial affairs. *Durable* refers to the fact that the authority that you give to another will be in effect even if you are incapacitated. Such a document provides another person that you appoint with the same powers and authority that you, yourself, have over your property. Your appointed person can sign checks, pay bills, sign contracts, and handle all of your affairs on your behalf. In general, there are two types of durable powers of attorney: one that is immediately in effect and that will *remain* in effect in the event of your incapacitation, and another that *only* goes into effect if you become incapacitated. For information on preparing a durable power of attorney for financial affairs, please see Chapter 7.

The combination of these five forms provides a comprehensive method by which you may provide, in advance, for a situation in which you may be unable to communicate your desires to your family, your friends, and your health care providers. It is an opportunity to carefully plan how you would like various medical situations to be handled should they arise.

Methods for Completing Your Advance Health Care Directive

Please note that there are two distinct methods provided in this book for completing an Advance Heatlh Care Directive. Either method is legal and either method may be selected. There are different reasons for choosing each method and these are outlined below:

Prepare Individual Forms

You may choose to complete one or more of the forms that comprise your Advance Health Care Directive separately. Chapters 3 through 7 provide individual copies of each of the five general forms that will comprise your Advance Health Care Directive: a Living Will, a Health Care Power of Attorney, a Designation of Primary Physician, an Organ Donation Form, and a Durable Power of Attorney for Financial Affairs.

This method may be chosen if:

• You desire to custom-tailor one or more of the forms to more closely fit your individual wishes and desires concerning your health care concerns, or

• The details of the state-specific statutory forms (explained below) do not fit your individual desires concerning your health care concerns, or

• You wish only to complete one or two of the forms and not the entire state-specific statutory form set that is provided for your state (see below).

These forms are provided on the enclosed CD in two separate formats: either as PDF forms that may be filled in on your computer, but not altered, or as text forms that may be carefully altered to more closely fit your individual wishes and desires. The individual forms have been prepared to meet the minimum legal requirements in all states and are legally-valid in all states. Please see the detailed instructions in Chapter 1 concerning how to complete either the PDF or text versions of these individual forms,

Prepare State-Specific Forms (and Durable Power of Attorney for Health Care, if desired)

The second method is to prepare a state-specific statutory form in Chapter 8. A '*state-specific statutory Advance Health Care Directive*' is a form that has been taken directly from the laws of your particular state. The legal effects of the language in such a document have been approved by the legislature of the state. This provides an advantage in that the legal language in such a 'statutory' form is generally familiar to health care providers in the particular state and they know that such language has been approved. This does not mean, however, that other 'non-statutory' forms are not legally valid in the state as well. Anyone may use a 'non-statutory' legal form, such as those in Chapters 3 through 7, with language that they find appropriate to their own situation, as long as the document meets certain minimum legal standards for a state which, of course, all forms in this book do meet.

The state-specific statutory advance health care directives that are contained in Chapter 8 of this book and on the CD (in fillable PDF format) have been prepared directly from the language in the statutes of each individual state. They are designed as a complete Advance Health Care Directive containing all appropriate forms. Each directive contain the following four forms:

- Living Will
- Selection of Health Care Agent (generally, by Health Care Power of Attorney)
- Designation of Primary Physician
- Organ Donation

Should you choose to use a state-specific form, you need not necessarily adopt all four sections of the document for your own use. You may select and complete any or all of the four separate sections of the form. For example, if you choose not to select a health care agent, you may use the other three parts of the form and not complete that section. Instructions for filling in the state-specific forms are contained later in this chapter. Many people find using a state-specific document easier than completing each separate form as an individual document. This method also provides a simple compact package that contains your entire Advance Health Care Directive with forms using legal language that most health care providers in your state are familiar with. More details regarding each specific form are provided in the specific chapter of this book relating to the particular form. In addition, state-specific requirements and explanations are also provided in the appendix of this book.

In a few states, the legislatures have not developed specific language for one or more of the forms. These few instances are noted under the state's heading in the appendix of this book. In addition, in such situations, an appropriate and legally-valid form has been added to the directives for those states. Any such forms have been prepared following any guidelines set out by the state's legislature.

Important Note: The state-specific statutory forms *do not* contain a durable power of attorney for financial affairs. As this form is not directly related to health care issues, it is left as a separate form located in Chapter 7. Should you desire to use this type of document to authorize someone to handle your financial affairs in the event of your disability or incapacitation, you should use the forms provided in Chapter 7.

Witness and Notary Requirements

All states have provided protections to ensure the validity of the Advance Health Care Directive. They have also provided legal protections against persons using undue influence to force or coerce someone into signing an Advance Health Care Directive. There are various requirements regarding who may be a witness to your signing of your Advance Health Care Directive. In general, these protections are for the purpose of ensuring that the witnesses have no actual or indirect stake in your death. These witnesses should have no connection with you from a health care or beneficiary standpoint. In most states, the witnesses must:

- Not be under 18 years of age (19 in Alabama)
- Not be related to you in any manner either by blood, marriage, or adoption
- Not be your attending physician
- Not be a patient or employee of your attending physician
- Not be a patient, physician, or employee of the health care facility in which you may be a patient
- Not be entitled to any portion of your estate upon your death under any laws of intestate succession, nor under your will or any codicil
- Not have a claim against any portion of your estate upon your death
- Not be directly financially responsible for your medical care
- Not have signed the Advance Health Care Directive for you, even at your direction
- Not be paid a fee for acting as a witness

In addition, please note that several states and the District of Columbia (Washington D.C.) have laws in effect regarding witnesses when the *declarant* (the person signing the Advance Health Care Directive) is a patient in a nursing home, boarding facility, hospital, or skilled or intermediate health care facility. In those situations, it is advisable to have a patient ombudsman, patient advocate, or the director of the health care facility act as the third witness to the signing of an Advance Health Care Directive.

These restrictions on who may be a witness to your signing of an Advance Health Care Directive require, in most cases, that the witnesses either be 1) friends who will receive nothing from you under your will, or 2) strangers. Please review the requirements for your own state in the Appendix of this book and in the witness statements on your particular state's form.

In addition, all of the forms included in this book, including all of the state-specific advance health care directives, are designed to be notarized. This is a requirement in most states for most forms and has been made mandatory on all of the forms in this book. The purpose of notarization in this instance is to add another level of protection against coercion or undue pressure being exerted to force anyone to sign any of these legal forms against their wishes. Sadly, such undue pressure has been applied in some cases to force senior citizens to sign legal documents against their own wishes. The requirement that one sign a document in front of a notary and in front of two additional witnesses can significantly lessen the opportunity for such abuse.

Preparing and Signing Your Advance Health Care Directive

① Select the appropriate form from the included forms in Chapters 3-7 or select a state-specific directive for your state from Chapter 8. Carefully read through each section of your Advance Health Care Directive. You may wish to make two copies of the form(s) that you choose. This will allow you to use one form as a draft copy and the other form for a final copy that you, your witnesses, and a notary will sign.

② If you are using a state-specific directive, you will need to initial your choices in the first section of the form as to which sections of the entire Advance Health Care Directive you wish to be effective. The choices are:

- Living Will
- Selection of Health Care Agent
- Designation of Primary Physician
- Organ Donation

Please note that you may choose to exclude any of the above portions of your form and the remaining portions will be valid. If you wish to exclude one or more portions, DO NOT place your initials in the space before the section that you wish to exclude. Be careful so that you are certain you are expressing your desires exactly as you wish on these very important matters. If you do not wish to use a particular main section of the entire form, cross out that section of the form clearly and do not initial that section in either the first paragraph of the Directive or in the paragraph directly before your signature near the end of the Directive. If you do not wish to use a particular paragraph within one of the four main sections of the form, cross out that paragraph also.

③ For all forms, make the appropriate choices in each section where indicated by initialing the designated place or filling in the appropriate information. Depending on which form that you use, you may have many choices to initial or you may have no choices to initial. Please carefully read through the paragraphs and clauses that require choices to be certain that you understand the choices that you will be making. If you wish to add additional instructions or limitations in the places indicated on the form, please type or clearly print your instructions. If you need to add additional pages, please use the form titled "Additional Information for Advance Health Care Directive" which is provided at the end of this chapter. If you need and use additional pages, be certain that you initial and date each added page and that you clearly label each additional page regarding which paragraph or section of the form to which it pertains.

④ In the form or section on Organ Donations, you may choose to either donate all of your organs or limit your donation to certain specific organs. Likewise, you may provide that the organs be used for any purpose or you may limit their use to certain purposes.

⑤ Finally, you will need to complete the signature and witness/notary sections of your forms. When you have a completed original with no erasures or corrections, staple all of the pages together in the upper left-hand corner. Do not sign this document or fill in the date yet. You should now assemble your witnesses and a Notary Public to witness your signature. As noted in the Appendix, be certain that your witnesses meet your specific state requirements. In addition, please note that several states and the District of Columbia have laws in effect regarding witnesses when the declarant is a patient in a nursing home, boarding facility, hospital, or skilled or intermediate health care facility. In those situations, it is advisable to have a patient ombudsman, patient advocate, or the director of the health care facility to act as the third witness to the signing of an Advance Health Care Directive. In order that your Advance Health Care Directive be accepted by all legal and medical authorities with as little difficulty as possible, it is highly recommended that you have your signing of this important document witnessed by both your appropriate witnesses and a Notary Public.

⑥ In front of all of the witnesses and the Notary Public, the following should take place in the order shown:

(a) There is no requirement that the witnesses know any of the terms of your Advance Health Care Directive or other legal forms, or that they read any of your Advance Health Care Directive or legal forms. All that is necessary is that they observe you sign your Advance Health Care Directive and that they also sign the Advance Health Care Directive as witnesses in each other's presence.

(b) You will sign your legal form at the end where indicated, exactly as your name is written on the form, in ink using a pen. At this time, if you are using a state-specific form, you should also again initial your choices as to which sections you have chosen (directly before your signature space). You will also need to fill in the date on the first page of the Directive or form, date and initial each Additional Information Page (if you have used any), and fill in your address after your signature. Once you have signed and completed all of the necessary information, pass your Advance Health Care Directive or other legal form to the first witness, who should sign and date the acknowledgment where indicated and also print his or her name.

(c) After the first witness has signed, have the Advance Health Care Directive or other legal form passed to the second witness, who should also sign and date the acknowledgment where indicated and print his or her name.

(d) Throughout this ceremony, you and all of the witnesses must remain together. The final step is for the Notary Public to sign in the space where indicated and complete the notarization block on the form.

(e) If you have chosen individuals to act as either your Health Care Agent (Durable Power of Attorney for Health Care) or as your Attorney-in-fact for Financial Affairs (Durable Power of Attorney for Financial Affairs), you should have them sign the form at the end where shown acknowledging that they accept their appointment.

⑦ When this step is completed, your Advance Health Care Directive or individual legal form that you have signed is a valid legal document. Have several photo-copies made and, if appropriate, deliver a copy to your attending physician to have placed in your medical records file. You should also provide a copy to any person who was selected as either your Health Care Agent or your Agent for Financial Affairs. You may also desire to give a copy to the person you have chosen as the executor of your will, your clergy, and your spouse or other trusted relative.

Revoking Your Advance Health Care Directive

These instructions apply to the state-specific statutory forms provided in this book. For revocation of individual legal forms in Chapters 3-7, please see revocation forms in those chapters. All states have provided methods for the easy revocation of Advance Health Care Directives and the forms that they contain. Since such forms provide authority to medical personnel to withhold life-support technology that will likely result in death to the patient, great care must be taken to insure that a change of mind by the patient is heeded. If revocation of your Advance Health Care Directive is an important issue, please consult your state's laws directly. For the revocation of an Advance Health Care Directive, any one of the following methods of revocation is generally acceptable:

- Physical destruction of the Advance Health Care Directive, such as tearing, burning, or mutilating the document.

- A written revocation of the Advance Health Care Directive by you or by a person acting at your direction. A form for this is provided at the end of this section.

- An oral revocation in the presence of a witness who signs and dates an affidavit confirming a revocation. This oral declaration may take in any manner (verbal or non-verbal). Most states allow for a person to revoke such a document by any indication (even non-verbal) of the intent to revoke an Advance Health Care Directive, regardless of his or her physical or mental condition. A form for this effect is included, titled "Witness Affidavit of Oral Revocation of Advance Health Care Directive."

To use the Revocation of Advance Health Care Directive form provided on the next page, simply fill in the appropriate information and sign it. Make sure that you provide a copy of this revocation to anyone or any health care facility that has a copy or original of the Advance Health Care Directive that you are revoking.

If it is necessary to use the Witness Affidavit of Oral Revocation of Advance Health Care Directive form, the witness should actually observe your indication of an intention to revoke your Advance Health Care Directive. This may take the form of any verbal or non-verbal direction, as long as your intent to revoke is clearly and unmistakably evident to the witness. This form does not need to be notarized to be effective. Make sure that you provide a copy of this revocation to anyone or any health care facility that has a copy or original of the Advance Health Care Directive that you are revoking.

Additional Information for Advance Health Care Directives

If you need to add additional pages to your advance health care directive, please use the form titled "Additional Information for Advance Health Care Directive" which is provided at the end of this chapter after the two revocation forms. If you need and use additional pages, be certain that you initial and date each added page and that you clearly label each additional page regarding which paragraph or section of the form to which it pertains. You should also note in the form itself that you are using additional pages by printing or writing "See Attached Additional Page" in the section of the form where you wish to insert additional instructions or information.

Revocation of Advance Health Care Directive

I, _____ , am the maker and signatory of an Advance Health Care Directive which was dated _____ , and which was executed by me for use in the State of _____ .

By this written revocation, I hereby entirely revoke such Advance Health Care Directive, any Living Will, any Durable Power of Attorney for Health Care, any Organ Donation, or any other appointment or designation of a person to make any health care decisions on my behalf. I intend that all of the above mentioned documents have no force or effect whatsoever.

BY SIGNING HERE I INDICATE THAT I UNDERSTAND THE PURPOSE AND EFFECT OF THIS DOCUMENT.

Signature _____ Date _____

Witness Affidavit of Oral Revocation of Advance Health Care Directive

I, _____ , herein referred to as the declarant, was the maker and signatory of an Advance Health Care Directive which was dated _____ , and which was executed by him or her for use in the State of _____ . By this written affidavit, I, _____ , the witness, hereby affirm that on the date of _____ , I personally witnessed the above-named declarant make known to me, through verbal and/or non-verbal methods, their clear and unmistakable intent to entirely revoke such Advance Health Care Directive, any Living Will, any Durable Power of Attorney for Health Care, any Organ Donation, or any other appointment or designation of a person to make any health care decisions on his or her behalf. It is my belief that the above-named declarant fully intended that all of the above-mentioned documents no longer have any force or effect whatsoever.

Witness Acknowledgment

The declarant is personally known to me and I believe him or her to be of sound mind and under no duress, fraud, or undue influence.

Witness Signature _____ Date _____

Printed Name of Witness _____

Additional Information for
Advance Health Care Directive

of _____ (name)

The following information is to be considered as a part of my Advance Health Care Directive *(insert additional information)*:

Initials of Declarant _____ Date _____

CHAPTER 3
Preparing a Living Will

In this chapter, you will be given instructions on how to prepare a *living will,* a document that states your desires regarding end-of-life medical care. A living will is a relatively new legal document that has been made necessary due to recent technological advances in the field of medicine. These advances can allow for the continued existence of a person on advanced life support systems long after any normal semblance of "life," as many people consider it, has ceased. The inherent problem that is raised by this type of extraordinary medical life support is that the person whose life is being artificially continued by such means may not wish to be kept alive beyond what they may consider to be the proper time for their life to end. However, since a person in such condition has no method of communicating their wishes to the medical or legal authorities in charge, a living will was developed that allows one to make these important decisions in advance of the situation. The purpose of a living will is to provide doctors and other health care workers with clear directions regarding how you would like your medical care handled toward the end of your life.

A living will makes it possible for you to specify, in advance, exactly what your preferences are regarding the use of life-sustaining medical procedures, if you are ever in a terminal medical condition or in a vegetative state, and are unable to give such directions yourself.

Terminal is generally defined as an incurable condition that will cause imminent death such that the use of life-sustaining procedures only serve to prolong the moment of death. Likewise, a *vegetative state* is generally defined as a complete and irreversible loss of cognitive brain function and consciousness. Thus, a living will comes into effect only when there is no medical hope for a recovery from a particular injury or illness which will prove fatal or leave one in a permanent and irreversible coma. *Life-sustaining procedures* are normally defined as any of the following: 1) cardiopulmonary resuscitation, or CPR (reviving a person when they stop breathing or their heart stops pumping), 2) artificial respiration (mouth-to-mouth breathing, manual breathing, or using a ventilator to breath for the person), 3) medicines to artificially change blood pressure and heart function, 4) artificial nutrition/hydration (such as giving tube feeding or fluids in the vein), 5) dialysis (using a kidney machine), and 6) certain surgical procedures such as amputation, feeding tube placement, removal of tumor, organ transplant, or other similar procedures. Pain medications are generally not considered life-sustaining procedures.

As more and more advances are made in the medical field in terms of the ability to prevent "clinical" death, the difficult situations envisioned by a living will are destined to occur more often. The legal acceptance of a living will is currently at the forefront of law. Living wills are accepted in all states, but they must adhere to certain legal conditions. A few states do not currently have specific legislation providing express statutory recognition of living wills, but courts in those states have ruled that living wills are legally valid. Although a living will does not address all possible contingencies regarding terminally-ill patients, it does provide a written declaration for the individual to make known her or his decisions on life-prolonging procedures. A living will declares your wishes not to be kept alive by artificial or mechanical means if you are suffering from a terminal condition and your death would be imminent without the use of such artificial means. It provides a legally-binding written set of instructions regarding your wishes about this important matter.

In most states, in order to qualify for the use of a living will, you must meet the following criteria:

• You must be at least 18 years of age
• You must be of "sound mind"
• You must be able to comprehend the nature of your action in signing such a document

A living will becomes valid when it has been properly signed and witnessed. However, it is very important to remember that as long as you are capable of making decisions and giving directions regarding your medical care, your stated wishes must be followed–*not* those directions that are contained in your living will. Your living will only comes into force when you are in a terminal or vegetative condition, with no likelihood of recovery, *and* are unable to provide directions yourself. Until that time, *you*–and not your living will–will provide the directions for your health care. Generally, a licensed physician is required to determine when your condition has become terminal or vegetative with no likelihood of recovering.

This chapter contains a general, standardized living will. Chapter 8 also contains state-specific living will forms as part of the state-specific statutory Advance Health Care Directives that have been taken directly from the most recent legislation regarding living wills in each state. A few states do not currently have specific legislation providing express statutory recognition of living wills. For those states, the living will (in the state-specific statutory Advance Health Care Directive in Chapter 8) has been prepared by legal professionals to comply with the basic requirements that courts in that state or other states have found important. In such states, be assured that courts, health care professionals, and physicians will be guided by this expression of your desires concerning life support as expressed in the living will prepared using this book. You may use either the general living will form or the state-specific statutory form (containing a living will or its equivalent) for your state. Please compare your state's form (in your state's Advance Health Care Directive in Chapter 8) with the standardized form in this chapter and select the appropriate form that you feel best expresses your wishes regarding health care in a terminal condition.

As noted in Chapter 1, the Federal Patient Self-Determination Act encourages all people to make their own decisions now about the type of medical care they wish to receive. This act also requires all health care agencies (hospitals, long-term care facilities, and home health agencies) receiving Medicare and Medicaid reimbursement to recognize a living will and health care power of attorney as advance directives. Under this Act, all health care agencies must ask you if you have advance directives and must give you materials with information about your rights under state law. The living will included in this chapter and/or the living will included in the state-specific Advance Health Care Directives in Chapter 8 must be recognized by all health care agencies.

Typical Living Wills Provisions

Nearly all states have passed legislation setting up a statutorily-accepted living will form. Those states that have not expressed a preference for a specific type of living will have, nevertheless, accepted living wills that adhere to general legal requirements. There are many different types of living wills, from very brief statements such as the following from the state of Illinois:

> "If at any time I should have an incurable and irreversible injury, disease, or illness judged to be a terminal condition by my attending physician who has personally examined me and has determined that my death is imminent except for death-delaying procedures, I direct that such procedures which would only prolong the dying process be withheld or withdrawn, and that I be permitted to die naturally with only the administration of medication, sustenance, or the performance of any medical procedure deemed necessary by my attending physician to provide me with comfort care."

to lengthy and elaborate multi-page forms with detailed and very specific instructions. All of the various state forms try to assure that a person's own wishes are followed regarding health care decisions. Many states have drafted their legislation with the intention that people prepare both a living will and a health care power of attorney (or similar form) which appoints a person of your choosing to act on your behalf in making health care decisions when you are unable to make such decisions for yourself. It is advisable that you prepare both of these advance health care forms in order to cover most, if not all, eventualities that may arise regarding your health care in difficult situations. In general, the purpose of your living will is to convey your wishes regarding life-prolonging treatment and artificially provided nutrition and hydration (food and water) if you no longer have the capacity to make your own decisions, have a terminal condition, or become permanently unconscious. Please also note that the basic living will included in this book contains a release of medical information under the federal HIPAA guidelines for privacy of medical information.

You should also read through this statement concerning the importance of the decisions that you make in a living will (this notice is also part of the living will itself):

Notice to the Adult Signing this Document:

This is an important legal document. This document directs the medical treatment you are to receive in the event you are unable to participate in your own medical decisions and you are in a terminal condition. This document may state what kind of treatment you want or do not want to receive. This document can control whether you live or die. Prepare this document carefully. If you use this form, read it completely.

You may want to seek professional help to make sure the form does what you intend and is completed without mistakes. This document will remain valid and in effect until and unless you revoke it. Review this document periodically to make sure it continues to reflect your wishes. You may amend or revoke this document at any time by notifying your physician and other health-care providers. You should give copies of this document to your physician and your family. This form is entirely optional. If you choose to use this form, please note that the form provides signature lines for you, the three witnesses whom you have selected and a notary public.

Instructions for Preparing and Signing a Living Will

If you desire that your life not be prolonged artificially when there is no reasonable chance for recovery and death is imminent, please follow the instructions below for completion of your living will. Use of this form is voluntary. However, if you do choose to use this form, the entire form is mandatory. It has been adapted to be valid in all states. Courts, health care professionals, members of your family, and physicians will be guided by this expression of your desires concerning life support. Please consult the Appendix for further information regarding recognition of living wills in your state.

1. Make a photo-copy or printout a copy of the entire living will form from this chapter. Using the photo-copy as a worksheet, please fill in the correct information in the appropriate blanks as noted below:
    ① Name of person making living will
    ② Name of person making living will
    ③ State whose laws will govern the living will
    ④ Any additional directions, terms or conditions that you wish to add
    ⑤ Number of pages of entire living will (fill in after printing out final copy)
    ⑥ Date of signing of living will (fill in upon signing)
    ⑦ Your signature and printed name (do not sign unless in front of a notary public)
    ⑧ Date, signatures and printed names of witnesses to signing of living will
    ⑨ The notary acknowledgment section (to be completed by notary public)

2. On clean, white, 8 1/2 x 11" paper, type or printout the entire living will exactly as shown with your information added. Carefully re-read this original living will to be certain that it exactly expresses your desires on this very important matter. When you have a clean, clear original version, staple all of the pages together in the upper left-hand corner. Do not yet sign this document or fill in the date.

3. You should now assemble three witnesses and a Notary Public to witness your signature. Note that the standardized living will provides for three witnesses so that it will be legally valid in all states. Most of the states require only two witnesses, although some will require three. As noted on the document itself, these witnesses should have no connection with you from a health care or beneficiary standpoint (exception: see note following). Specifically, the witnesses must:

- Be at least 19 years of age
- Not be related to you in any manner: by blood, marriage, or adoption
- Not be your attending physician, or a patient or employee of your attending physician; or a patient, physician, or employee of the health care facility in which you may be a patient. However, please see below.
- Not be entitled to any portion of your estate on your death under any laws of intestate succession, nor under your will or any codicil
- Have no claim against any portion of your estate on your death
- Not be directly financially responsible for your medical care
- Not have signed the living will for you, even at your direction
- Not be paid a fee for acting as a witness

Please note that a few states have laws in effect regarding witnesses when the declarant is a patient in a nursing home, boarding facility, hospital, or skilled or intermediate health care facility. In those situations, it is advisable to have a patient ombudsman, patient advocate, or the director of the health care facility to act as the third witness to the signing of a living will. Please check the Appendix for your state's requirements.

4. In front of all of the witnesses and in front of the Notary Public, the following should take place in the order shown:

- You will then sign your living will at the end, exactly as your name is typewritten on your living will, where indicated, in ink using a pen.

- After you have signed, pass your living will to the first witness, who should sign where indicated and fill in his or her address.

- After the first witness has signed, have the living will passed to the second witness, who should also sign where indicated.

- If you are using a living will that requires a third witness, then after the second witness has signed, have the living will passed to the third and final witness, who also signs where indicated and fills in his or her address. Throughout this ceremony, you and all of the witnesses must remain together.

The final step is for the notary public to sign in the space indicated. When this step is completed, your living will is a valid legal document. Have several copies made and, if appropriate, deliver a copy to your attending physician to have placed in your medical records file. You may also desire to give a copy to the person you have chosen as the executor of your will, a copy to your clergy, and a copy to your spouse or other trusted relative.

Living Will Declaration and Directive to Physicians of ①_____

Notice to Adult Signing This Document: This is an important legal document. This document directs the medical treatment you are to receive in the event you are unable to participate in your own medical decisions and you are in a terminal condition. This document may state what kind of treatment you want or do not want to receive. This document can control whether you live or die. Prepare this document carefully. If you use this form, read it completely. You may want to seek professional help to make sure the form does what you intend and is completed without mistakes. This document will remain valid and in effect until and unless you revoke it. Review this document periodically to make sure it continues to reflect your wishes. You may amend or revoke this document at any time by notifying your physician and other health-care providers. You should give copies of this document to your physician and your family. This form is entirely optional. If you choose to use this form, please note that the form provides signature lines for you, the three witnesses whom you have selected and a notary public.

② I, _____ , being of sound mind, willfully and voluntarily make known my desire that my life not be artificially prolonged under the circumstances set forth below, and, ③ pursuant to any and all applicable laws in the State of _____ , I declare that:

If at any time I should have an incurable injury, disease, or illness which has been certified as a terminal condition by my attending physician and one additional physician, both of whom have personally examined me, and such physicians have determined that there can be no recovery from such condition and my death is imminent, and where the application of life prolonging procedures would serve only to artificially prolong the dying process, then:

I direct that such procedures be withheld or withdrawn, and that I be permitted to die naturally with only the administration of medication, the administration of nutrition and/or hydration, or the performance of any medical procedure deemed necessary to provide me with comfort, care, or to alleviate pain.

If at any time I should have been diagnosed as being in a persistent vegetative state which has been certified as incurable by my attending physician and one additional physician, both of whom have personally examined me, and such physicians have determined that there can be no recovery from such condition, and where the application of life prolonging procedures would serve only to artificially prolong the dying process, then:

I direct that such procedures be withheld or withdrawn, and that I be permitted to die naturally with only the administration of medication, the administration of nutrition and/or hydration, or the performance of any medical procedure deemed necessary to provide me with comfort, care, or to alleviate pain.

In the absence of my ability to give directions regarding my treatment in the above situations, including directions regarding the use of such life prolonging procedures, then:

It is my intention that this declaration shall be honored by my family, my physician, and any court of law, as the final expression of my legal right to refuse medical and surgical treatment. I declare that I fully accept the consequences for such refusal.

④ If I have any additional directions, I will state them here:

If I have also signed a Health Care Power of Attorney, Appointment of Health Care Agent, or Health Care Proxy, I direct the person who I have appointed with such instrument to follow the directions that I have made in this document. I intend for my agent to be treated as I would be with respect to my rights regarding the use and disclosure of my individually identifiable health information or other medical records. This release authority applies to any information governed by the Health Insurance Portability and Accountability Act of 1996 (aka HIPAA), 42 USC 1320d and 45 CFR 160-164.

If I am diagnosed as pregnant, this document shall have no force and effect during my pregnancy.

I understand the full importance of this declaration, and I am emotionally and mentally competent to make this declaration and Living Will. I also understand that I may revoke this document at any time.

⑤ I publish and sign this Living Will and Directive to Physicians, consisting of _____
⑥ typewritten pages, on _____, 20_____ , and declare that I do so freely, for the purposes expressed, under no constraint or undue influence, and that I am of sound mind and of legal age.

⑦ _____
Declarant's Signature

_____
Printed Name of Declarant

⑧ On _____, 20_____ , in the presence of all of us, the above-named Declarant published and signed this Living Will and Directive to Physicians, and then at the Declarant's request, and in the Declarant's presence, and in each other's presence, we all signed below as witnesses, and we each declare, under penalty of perjury, that, to the best of our knowledge:

1.   The Declarant is personally known to me and, to the best of my knowledge, the Declarant signed this instrument freely, under no constraint or undue influence, and is of sound mind and memory and legal age, and fully aware of the possible consequences of this action.

2.   I am at least 19 years of age and I am not related to the Declarant in any manner: by blood, marriage, or adoption.

3.   I am not the Declarant's attending physician, or a patient or employee of the Declarant's attending physician; or a patient, physician, or employee of the health care facility in which the Declarant is a patient, unless such person is required or allowed to witness the execution of this document by the laws of the state in which this document is executed.

4.   I am not entitled to any portion of the Declarant's estate on the Declarant's death under the laws of intestate succession of any state or country, nor under the Last Will and Testament of the Declarant or any Codicil to such Last Will and Testament.

5.   I have no claim against any portion of the Declarant's estate on the Declarant's death.

6.   I am not directly financially responsible for the Declarant's medical care.

7.   I did not sign the Declarant's signature for the Declarant or on the direction of the Declarant, nor have I been paid any fee for acting as a witness to the execution of this document.

_____
Signature of Witness #1

_____
Printed name of Witness #1

_____
Address of Witness #1

_____
Signature of Witness #2

_____
Printed name of Witness #2

_____
Address of Witness #2

Signature of Witness #3

Printed name of Witness #3

Address of Witness #3

⑨ County of _____
State of _____

On _____ , 20_____ , before me personally appeared _____ ,
the Declarant, and _____ , the first witness, _____ , the
second witness, _____ , the third witness, and, being first sworn on oath
and under penalty of perjury, state that, in the presence of all the witnesses, the Declarant
published and signed the above Living Will Declaration and Directive to Physicians, and then,
at Declarant's request, and in the presence of the Declarant and of each other, each of the
witnesses signed as witnesses, and stated that, to the best of their knowledge, the Declarant
signed said Living Will Declaration and Directive to Physicians freely, under no constraint
or undue influence, and is of sound mind and memory and legal age and fully aware of the
potential consequences of this action. The witnesses further state that this affidavit is made
at the direction of and in the presence of the Declarant.

Signature of Notary Public

Printed name of Notary Public

Notary Public,
In and for the County of _____
State of _____
My commission expires: _____   Notary Seal

Instructions for Revoking a Living Will

All states which have recognized living wills have provided methods for the easy revocation of them. Since they provide authority for medical personnel to withhold life-support technology which will likely result in death to the patient, great care must be taken to insure that a change of mind by the patient is heeded.

If revocation of your living will is an important issue, please consult your state's law directly. The name of your particular state's law relating to living wills is provided in the Appendix of this book.

For the revocation of a living will, any one of the following methods of revocation is generally acceptable:

- Physical destruction of the living will, such as tearing, burning, or mutilating the document.

- A written revocation of the living will by you or by a person acting at your direction. A form for this is provided at the end of this chapter.

- An oral revocation in the presence of a witness who signs and dates a writing confirming a revocation. This oral declaration may take any manner. Most states allow for a person to revoke such a document by any indication (even non-verbal) of the intent to revoke a living will, regardless of their physical or mental condition.

To use the Revocation of Living Will form provided on the next page, simply fill in the following information:

① Name of person revoking living will
② Date of original living will
③ Date of signing revocation of living will
④ Signature and printed name of person revoking living will

Revocation of Living Will

① I, _____ , am the Declarant and maker of a Living Will and Directive to
② Physicians, dated _____ , 20_____ .

By this written revocation, I hereby entirely revoke such Living Will and Directive to Physicians and intend that it no longer have any force or effect whatsoever.

③ Dated _____ , 20_____ .

④ _____
Declarant's Signature

_____
Printed Name of Declarant

CHAPTER 4
Preparing a Health Care Power of Attorney

A *power of attorney* is a document that is used to allow one person to give authority to another person to act on their behalf. The person signing the power of attorney grants legal authority to another to "stand in their shoes" and act legally for them. The person who receives the power of attorney is called an *attorney-in-fact*. This title and the power of attorney form does not mean that the person receiving the power has to be a lawyer. Power of attorney forms are useful documents for many occasions. They can be used to authorize someone else to sign certain documents if you can not be present when the signatures are necessary. Traditionally, property matters were the type of actions handled with powers of attorney. Increasingly, however, people are using a specific type of power of attorney to authorize other persons to make health care decisions on their behalf in the event of a disability which makes the person unable to communicate their wishes to doctors or other health care providers. This broad type of power of attorney is called a *health care power of attorney*. It is different from *durable power of attorney*, which gives another person the authority to sign legal papers, transact business, buy or sell property, etc. but is intended to remain in effect even if a person becomes disabled or incompetent. A durable power of attorney does not confer authority on another person to make health care decisions on someone else's behalf. Only a health care power of attorney can do that.

Health care powers of attorney are useful documents that go beyond the provisions of a living will, provide for health care options that living wills do not cover, and are important additions to the use of a living will. Basically, a health care power of attorney allows you to appoint someone to act for you in making health care decisions when you are unable to make them for yourself. A living will does not provide for this. Also, a health care power of attorney generally applies to all medical decisions (unless you specifically limit the power). Most living wills only apply to certain decisions regarding life support at the end of your life and are most useful in "terminal illness" or "permanent unconsciousness" situations.

Additionally, a health care power of attorney can provide your chosen agent with a valuable flexibility in making decisions regarding medical choices that may arise. Often, during the course of medical treatment, unforeseen situations may occur that require immediate decision-making. If you are unable to communicate your desires regarding such choices, the appointment of a *health care representative* for you (appointed with a health care power of attorney) will allow such decisions to be made on your behalf by a trusted person.

Finally, a health care power of attorney can provide specific detailed instructions regarding what you would like done by your attending physician in specific circumstances. Generally, living wills are limited to options for the withholding of life support. In order to be certain that you have made provisions for most potential health care situations, it is recommended you prepare both a living will and a health care power of attorney. Not everyone, however, has a trusted person available to serve as their health care representative. In these situations, the use of a living will alone will be necessary. It is, of course, possible to add additional instructions to any living will to clearly and specifically indicate your desires.

Your health care representative can be a relative or close friend. It should be someone who knows you very well and whom you trust completely. Your representative should be someone who is not afraid to ask questions of health care providers and is able to make difficult decisions. Your representative may need to be assertive on your behalf. You should discuss your choice with your representative and make certain that he or she understands the responsibilities involved.

All states have enacted legislation regarding this type of form and recognize the validity of this type of legal document. In some states, they are called Appointment of Health Care Agent; in others, they are referred to as a Health Care Proxy. The form included in this book is officially titled Health Care Power of Attorney and Appointment of Health Care Agent and Proxy, and is designed to be legally valid in all states. Information regarding each state's provisions are included in the Appendix under the listing "Other Directives".

The health care power of attorney included in this chapter is intended to be used to confer a very powerful authority to another person. In some cases, this may actually mean that you are giving that other person the power of life or death over you. This is not a power that should be conferred lightly. Very serious thought should be given to both who you appoint as your health care attorney-in-fact (the person you authorize to act on your behalf) and to any specific directions that you may want to give to that person regarding health care decisions. You may, of course, revoke your health care power of attorney at any time prior to your incapacitation (and even during any incapacitation if you are able to make your desire to revoke the power known). Remember, however, that should you become disabled or incapacitated and unable to communicate your wishes to anyone, you may be unable to communicate your desire to revoke your health care power of attorney.

Please note that this form provides a release for your health care representative to receive your medical records under the federal HIPAA regulations relating to the privacy of health care records. Also, at the beginning of the form is a notice that clearly explains the importance of caution in the use of this form and is applicable to all states. Please read it carefully before you sign your health care power of attorney.

This chapter contains a general, standardized health care power of attorney. Chapter 8 also contains state-specific health care power of attorney forms as part of the state-specific statutory Advance Health Care Directives that have been taken directly from the most recent legislation regarding health care powers of attorney in each state. A few states do not currently have specific legislation providing express statutory recognition of health care powers of attorney. For those states, a health care power of attorney (in the state-specific Advance Health Care Power of Attorney in Chapter 8) has been prepared by legal professionals to comply with the basic requirements that courts in that state or other states have found important. In such states, be assured that courts, health care professionals, and physicians will be guided by this expression of your desires concerning life support as expressed in the health care power of attorney prepared using this book. You may use either the general health care power of attorney form or the state-specific statutory form for your state. Please compare your state's form (in your state's Advance Health Care Directive in Chapter 8) with the standardized form in this chapter and select the appropriate form that you feel best expresses your wishes regarding the appointment of a health care agent to make your health care decisions for you if you are unable to make those decisions for yourself.

As noted in Chapter 1, the Federal Patient Self-Determination Act encourages all people to make their own decisions about the type of medical care they wish to receive. This act also requires all health care agencies (hospitals, long-term care facilities, and home health agencies) receiving Medicare and Medicaid reimbursement to recognize a living will and health care power of attorney as advance directives. Under this Act, all health care agencies must ask you if you have advance directives and must give you materials with information about your rights under state law. The health care power of attorney included in this chapter and/or the health care power of attorney included in the state-specific Advance Health Care Directives in Chapter 8 must be recognized by all health care agencies.

Instructions for Health Care Power of Attorney

This form should be used for providing a health care power of attorney to another person whom you chose to have the authority to make health care decisions for you in the event that you become incapacitated.

To complete this form, you will need the following information:

①　Name of person granting power of attorney
　　Address of person granting power of attorney
②　Name of person appointed as the "health care representative" (same as the "attorney-in-fact for health care decisions")
　　Address of person appointed as the "health care representative" (same as the "attorney-in-fact for health care decisions")
③　State whose laws will govern the powers granted
④　Signature of person granting power of attorney. NOTE: You should only sign this section if you have carefully read and agree with the statement that grants your health care representative the authority to order the withholding of medical care when you are diagnosed as being in a persistent vegetative state.
⑤　Any additional terms or conditions that you wish to add
⑥　Date of signing of health care power of attorney
⑦　Your signature and printed name (do not sign unless in front of a notary public)
⑧　Signature and printed name of witnesses (signed in front of a notary)
⑨　The notary acknowledgment section (to be completed by notary public)
⑩　Signature and printed name of person appointed as health care representative

Health Care Power of Attorney and Appointment of Health Care Agent and Proxy

Notice to Adult Signing this Document: This is an important legal document. Before executing this document, you should know these facts:

This document gives the person you designate (the attorney in fact) the power to make MOST health care decisions for you if you lose the capacity to make informed health care decisions for yourself. This power is effective only when your attending physician determines that you have lost the capacity to make informed health care decisions for yourself and, notwithstanding this document, as long as you have the capacity to make informed health care decisions for yourself, you retain the right to make all medical and other health care decisions for yourself.

You may include specific limitations in this document on the authority of the attorney in fact to make health care decisions for you. Subject to any specific limitations you include in this document, if your attending physician determines that you have lost the capacity to make an informed decision on a health care matter, the attorney in fact GENERALLY will be authorized by this document to make health care decisions for you to the same extent as you could make those decisions yourself, if you had the capacity to do so.

The authority of the attorney in fact to make health care decisions for you GENERALLY will include the authority to give informed consent, to refuse to give informed consent, or to withdraw informed consent to any care, treatment, service, or procedure to maintain, diagnose, or treat a physical or mental condition.

Additionally, when exercising authority to make health care decisions for you, the attorney in fact will have to act consistently with your desires or, if your desires are unknown, to act in your best interest. You may express your desires to the attorney in fact by including them in this document or by making them known to the attorney in fact in another manner.

When acting pursuant to this document, the attorney in fact GENERALLY will have the same rights that you have to receive information about proposed health care, to review health care records, and to consent to the disclosure of health care records. You can limit that right in this document if you so choose.

GENERALLY, you may designate any competent adult as the attorney in fact under this document. You have the right to revoke the designation of the attorney in fact and the right to revoke this entire document at any time and in any manner. Any such revocation generally will be effective when you express your intention to make the revocation. However, if you made your attending physician aware of this document, any such revocation will be effective only when you communicate it to your attending physician, or when a witness to the revocation or other health care personnel to whom the revocation is communicated by such a witness commu-

nicates it to your attending physician. If you execute this document and create a valid Health Care Power of Attorney with it, this will revoke any prior, valid power of attorney for health care that you created, unless you indicate otherwise in this document. This document is not valid as a Health Care Power of Attorney unless it is acknowledged before a notary public or is signed by at least two adult witnesses who are present when you sign or acknowledge your signature. No person who is related to you by blood, marriage, or adoption may be a witness. The attorney in fact, your attending physician, and the administrator of any nursing home in which you are receiving care also are ineligible to be witnesses. If there is anything in this document that you do not understand, you should ask a lawyer to explain it to you.

① I, _____ ,

    residing at _____ ,

    appoint the following person as my attorney-in-fact for health care decisions, my health care agent, and confer upon this person my health care proxy. This person shall hereafter referred to as my "health care

② representative": _____ ,

    residing at _____ .

    I grant my health care representative the maximum power under law to perform any acts on my behalf

③ regarding health care matters that I could do personally under the laws of the State of _____, including specifically the power to make any health decisions on my behalf, upon the terms and conditions set forth below. My health care representative accepts this appointment and agrees to act in my best interest as he or she considers advisable. This health care power of attorney and appointment of health care agent and proxy may be revoked by me at any time and is automatically revoked on my death. However, this power of attorney shall not be affected by my present or future disability or incapacity.

This health care power of attorney and appointment of health care agent and proxy has the following terms and conditions:

If I have signed a Living Will or Directive to Physicians, and it is still in effect, I direct that my health care representative abide by the directions that I have set out in that document.

If at any time I should have an incurable injury, disease, or illness which has been certified as a terminal condition by my attending physician and one additional physician, both of whom have personally examined me, and such physicians have determined that there can be no recovery from such condition and my death is imminent, and where the application of life prolonging procedures would serve only to artificially prolong the dying process, then:

I direct my health care representative to assure that such procedures be withheld or withdrawn, and that I be permitted to die naturally with only the administration of medication, the administration of nutrition and/or hydration, or the performance of any medical procedure deemed necessary to provide me with comfort, care, or to alleviate pain.

If at any time I should have been diagnosed as being in a persistent vegetative state which has been certified as incurable by my attending physician and one additional physician, both of whom have personally examined me, and such physicians have determined that there can be no recovery from such condition, and where the application of life prolonging procedures would serve only to artificially prolong the dying process, then

I direct that my health care representative assure that such procedures be withheld or withdrawn, and that I be permitted to die naturally with only the administration of medication, the administration of nutrition and/or hydration, or the performance of any medical procedure deemed necessary to provide me with comfort, care, or to alleviate pain.

THE FOLLOWING INSTRUCTIONS (IN BOLDFACE TYPE) ONLY APPLY
④ **IF I HAVE SIGNED MY NAME IN THIS SPACE: _____**

However, if at any time I should have been diagnosed as being in a persistent vegetative state which has been certified as incurable by my attending physician and one additional physician, both of whom have personally examined me, and such physicians have determined that there can be no recovery from such condition, I also direct that my health care representative have sole authority to order the withholding of any aid, including the administration of nutrition, hydration, and any other medical procedure deemed necessary to provide me with comfort, care, or to alleviate pain.

If I am able to communicate in any manner, including even blinking my eyes, I direct that my health care representative try and discuss with me the specifics of any proposed health care decision.

⑤ If I have any further terms or conditions, I state them here:

I have discussed my health care wishes with the person whom I have herein appointed as my health care representative, I am fully satisfied that the person who I have herein appointed as my health care representative will know my wishes with respect to my health care and I have full faith and confidence in their good judgement.

I further direct that my health care representative shall have full authority to do the following, should I lack the capacity to make such a decision myself, provided however, that this listing shall in no way limit the full authority that I give my health care representative to make health care decisions on my behalf:

a. to give informed consent to any health care procedure;

b. to sign any documents necessary to carry out or withhold any health care procedures on my behalf, including any waivers or releases of liabilities required by any health care provider;

c. to give or withhold consent for any health care or treatment;

d. to revoke or change any consent previously given or implied by law for any health care treatment;

e. to arrange for or authorize my placement or removal from any health care facility or institution;

f. to require that any procedures be discontinued, including the withholding of any medical treatment and/or aid, including the administration of nutrition, hydration, and any other medical procedure deemed necessary to provide me with comfort, care, or to alleviate pain, subject to the conditions earlier provided in this document;

g. to authorize the administration of pain-relieving drugs, even if they may shorten my life.

I desire that my wishes with respect to all health care matters be carried out through the authority that I have herein provided to my health care representative, despite any contrary wishes, beliefs, or opinions of any members of my family, relatives, or friends.

I have read the Notice that precedes this document. I understand the full importance of this appointment, and I am emotionally and mentally competent to make this appointment of health care representative.

I intend for my health care representative to be treated as I would be with respect to my rights regarding the use and disclosure of my individually identifiable health information or other medical records. This release authority applies to any information governed by the Health Insurance Portability and Accountability Act of 1996 (aka HIPAA), 42 USC 1320d and 45 CFR 160-164.

⑥ Dated _____ , 20_____

⑦ _____
Signature of person granting health care power of attorney and appointing health care representative

_____
Printed name of person granting health care power of attorney and appointing health care representative

⑧ **Witness Attestation**

I, _____(printed name), the first witness, and

I, _____(printed name), the second witness, sign my name to the foregoing power of attorney being first duly sworn and do declare to the undersigned authority that the principal signs and executes this instrument as his/her power of attorney and that he/she signs it willingly, or willingly directs another to sign for him/her, and that I, in the presence and hearing of the principal, sign this power of attorney as witness to the principal's signing and that to the best of my knowledge the principal is eighteen years of age or older, of sound mind and under no constraint or undue influence. I am not related to the principal, nor am I entitled to any portion of the principal's estate. I also do not provide health care services to the principal and am not financially responsible for the principal's health care.

_____   _____
Signature of First Witness   Address of First Witness

_____   _____

Signature of Second Witness   Address of Second Witness

⑨ **Notary Acknowledgment**

    State of _____

    County of _____

    On _____ , 20_____ , _____ came before me personally and, under oath, stated that he/she is the person described in the above document and he/she signed the above document in my presence.

    _____

    Notary Signature

    Notary Public
    In and for the County of _____
    State of _____
    My commission expires: _____   Notary Seal

    I accept my appointment as health care attorney-in-fact and health care representative.

⑩ _____

    Signature of person granted health care power of attorney and appointed as health care representative

    _____

    Printed name of person granted health care power of attorney and appointed as health care representative

Instructions for Revocation of Health Care Power of Attorney

On the following page, there is included a Revocation of Health Care Power of Attorney. You have the right at any time to revoke your Health Care Power of Attorney. Remember, however, that should you become disabled or incapacitated and unable to communicate your wishes to anyone, you may be unable to communicate your desire to revoke your Health Care Power of Attorney. In any event, if you choose to revoke your health care power of attorney, a copy of this revocation should be provided to the person to whom the power was originally given. Copies should also be given to any party that may have had dealings with the attorney-in-fact before the revocation and to any party with whom the attorney-in-fact may be expected to attempt to deal with after the revocation, for example, your family physician.

This form should be filled out and signed by the person revoking the health care power of attorney. It should also be notarized.

1. Name and address of person granting original health care power of attorney
2. Date of original health care power of attorney (that is now being revoked)
3. Name and address of person originally appointed as the "health care representative"
4. Date of signing of Revocation of Health Care Power of Attorney
5. Your signature and printed name (do not sign unless in front of a notary public)
6. The notary acknowledgment section (to be completed by notary public)

Revocation of Health Care Power of Attorney

① I, _____ , of _____
_____
② revoke the Health Care Power of Attorney dated _____ , 20_____ ,
③ which was granted to _____ , of _____
_____ _____ , to act as my attorney-in-fact
for health care decisions and I revoke any appointment of the above person as my health
care agent, health care representative, or health care proxy.

④ Dated _____ , 20___

⑤ _____
Signature of person revoking power of attorney

_____
Printed name of person revoking power of attorney

⑥ **Notary Acknowledgment**

State of _____
County of _____

On _____ , 20_____ , _____ came before me personally and,
under oath, stated that he/she is the person described in the above document and he/she
signed the above document in my presence.

_____
Notary Signature

Notary Public
In and for the County of _____
State of _____
My commission expires: _____   Notary Seal

CHAPTER 5
Preparing a Designation of Primary Physician

This form allows you to make known your personal choice of the doctor whom you would like to care for you should you be unable to make known your choice. Generally, people desire that their personal family physician be designated as their primary physician since this person is most aware of their personal wishes and desires concerning health care issues. This form may also be useful in conjunction with other estate planning forms that may call for a certification by a primary physician of a person's disability or incapacitation, such as with a durable power of attorney or health care power of attorney. The use of this form is optional. You should keep a copy of this document attached to any such form that may require action by your primary physician. In addition, you should request that a copy of this document be placed into your main medical files. This form need not be acknowledged by a notary public.

The state-specific Advance Health Care Directive in Chapter 8 contains a Designation of Primary Physician. If you chose to use your state's form from Chapter 8, it is not necessary to prepare this individual form.

Instructions for Designation of Primary Physician

To complete this form, fill in the following information:

① Your name and address
② Name and address of doctor selected as your primary physician
③ Date of signing of Designation of Primary Physician
④ Your signature and printed name

Designation of Primary Physician

① I, _____ ,
address:

do hereby designate the following doctor as my primary physician for all medical issues:

② _____ ,
address:

③ Date _____

④ _____
       Signature of person designating primary physician

_____
       Printed name of person designating primary physician

CHAPTER 6
Preparing an Organ Donation Form

The use of a form of this type allows you to make a donation of your organs for medical use after your death. Using this form, you may make choices about whether and how you may wish any of your organs to be donated for medical, scientific, or educational uses after your death. All states have versions of a state law usually referred to as an "Anatomical Gift Act," which provides that individuals may make personal choices about whether and how to provide for the gift of their organs after death. Because of the many lives that can be saved though the use of transplanted donated organs, many states actually actively encourage such donations. This form allows for a selection of which of your organs or body parts you wish to donate and a selection of how those items that you have chosen to donate may be used (such as for any purpose, for research, therapy, transplantation, medical education, or other limitations on their use).

Please read through this carefully and make your appropriate decisions. You may choose to select the donation of your whole body or only of specific parts. You may also choose to allow your donation to be used for any medical or scientific purpose or you may limit the uses of your donation in any way. Naturally, the use of this form is entirely optional. If you do complete this form, it is a good idea to leave a copy of this form with your will and/or living trust and, additionally, to have a copy placed in your main medical file of your primary family physician. As the viability of organs for donation is very time-sensitive, it may also be a good idea to inform your closest relatives of your decision regarding the use of your organs after your death. This form is designed to be notarized.

Please note that this form specifically states that such donation be made regardless of the objections of any family member. This clause is included because there have been many successful efforts by surviving family members to prevent organ donations after the death of a person who has signed a valid organ donation form. This clause makes known your desire that such donations are your strong personal desire, regardless of the objections of any family members.

Also note that you should be certain that the choices that you make using this document should be identical to any choices that you may have made in any other document, including in your will or on a driver's license organ donation designation.

The state-specific Advance Health Care Directive in Chapter 8 contains an Organ Donation Form. If you chose to use your state's form from Chapter 8, it is not necessary to prepare this individual form.

Instructions for Organ Donation Form

To complete this form, fill in the following information:

① Your name and address
② Initial your selection of either any organs/parts or which specific organs or parts
③ Initial your selection of either any purposes or which specific purposes limitations on the use of your organs or parts
④ Date of signing of organ donation form
⑤ Your signature and printed name (Sign in front of notary public)
⑥ The notary acknowledgement section is completed by a notary public

Organan Donation Form

① I, _____ ,
address:

being of sound mind, do hereby donate the following organs for the noted medical purposes, and I specifically intend that such donations take place regardless of any objections of any of my family members:

② In the event of my death, I have placed my *initials* next to the following part(s) of my body that I wish donated for the purposes that I have *initialed* below:

[   ] any organs or parts **OR**

[   ] eyes   [   ] bone and connective tissue   [   ] skin
[   ] heart   [   ] kidney(s)   [   ] liver
[   ] lung(s)   [   ] pancreas   [   ] other _____

③ for the purposes of:

[   ] any purpose authorized by law **OR**

[   ] transplantation   [   ] research   [   ] therapy
[   ] medical education   [   ] other limitations

④ Dated _____

⑤ _____
   Signature of person donating organs

   _____
   Printed name of person donating organs

⑥ Notary Acknowledgement

   State of _____
   County of _____

   On _____ , 20_____ , _____ came before me personally and, under oath, stated that he/she is the person described in the above document and he/she signed the above document in my presence.

   _____
   Notary Public
   In and for the County of _____   State of _____
   My commission expires: _____   Notary Seal

CHAPTER 7
Preparing a Durable Unlimited Power of Attorney for Financial Affairs

A power of attorney is a document that is used to allow one person to give authority to another person to act on their behalf. The person signing the power of attorney grants legal authority to another to "stand in their shoes" and act legally for them. The person who receives the power of attorney is called an *attorney-in-fact*. This title and the power of attorney form does not mean that the person receiving the power has to be a lawyer. If you appoint your spouse or a trused relative or friend, then that person is your "attorney-in-fact".

Power of attorney forms are useful documents for many occasions. They can be used to authorize someone else to sign certain documents if you can not be present when the signatures are necessary. Traditionally, property matters were the type of actions handled with powers of attorney. A *durable unlimited power of attorney for financial affairs* is a specific type of power of attorney that gives another person the authority to sign legal papers, transact business, buy or sell property, etc., and is only effective in one of two scenarios: (1) it may be written so that it *remains* in effect *even* if a person becomes disabled or incompetent, or (2) it may be written so that it *only* goes into effect *if and when* a person becomes disabled or incompetent. A durable power of attorney does not confer authority on another person to make health care decisions on someone else's behalf. Only a *health care* power of attorney can do that. There are two durable power of attorney forms contained in this book: one is written for the (1) scenario above (remains in effect if a person becomes incapacitated) and the other is written for the (2) scenario (it will only go into effect when and if a person becomes incapacitated). Note that a limited power of attorney for financial affairs is also possible to create for granting authority to act in specific situation or for particular transactions. However, because of its limited scope, this type of power of attorney is not as practical in estate planning situations. If you wish to limit the powers that you grant in your power of attorney, please consult an attorney.

A durable unlimited power of attorney for financial affairs allows you to appoint an agent (who is then referred to as an 'attorney-in-fact') to handle your financial affairs during a period that you are unable to handle them yourself. With this form, you are giving another person the right to manage your financial and business matters on your behalf. They are given the power to act as you could, if you were able. If there is someone available who can be trusted implicitly to act on your behalf, the appointment of such a person can eliminate many problems that may arise if you are unable to handle your own affairs. The appointment of an agent for your financial affairs allows for the paying of bills, writing of checks, etc. while you are unable to do so yourself.

You should appoint someone whom you trust completely. With the forms in this book, you are granting the appointed agent very broad powers to handle your affairs. You will give your agent the maximum power under law to perform the following specific acts on your behalf: all acts relating to any and all of your financial and/or business affairs, including all banking and financial institution transactions, all real estate transactions, all insurance and annuity transactions, all claims and litigation, and all business transactions. Your attorney-in-fact (agent) is granted full power to act on your behalf in the same manner as if you were personally present.

The first durable power of attorney for financial affairs that is provided immediately appoints your chosen attorney-in-fact and that appointment will remain in effect *even if* you become incapacitated. The second durable power of attorney for financial affairs that is provided will become effective *only* upon your disability, as certified by your primary physician or, if your primary physician is not available, by any other attending physician. Neither power of attorney grants any power or authority to your designated attorney-in-fact regarding health care decisions. Only the health care power of attorney can confer those powers. You may, of course, choose to select the very same person to act as both your health care representative and your agent for financial affairs.

By accepting their appointment, your agent agrees to act in your best interest as he or she considers advisable. A durable power of attorney for financial matters may be revoked at any time and is automatically revoked on your death. The durable powers of attorney included in this chapter are intended to be used to confer a very powerful authority to another person. You will be providing another person with the power to handle all of your affairs (other than health care decisions). This is not a power that should be conferred lightly. Very serious thought should be given to both who you appoint as your attorney-in-fact (the person you authorize to act on your behalf) and to any specific directions that you may want to give to that person regarding financial decisions. You do not have to appoint anyone to handle your financial affairs, but it is often very useful to do so.

At the beginning of each of the documents are notices regarding the use of a durable power of attorney. They clearly explain the importance of caution in the use of this form and are applicable to all states. Please read each carefully to decide which of these forms are appropriate for your situation. Please note that this form provides a release for your attorney-in-fact to receive your medical records under the federal HIPAA regulations relating to the privacy of health care records. This does not confer any authority for your attorney-in-fact to make health care decisions on your behalf. The HIPPAA release is for the purpose of allowing your attorney-in-fact to have access to your medical files for the purpose of paying or examining medical bills and charges.

Please also note that the state-specific statutory Advance Health Care forms in Chapter 8 *do not* contain a Durable Power of Attorney for Financial Affairs. If you wish to have this type of document as part of your advance health care plans, you will need to complete one of the two types of forms that are contained in this chapter.

Instructions for Durable Unlimited Power of Attorney for Financial Affairs

(1) Goes into effect immediately and remains in effect even upon your Incapacitation

This form should be used only in situations where you desire to authorize another person to act for you in *all* transactions immediately and you wish the power to remain in effect in the event that you become incapacitated and unable to handle your own affairs. The grant of power under this document is unlimited (except for health care decisions). This form gives the person whom you designate as your "attorney-in-fact" broad powers to handle your property during your lifetime, which may include powers to mortgage, sell, or otherwise dispose of any real or personal property without advance notice to you or approval by you. This document does not authorize anyone to make medical or other health care decisions. You must execute a health care power of attorney to accomplish this. This form does provide a HIPPA medical records privacy release that will allow the person that you appoint to access any hospital or medical bills or records on you behalf. This form also provides that you will also name a successor attorney-in-fact who will have the same powers as the original person appointed, but who will only have the powers if the original person appointed is unable to perform the necessary tasks required by the power of attorney. The authority granted by this power of attorney may be revoked by you at any time and is automatically revoked if you die. If there is anything about this form that you do not understand, you should ask a lawyer to explain it to you. To complete this form, fill in the following:

① Name and address of person granting power (principal)
② Name and address of person granted power (attorney-in-fact)
③ Name and address of successor to person originally granted power (successor attorney-in-fact)
④ Date and printed name of principal
⑤ Signature of principal (signed in front of Notary Public)
⑥ Witness printed names and signatures (signed in front of Notary Public)
⑦ Notary acknowledgement should be completed by the Notary Public

The following should be completed by the person you have appointed as attorney-in-fact:

⑧ Printed name and signature of attorney-in-fact and successor attorney-in-fact

Durable Unlimited Power of Attorney For Financial Affairs

Effective Immediately

Notice to Adult Signing this Document: This is an important document. Before signing this document, you should know these important facts. By signing this document, you are not giving up any powers or rights to control your finances and property yourself. In addition to your own powers and rights, you are giving another person, your attorney-in-fact, broad powers to handle your finances and property, which may include powers to encumber, sell or otherwise dispose of any real or personal property without advance notice to you or approval by you. THE POWERS GRANTED UNDER THIS DOCUMENT ARE EFFECTIVE IMMEDIATELY AND WILL REMAIN IN EFFECT IF YOU BECOME DISABLED OR INCAPACITATED. This document does not authorize anyone to make medical or other health care decisions for you. If you own complex or special assets such as a business, or if there is anything about this form that you do not understand, you should ask a lawyer to explain this form to you before you sign it. If you wish to change your durable unlimited power of attorney, you must complete a new document and revoke this one. You have the right to revoke the designation of the attorney-in-fact and the right to revoke this entire document at any time and in any manner. You may revoke this document at any time by destroying it, by directing another person to destroy it in your presence or by signing a written and dated statement expressing your intent to revoke this document. If you revoke this document, you should notify your attorney-in-fact and any other person to whom you have given a copy of the form. You also should notify all parties having custody of your assets. These parties have no responsibility to you unless you actually notify them of the revocation. If your attorney-in-fact is your spouse and your marriage is annulled, or you are divorced after signing this document, this document may become invalid. Since some third parties or some transactions may not permit use of this document, it is advisable to check in advance, if possible, for any special requirements that may be imposed. You should sign this form only if the attorney-in- fact you name is reliable, trustworthy and competent to manage your affairs. Generally, you may designate any competent adult as the attorney-in-fact under this document.

① I, _____ ,of

   (address) _____ ,as

② principal, do appoint _____ of

   (address) _____ ,as

my attorney-in- fact to act in my name, place and stead in any way which I myself could do, if I were personally present, with respect to all of the following matters to the extent that I am permitted by law to act through an agent: I grant my attorney-in-fact the maximum power under law to perform any act on my behalf that I could do personally, including but not limited to, all acts relating to any and all of my financial transactions and/or business affairs including all banking and financial institution transactions, all real estate or personal property transactions, all insurance or annuity transactions, all claims and litigation, and any and all business transactions. This power of attorney shall become effective immediately and shall remain in full effect upon my disability or incapacitation. This power of attorney grants no power or authority regarding healthcare decisions to my designated attorney-in-fact.

③   If the attorney-in-fact named above is unable or unwilling to serve, then I appoint

_____, of
_____ (address),
to be my successor attorney-in-fact for all purposes hereunder.

My attorney-in-fact is granted full and unlimited power to act on my behalf in the same manner as if I were personally present. My attorney-in-fact accepts this appointment and agrees to act in my best interest as he or she considers advisable. To induce any third party to rely upon this power of attorney, I agree that any third party receiving a signed copy or facsimile of this power of attorney may rely upon such copy, and that revocation or termination of this power of attorney shall be ineffective as to such third party until actual notice or knowledge of such revocation or termination shall have been received by such third party. I, for myself and for my heirs, executors, legal representatives and assigns, agree to indemnify and hold harmless any such third party from any and all claims that may arise against such third party by reason of such third party having relied on the provisions of this power of attorney. This power of attorney may be revoked by me at any time and is automatically revoked upon my death. My attorney-in-fact shall not be compensated for his or her services nor shall my attorney-in-fact be liable to me, my estate, heirs, successors, or assigns for acting or refraining from acting under this document, except for willful misconduct or gross negligence. Revocation of this document is not effective unless a third party has actual knowledge of such revocation.

I intend for my attorney-in-fact under this Power of Attorney to be treated as I would be with respect to my rights regarding the use and disclosure of my individually identifiable health information or other medical records. This release authority applies to any information governed by the Health Insurance Portability and Accountability Act of 1996 (aka HIPAA), 42 USC 1320d and 45 CFR 160-164.

Signature and Declaration of Principal

④   I, _____(printed name), the principal, sign my name to this power of attorney this _____ day of _____and, being first duly sworn, do declare to the undersigned authority that I sign and execute this instrument as my power of attorney and that I sign it willingly, or willingly direct another to sign for me, that I execute it as my free and voluntary act for the purposes expressed in the power of attorney and that I am eighteen years of age or older, of sound mind and under no constraint or undue influence ,and that I have read and understand the contents of the notice at the beginning of this document.

⑤   _____

Signature of Principal

Witness Attestation

⑥ I, _____ (printed name), the first witness, and
I, _____ (printed name), the second witness,
sign my name to the foregoing power of attorney being first duly sworn and do declare to the undersigned authority that the principal signs and executes this instrument as his/her power of attorney and that he/she signs it willingly, or willingly directs another to sign for him/her, and that I, in the presence and hearing of the principal, sign this power of attorney as witness to the principal's signing and that to the best of my knowledge the principal is eighteen years of age or older, of sound mind and under no constraint or undue influence.

_____   _____
Signature of First Witness   Signature of Second Witness

Notary Acknowledgment

⑦ The State of _____
County of _____
Subscribed, sworn to and acknowledged before me by _____,
the principal, and subscribed and sworn to before me by _____, the
first witness, and _____, the second witness on this date _____.

_____
Notary Public Signature
Notary Public, In and for the County of _____State of _____
My commission expires: _____   Notary Seal

Acknowledgment and Acceptance of Appointment as Attorney-in-Fact

⑧ I, _____, (printed name) have read the attached power of attorney and am the person identified as the attorney-in-fact for the principal. I hereby acknowledge that I accept my appointment as Attorney-in-Fact and that when I act as agent I shall exercise the powers for the benefit of the principal; I shall keep the assets of the principal separate from my assets; I shall exercise reasonable caution and prudence; and I shall keep a full and accurate record of all actions, receipts and disbursements on behalf of the principal.

_____   _____
Signature of Attorney-in-Fact   Date

Acknowledgment and Acceptance of Appointment as Successor Attorney-in-Fact

⑧ I, _____, (printed name) have read the attached power of attorney and am the person identified as the successor attorney-in-fact for the principal. I hereby acknowledge that I accept my appointment as Successor Attorney-in-Fact and that, in the absence of a specific provision to the contrary in the power of attorney, when I act as agent I shall exercise the powers for the benefit of the principal; I shall keep the assets of the principal separate from my assets; I shall exercise reasonable caution and prudence; and I shall keep a full and accurate record of all actions, receipts and disbursements on behalf of the principal.

_____   _____
Signature of Successor Attorney-in-Fact   Date

Instructions for Durable Unlimited Power of Attorney for Financial Affairs

(2) Goes into effect only upon your incapacitation as certified by your primary physician, or another physician, if your primary physician is not available.

This form should be used only in situations where you desire to authorize another person to act for you in *all* transactions but you desire that the powers granted will not take effect until you become incapacitated and unable to handle your own affairs. This documents also provides that your incapacitation must be certified by your primary physician, or another attending physician if your primary physician is not available. The grant of power under this document is unlimited (except for health care decisions). This form gives the person whom you designate as your "attorney-in-fact" broad powers to handle your property during your incapacitation, which may include powers to mortgage, sell, or otherwise dispose of any real or personal property without advance notice to you or approval by you. This document does not authorize anyone to make medical or other health care decisions. You must execute a health care power of attorney to accomplish this. This form does provide a HIPPA medical records privacy release that will allow the person that you appoint to access any hospital or medical bills or records on you behalf. This form also provides that you will also name a successor attorney-in-fact who will have the same powers as the original person appointed, but who will only have the powers if the original person appointed is unable to perform the necessary tasks required by the power of attorney. The authority granted by this power of attorney may be revoked by you at any time and is automatically revoked if you die. If there is anything about this form that you do not understand, you should ask a lawyer to explain it to you. Please note that this form provides a release for your attorney-in-fact to receive your medical records under the federal HIPAA regulations relating to the privacy of health care records.

To complete this form, fill in the following:

① Name and address of person granting power (principal)
② Name and address of person granted power (attorney-in-fact)
③ Name and address of successor to person originally granted power (successor attorney-in-fact)
④ Date and printed name of principal
⑤ Signature of principal (signed in front of Notary Public)
⑥ Witness printed names and signatures (signed in front of Notary Public)
⑦ Notary acknowledgement should be completed by the Notary Public.

The following should be completed by the person you have appointed as attorney-in-fact:

⑧ Printed name and signature and of attorney-in-fact and successor attorney-in-fact

Durable Unlimited Power of Attorney
Effective Only Upon Disability

Notice to Adult Signing this Document: This is an important document. Before signing this document, you should know these important facts. By signing this document, you are not giving up any powers or rights to control your finances and property yourself. In addition to your own powers and rights, you are giving another person, your attorney-in-fact, broad powers to handle your finances and property, which may include powers to encumber, sell or otherwise dispose of any real or personal property without advance notice to you or approval by you. THE POWERS GRANTED UNDER THIS DOCUMENT WILL ONLY GO INTO EFFECT IF YOU BECOME DISABLED OR INCAPACITATED, AS CERTIFIED BY YOUR PRIMARY PHYSICIAN, OR BY ANOTHER ATTENDING PHYSICIAN, IF YOUR PRIMARY PHYSICIAN IS NOT AVAILABLE. This document does not authorize anyone to make medical or other health care decisions for you. If you own complex or special assets such as a business, or if there is anything about this form that you do not understand, you should ask a lawyer to explain this form to you before you sign it. If you wish to change your durable unlimited power of attorney, you must complete a new document and revoke this one. You have the right to revoke the designation of the attorney-in-fact and the right to revoke this entire document at any time and in any manner. You may revoke this document at any time by destroying it, by directing another person to destroy it in your presence or by signing a written and dated statement expressing your intent to revoke this document. If you revoke this document, you should notify your attorney-in-fact and any other person to whom you have given a copy of the form. You also should notify all parties having custody of your assets. These parties have no responsibility to you unless you actually notify them of the revocation. If your attorney-in-fact is your spouse and your marriage is annulled, or you are divorced after signing this document, this document may become invalid. Since some third parties or some transactions may not permit use of this document, it is advisable to check in advance, if possible, for any special requirements that may be imposed. You should sign this form only if the attorney-in-fact you name is reliable, trustworthy and competent to manage your affairs. Generally, you may designate any competent adult as the attorney-in-fact under this document.

① I, _____, of
(address) _____, as principal,
② do appoint _____ of
(address) _____, as
my attorney-in-fact to act in my name, place and stead in any way which I myself could do, if I were personally present, with respect to all of the following matters to the extent that I am permitted by law to act through an agent: I grant my attorney-in-fact the maximum power under law to perform any act on my behalf that I could do personally, including but not limited to, all acts relating to any and all of my financial transactions and/or business affairs including all banking and financial institution transactions, all real estate or personal prop-

erty transactions, all insurance or annuity transactions, all claims and litigation, and any and all business transactions. This power of attorney shall only become effective upon my disability or incapacitation, as certified by my primary physician, or if my primary physician is not available, by any other attending physician. This power of attorney grants no power or authority regarding healthcare decisions to my designated attorney-in-fact.

If the attorney-in-fact named above is unable or unwilling to serve, then I appoint

③ _____, of
_____ (address),
to be my successor attorney-in-fact for all purposes hereunder.

My attorney-in-fact is granted full and unlimited power to act on my behalf in the same manner as if I were personally present. My attorney-in-fact accepts this appointment and agrees to act in my best interest as he or she considers advisable. To induce any third party to rely upon this power of attorney, I agree that any third party receiving a signed copy or facsimile of this power of attorney may rely upon such copy, and that revocation or termination of this power of attorney shall be ineffective as to such third party until actual notice or knowledge of such revocation or termination shall have been received by such third party. I, for myself and for my heirs, executors, legal representatives and assigns, agree to indemnify and hold harmless any such third party from any and all claims that may arise against such third party by reason of such third party having relied on the provisions of this power of attorney. This power of attorney may be revoked by me at any time and is automatically revoked upon my death. My attorney-in-fact shall not be compensated for his or her services nor shall my attorney-in-fact be liable to me, my estate, heirs, successors, or assigns for acting or refraining from acting under this document, except for willful misconduct or gross negligence. Revocation of this document is not effective unless a third party has actual knowledge of such revocation.

I intend for my attorney-in-fact under this Power of Attorney to be treated as I would be with respect to my rights regarding the use and disclosure of my individually identifiable health information or other medical records. This release authority applies to any information governed by the Health Insurance Portability and Accountability Act of 1996 (aka HIPAA), 42 USC 1320d and 45 CFR 160-164.

Signature and Declaration of Principal

④ I, _____ (printed name), the principal, sign my name to this power of attorney this _____ day of _____ and, being first duly sworn, do declare to the undersigned authority that I sign and execute this instrument as my power of attorney and that I sign it willingly, or willingly direct another to sign for me, that I execute it as my free and voluntary act for the purposes expressed in the power of attorney and that I am eighteen years of age or older, of sound mind and under no constraint or undue influence ,and that I have read and understand the contents of the notice ⑤ at the beginning of this document.

_____
Signature of Principal

Witness Attestation

⑥ I, _____ (printed name), the first witness, and
I, _____ (printed name), the second witness, sign my name to the foregoing power of attorney being first duly sworn and do declare to the undersigned authority that the principal signs and executes this instrument as his/her power of attorney and that he/she signs it willingly, or willingly directs another to sign for him/her, and that I, in the presence and hearing of the principal, sign this power of attorney as witness to the principal's signing and that to the best of my knowledge the principal is eighteen years of age or older, of sound mind and under no constraint or undue influence.

_____   _____
Signature of First Witness   Signature of Second Witness

Notary Acknowledgment

⑦ The State of _____
County of _____
Subscribed, sworn to and acknowledged before me by _____,the principal, and subscribed and sworn to before me by _____, the first witness, and _____,the second witness on this date _____.

_____
Notary Public Signature
Notary Public, In and for the County of _____ State of _____
My commission expires: _____ Notary Seal

Acknowledgment and Acceptance of Appointment as Attorney-in-Fact

⑧ I, _____ (printed name) have read the attached power of attorney and am the person identified as the attorney-in-fact for the principal. I hereby acknowledge that I accept my appointment as Attorney-in-Fact and that when I act as agent I shall exercise the powers for the benefit of the principal; I shall keep the assets of the principal separate from my assets; I shall exercise reasonable caution and prudence; and I shall keep a full and accurate record of all actions, receipts and disbursements on behalf of the principal.

_____   _____
Signature of Attorney-in-Fact   Date

Acknowledgment and Acceptance of Appointment as Successor Attorney-in-Fact

⑧ I, _____ (printed name) have read the attached power of attorney and am the person identified as the successor attorney-in-fact for the principal. I hereby acknowledge that I accept my appointment as Successor Attorney-in-Fact and that, in the absence of a specific provision to the contrary in the power of attorney, when I act as agent I shall exercise the powers for the benefit of the principal; I shall keep the assets of the principal separate from my assets; I shall exercise reasonable caution and prudence; and I shall keep a full and accurate record of all actions, receipts and disbursements on behalf of the principal.

_____   _____
Signature of Successor Attorney-in-Fact   Date

Instructions for Revocation of Durable Unlimited Power of Attorney for Financial Affairs

On the following page, there is included a Revocation of Durable Unlimited Power of Attorney. You have the right at any time to revoke your durable unlimited power of attorney. Remember, however, that should you become disabled or incapacitated and unable to communicate your wishes to anyone, you may be unable to communicate your desire to revoke your Durable Unlimited Power of Attorney. In any event, if you choose to revoke your power of attorney, a copy of this revocation should be provided to the person to whom the power was originally given. Copies should also be given to any party that may have had dealings with the attorney-in-fact before the revocation and to any party with whom the attorney-in-fact may be expected to attempt to deal with after the revocation, for example, your bank or other financial institutions.

This form should be filled out and signed by the person revoking the Durable Unlimited Power of Attorney. It should also be notarized.

① Name and address of person granting original durable unlimited power of attorney
② Date of original durable unlimited power of attorney (that is now being revoked)
③ Name and address of person originally appointed as the "attorney-in-fact"
④ Date of signing of Revocation of Durable Unlimited Power of Attorney
⑤ Your signature and printed name (do not sign unless in front of a notary public)
⑥ The notary acknowledgment section (to be completed by notary public)

Revocation of Durable Unlimited Power of Attorney For Financial Affairs

① I, _____ , of_____
_____

② revoke the Durable Unlimited Power of Attorney dated _____ , 20_____ ,
③ which was granted to _____ , of _____
_____ , to act as my attorney-in-fact
for financial affairs and I revoke any appointment of the above person as my attorney-in-fact.

④ Dated _____ , 20_____

⑤ _____
Signature of person revoking power of attorney

_____
Printed name of person revoking power of attorney

⑥ **Notary Acknowledgment**

State of _____
County of _____

On _____ , 20_____ , _____ came before me personally and, under oath, stated that he/she is the person described in the above document and he/she signed the above document in my presence.

_____
Notary Signature

Notary Public
In and for the County of _____
State of _____
My commission expires: _____   Notary Seal

CHAPTER 8
State-Specific Statutory Advance Health Care Directives

A '***state-specific statutory Advance Health Care Directive***' is a form that has been prepared based on the the laws of your particular state. The legal effects of the language in such a document have been approved by the legislature of the state. This provides an advantage in that the legal language in such a 'statutory' form is generally familiar to health care providers in the particular state and they know that such language has been approved. This does not mean, however, that other 'non-statutory' forms are not legally valid in the state as well. Anyone may use a 'non-statutory' legal form, such as those in Chapters 3 through 7, with language that they find appropriate to their own situation, as long as the document meets certain minimum legal standards for a state which, of course, all forms in this book do meet.

The state-specific statutory advance health care directives that are contained in this chapter and on the CD (in fillable PDF format) have been designed as a complete Advance Health Care Directive containing all appropriate forms (see note below). Each directive contain the following four forms:

- Living Will
- Selection of Health Care Agent (generally, by Health Care Power of Attorney)
- Designation of Primary Physician
- Organ Donation

Should you choose to use a state-specific form, you need not necessarily adopt all four sections of the document for your own use. You may select and complete any or all of the four separate sections of the form. Instructions for filling in the state-specific forms are found on pages 15-17 in Chapter 2. Many people find using a state-specific document easier than completing each separate form as an individual document. This method also provides a simple compact package that contains your entire Advance Health Care Directive with forms using legal language that most health care providers in your state are familiar with. More details regarding each specific form are provided in the specific chapter of this book relating to the particular form. In addition, state-specific requirements and explanations are also provided in the appendix of this book. In a few states, the legislatures have not developed specific language for one or more of the forms. These few instances are noted under the state's heading in the appendix of this book. In addition, in such situations, an appropriate and legally-valid form has been added to the directives for those states. Any such forms have been prepared legal professionals following any guidelines set out by the state's legislature.

Important Note: The state-specific statutory forms in this chapter *do not* contain a durable power of attorney for financial affairs. As this form is not directly related to health care issues, it is left as a separate form located in Chapter 7. Should you desire to use this type of document to authorize someone to handle your financial affairs in the event of your disability or incapacitation, you should use the forms provided in Chapter 7.

Alabama Advance Health Care Directive

On this date of _____ , I, _____ , do hereby sign, execute, and adopt the following as my Advance Health Care Directive. I direct any and all persons or entities involved with my health care in any manner that these decisions are my wishes and were adopted without duress or force and of my own free will.

I have placed my initials next to the sections of this Directive that I have adopted:

[   ]   Living Will
[   ]   Selection of Health Care Agent (Health Care Proxy)
[   ]   Designation of Primary Physician
[   ]   Organ Donation

This form may be used in the State of Alabama to make your wishes known about what medical treatment or other care you would or would not want if you become too sick to speak for yourself. You are not required to have an advance directive. If you do have an advance directive, be sure that your doctor, family, and friends know you have one and know where it is located.

Living Will

I, being of sound mind and at least 19 years old, would like to make the following wishes known. I direct that my family, my doctors and health care workers, and all others follow the directions I am writing down. I know that at any time I can change my mind about these directions by tearing up this form and writing a new one. I can also do away with these directions by tearing them up and by telling someone at least 19 years of age of my wishes and asking him or her to write them down.

I understand that these directions will only be used if I am not able to speak for myself.

IF I BECOME TERMINALLY ILL OR INJURED: Terminally ill or injured is when my doctor and another doctor decide that I have a condition that cannot be cured and that I will likely die in the near future from this condition.

Life sustaining treatment - Life sustaining treatment includes drugs, machines, or medical procedures that would keep me alive but would not cure me. I know that even if I choose not to have life sustaining treatment, I will still get medicines and treatments that ease my pain and keep me comfortable.

Place your initials by either "yes" or "no":

I want to have life sustaining treatment if I am terminally ill or injured. _____ Yes _____ No

Artificially provided food and hydration (Food and water through a tube or an IV) - I understand that if I am terminally ill or injured I may need to be given food and water through a tube or an IV to keep me alive if I can no longer chew or swallow on my own or with someone helping me.

Place your initials by either "yes" or "no":

I want to have food and water provided through a tube or an IV if I am terminally ill or injured. _____ Yes _____ No

IF I BECOME PERMANENTLY UNCONSCIOUS: Permanent unconsciousness is when my doctor and another doctor agree that within a reasonable degree of medical certainty I can no longer think, feel anything, knowingly move, or be aware of being alive. They believe this condition will last indefinitely without hope for improvement and have watched me long enough to make that decision. I understand that at least one of these doctors must be qualified to make such a diagnosis.

Life sustaining treatment - Life sustaining treatment includes drugs, machines, or other medical procedures that would keep me alive but would not cure me. I know that even if I choose not to have life sustaining treatment, I will still get medicines and treatments that ease my pain and keep me comfortable.

Place your initials by either "yes" or "no":

I want to have life-sustaining treatment if I am permanently unconscious. _____ Yes _____ No

Artificially provided food and hydration (Food and water through a tube or an IV) - I understand that if I become permanently unconscious, I may need to be given food and water through a tube or an IV to keep me alive if I can no longer chew or swallow on my own or with someone helping me.

Place your initials by either "yes" or "no":

I want to have food and water provided through a tube or an IV if I am permanently unconscious. _____ Yes _____ No

OTHER DIRECTIONS:

Please list any other things you want done or not done.

In addition to the directions I have listed on this form, I also want the following:

If you do not have other directions, place your initials below:

_____ No, I do not have any other directions.

Selection of Health Care Agent (Health Care Proxy)

If I need someone to speak for me.

This form can be used in the State of Alabama to name a person you would like to make medical or other decisions for you if you become too sick to speak for yourself. This person is called a health care proxy. You do not have to name a health care proxy. The directions in this form will be followed even if you do not name a health care proxy.

Place your initials by only one answer:

_____ I do not want to name a health care proxy. (If you check this answer, go to next section).

_____ I do want the person listed below to be my health care proxy. I have talked with this person about my wishes.

First choice for proxy: _____

Relationship to me: _____

Address: _____

City: _____ State: _____ Zip: _____

Day-time phone number: _____

Night-time phone number: _____

If this person is not able, not willing, or not available to be my health care proxy, this is my next choice:

Second choice for proxy: _____

Relationship to me: _____

Address: _____

City: _____ State: _____ Zip: _____

Day-time phone number: _____

Night-time phone number: _____

Instructions for Proxy

Place your initials by either "yes" or "no":

I want my health care proxy to make decisions about whether to give me food and water through a tube or an IV. _____ Yes _____ No

Place your initials by only one of the following:

_____ I want my health care proxy to follow only the directions as listed on this form.

_____ I want my health care proxy to follow my directions as listed on this form and to make any decisions about things I have not covered in the form.

_____ I want my health care proxy to make the final decision, even though it could mean doing something different from what I have listed on this form.

Other Provisions

The things listed on this form are what I want. I also understand the following:

If my doctor or hospital does not want to follow the directions I have listed, they must see that I get to a doctor or hospital who will follow my directions. If I am pregnant, or if I become pregnant, the choices I have made on this form will not be followed until after the birth of the baby.

If the time comes for me to stop receiving life sustaining treatment or food and water through a tube or an IV, I direct that my doctor talk about the good and bad points of doing this, along with my wishes, with my health care proxy, if I have one, and with the following people:

_____

In the absence of my ability to give directions regarding the use of life-sustaining treatment, it is my intention that this advance directive for health care shall be honored by my family, my physician(s), and health care provider(s) as the final expression of my legal right to refuse medical or surgical treatment and accept the consequences from such refusal. I understand the full import of this declaration and I am emotionally and mentally competent to make this advance directive for health care.

Nothing in this directive shall be construed to exclude from consultation or notification any relative of mine about my health condition or dying. Written directives by me as to whether to notify or consult with certain family members shall be respected by health care workers, attorneys-in-fact, or surrogates.

I understand that I may revoke this directive at any time.

Designation of Primary Physician

I designate the following physician as my primary physician: _____ (name)
_____ (address)
_____ (phone).

OPTIONAL- DESIGNATION OF ALTERNATE PRIMARY PHYSICIAN: If the physician I have designated above is not willing, able, or reasonably available to act as my primary physician, I designate the following physician as my primary physician:
_____ (name)
_____ (address)
_____ (phone).

Organ Donation

In the event of my death, I have placed my initials next to the following part(s) of my body that I wish donated for the purposes **that I have initialed below**:

[   ] any organs or parts **OR**
[   ] eyes   [   ] bone and connective tissue   [   ] skin
[   ] heart   [   ] kidney(s)   [   ] liver
[   ] lung(s)   [   ] pancreas   [   ] other _____
for the purposes of:
[   ] any purpose authorized by law **OR**
[   ] transplantation   [   ] research   [   ] therapy
[   ] medical education   [   ] other limitations _____

Signature

I sign this Advance Health Care Directive, consisting of the following sections, **which I have initialed below and have elected to adopt:**

[   ] Living Will
[   ] Selection of Health Care Agent (Health Care Proxy)
[   ] Designation of Primary Physician
[   ] Organ Donation

BY SIGNING HERE I INDICATE THAT I UNDERSTAND THE PURPOSE AND EFFECT OF THIS DOCUMENT.

Signature _____   Date _____

City, County, and State of Residence _____

Notary Acknowledgment

State of _____

County of _____

On _____ , _____ came before me personally and, under oath, stated that he or she is the person described in the above document and he or she signed the above document in my presence. I declare under penalty of perjury that the person whose name is subscribed to this instrument appears to be of sound mind and under no duress, fraud, or undue influence.

_____
Notary Public
My commission expires _____

Witness Acknowledgment

The declarant is personally known to me and I believe him or her to be of sound mind and under no duress, fraud, or undue influence. I did not sign the declarant's signature above and I am not appointed as the health care agent or attorney-in-fact. I am at least eighteen (19) years of age and I am not related to the declarant by blood, adoption, or marriage, nor entitled to any portion of the estate. I am not directly financially responsible for declarant's medical care. I am not a health care provider of the declarant or an employee of the health facility in which the declarant is a patient.

Witness Signature _____ Date _____

Printed Name of Witness _____

Second Witness Signature _____ Date _____

Printed Name of Second Witness _____

Signature of First Choice for Health Care Proxy

I, _____, am willing to serve as the health care proxy.

Proxy Signature: _____ Date: _____

Signature of Second Choice for Health Care Proxy:

I, _____, am willing to serve as the health care proxy if the first choice cannot serve.

Proxy Signature: _____ Date: _____

Alaska Advance Health Care Directive

On this date of _____ , I, _____ , do hereby sign, execute, and adopt the following as my Advance Health Care Directive. I direct any and all persons or entities involved with my health care in any manner that these decisions are my wishes and were adopted without duress or force and of my own free will.

I have placed my initials next to the sections of this Directive that I have adopted:

[   ] Living Will (Instructions for Health Care)
[   ] Selection of Health Care Agent (Durable Power of Attorney for Health Care Decisions)
[   ] Designation of Primary Physician
[   ] Organ Donation

Living Will (Instructions For Health Care)

If you are satisfied to allow the person that you select later in this document as your health care agent to determine what is best for you in making health care decisions, you do not need to fill out this part of the form. If you do fill out this part of the form, you may strike any wording you do not want. There is a state protocol that governs the use of do not resuscitate orders by physicians and other health care providers. You may obtain a copy of the protocol from the Alaska Department of Health and Social Services. A 'do not resuscitate order' means a directive from a licensed physician that emergency cardiopulmonary resuscitation should not be administered to you.

END-OF-LIFE DECISIONS. Except to the extent prohibited by law, I direct that my health care providers and others involved in my care provide, withhold, or withdraw treatment in accordance with the choice I have marked below: **(Initial only one box.)**

[   ] Choice To Prolong Life: I want my life to be prolonged as long as possible within the limits of generally accepted health care standards; OR

[   ] Choice Not To Prolong Life: I want comfort care only and I do not want my life to be prolonged with medical treatment if, in the judgment of my physician, I have **(check all choices that represent your wishes)**

   [   ] a condition of permanent unconsciousness: a condition that, to a high degree of medical certainty, will last permanently without improvement; in which, to a high degree of medical certainty, thought, sensation, purposeful action, social interaction, and awareness of myself and the environment are absent; and for which, to a high degree of medical certainty, initiating or continuing life-sustaining procedures for me, in light of my medical outcome, will provide only minimal medical benefit for me; or

   [   ] a terminal condition: an incurable or irreversible illness or injury that without the administration of life-sustaining procedures will result in my death in a short period of time, for which there is no reasonable prospect of cure or recovery, that imposes severe pain or otherwise imposes an inhumane burden on me, and for which, in light of my medical condition, initiating or continuing life-sustaining procedures will provide only minimal medical benefit;

[   ] Additional instructions:

Artificial Nutrition and Hydration. If I am unable to safely take nutrition, fluids, or nutrition and fluids **(Initial your choices and/or write your instructions)**.

[   ] I wish to receive artificial nutrition and hydration indefinitely;

[   ] I wish to receive artificial nutrition and hydration indefinitely, unless it clearly increases my suffering and is no longer in my best interest;

[   ] I wish to receive artificial nutrition and hydration on a limited trial basis to see if I can improve;

[   ] In accordance with my choices above, I do not wish to receive artificial nutrition and hydration.

[   ] Other instructions:

Relief from Pain. **(Initial your choices and/or write your instructions)**.

[   ] I direct that adequate treatment be provided at all times for the sole purpose of the alleviation of pain or discomfort; or

[   ] I give these instructions:

(Write your instructions if applicable). Should I become unconscious and I am pregnant, I direct that:

OTHER WISHES. (If you do not agree with any of the optional choices above and wish to write your own, or if you wish to add to the instructions you have given above, you may do so here.)
I direct that

Conditions or limitations:

(Add additional sheets if needed.)

Selection of Health Care Agent
(Durable Power of Attorney for Health Care Decisions)

DESIGNATION OF AGENT: I designate the following individual as my agent to make health care decisions for me:

_____ (name of individual you choose as agent)

_____ (address)

_____ (home telephone) (work telephone)

OPTIONAL - DESIGNATION OF ALTERNATE AGENT: If I revoke my agent's authority or if my agent is not willing, able, or reasonably available to make a health care decision for me, I designate as my first alternate agent

_____ (name of individual you choose as first alternate agent)

_____ (address)

_____ (home telephone) (work telephone)

OPTIONAL - DESIGNATION OF SECOND ALTERNATE AGENT: If I revoke the authority of my agent and first alternate agent or if neither is willing, able, or reasonably available to make a health care decision for me, I designate as my second alternate agent

_____ (name of individual you choose as second alternate agent)

_____ (address)

_____ (home telephone) (work telephone)

AGENT'S AUTHORITY. My agent is authorized and directed to follow my individual instructions and my other wishes to the extent known to the agent in making all health care decisions for me. If these are not known, my agent is authorized to make these decisions in accordance with my best interest, including decisions to provide, withhold, or withdraw artificial hydration and nutrition and other forms of health care to keep me alive, except as I state here:

(Add additional sheets if needed.)

Under this authority, 'best interest' means that the benefits to you resulting from a treatment outweigh the burdens to you resulting from that treatment after assessing
(1) the effect of the treatment on your physical, emotional, and cognitive functions; and
(2) the degree of physical pain or discomfort caused to you by the treatment or the withholding or withdrawal of the treatment; and
(3) the degree to which your medical condition, the treatment, or the withholding or withdrawal of treatment, results in a severe and continuing impairment; and
(4) the effect of the treatment on your life expectancy; and
(5) your prognosis for recovery, with and without the treatment; and
(6) the risks, side effects, and benefits of the treatment or the withholding of treatment; and
(7) your religious beliefs and basic values, to the extent that these may assist in determining benefits and burdens.

WHEN AGENT'S AUTHORITY BECOMES EFFECTIVE. Except in the case of mental illness, my agent's authority becomes effective when my primary physician determines that I am unable to make my own health care decisions unless I mark the following box. In the case of mental illness, unless I mark the following box, my agent's authority becomes effective when a court determines I am unable to make my own decisions, or, in an emergency, if my primary physician or another health care provider determines I am unable to make my own decisions. If I mark this box, my agent's authority to make health care decisions for me takes effect immediately.

AGENT'S OBLIGATION. My agent shall make health care decisions for me in accordance with this durable power of attorney for health care, AND any instructions I give in my living will portion of this form, and my other wishes to the extent known to my agent. To the extent my wishes are unknown, my agent shall make health care decisions for me in accordance with what my agent determines to be in my best interest. In determining my best interest, my agent shall consider my personal values to the extent known to my agent.

NOMINATION OF GUARDIAN. If a guardian of my person needs to be appointed for me by a court, I nominate the agent designated in this form. If that agent is not willing, able, or reasonably available to act as guardian, I nominate the alternate agents whom I have named above, in the order designated.

Designation of Primary Physician

I designate the following physician as my primary physician: _____ (name)
_____ (address)
_____ (phone).

OPTIONAL- DESIGNATION OF ALTERNATE PRIMARY PHYSICIAN: If the physician I have designated above is not willing, able, or reasonably available to act as my primary physician, I designate the following physician as my primary physician:
_____ (name)
_____ (address)
_____ (phone).

Organ Donation

In the event of my death, I have placed my initials next to the following part(s) of my body that I wish donated for the purposes **that I have initialed below:**

[   ] any organs or parts **OR**
[   ] eyes   [   ] bone and connective tissue   [   ] skin
[   ] heart   [   ] kidney(s)   [   ] liver
[   ] lung(s)   [   ] pancreas   [   ] other _____

for the purposes of:
[   ] any purpose authorized by law **OR**
[   ] transplantation   [   ] research   [   ] therapy
[   ] medical education   [   ] other limitations _____

Signature

I sign this Advance Health Care Directive, consisting of the following sections, **which I have initialed below and have elected to adopt:**

[   ] Living Will (Instructions for Health Care)
[   ] Selection of Health Care Agent (Durable Power of Attorney for Health Care Decisions)
[   ] Designation of Primary Physician
[   ] Organ Donation

BY SIGNING HERE I INDICATE THAT I UNDERSTAND THE PURPOSE AND EFFECT OF THIS DOCUMENT.

Signature _____   Date _____

City, County, and State of Residence _____

Notary Acknowledgment

State of _____

County of _____

On _____ , _____ came before me personally and, under oath, stated that he or she is the person described in the above document and he or she signed the above document in my presence. I declare under penalty of perjury that the person whose name is subscribed to this instrument appears to be of sound mind and under no duress, fraud, or undue influence.

_____
Notary Public
My commission expires _____

Witness Acknowledgment

The declarant is personally known to me and I believe him or her to be of sound mind and under no duress, fraud, or undue influence. I did not sign the declarant's signature above and I am not appointed as the health care agent or attorney-in-fact. I am at least eighteen (18) years of age and I am not related to the declarant by blood, adoption, or marriage, entitled to any portion of the estate of the declarant, or directly financially responsible for declarant's medical care. I am not a health care provider of the declarant or an employee of the health facility in which the declarant is a patient.

Witness Signature _____ Date _____

Printed Name of Witness _____

Second Witness Signature _____ Date _____

Printed Name of Second Witness _____

Acceptance of Health Care Agent(s) and Attorney(s)-in-Fact for Health Care Decisions.

I accept my appointment as Health Care Agent and Attorney-in-Fact for Health Care Decisions:

Signature of Agent _____ Date _____

Signature of First Alternate Agent _____ Date _____

Signature of Second Alternate Agent _____ Date _____

Arizona Advance Health Care Directive

On this date of _____ , I, _____ , do hereby sign, execute, and adopt the following as my Advance Health Care Directive. I direct any and all persons or entities involved with my health care in any manner that these decisions are my wishes and were adopted without duress or force and of my own free will.

I have placed my initials next to the sections of this Directive that I have adopted:

[   ]   Living Will
[   ]   Selection of Health Care Agent (Health Care Power of Attorney)
[   ]   Designation of Primary Physician
[   ]   Organ Donation

Living Will

Some general statements concerning your health care options are outlined below. If you agree with one of the statements, you should *initial* that statement. Read all of these statements carefully before you initial your selection. You can also write your own statement concerning life-sustaining treatment and other matters relating to your health care. **You may initial any combination of paragraphs (1), (2), (3), and (4), but if you initial paragraph (5), the others should not be initialed.**

[   ]   1. If I have a terminal condition I do NOT want my life to be prolonged and I do NOT want life-sustaining treatment, beyond comfort care, that would serve only to artificially delay the moment of my death.

[   ]   2. If I am in a terminal condition or an irreversible coma or a persistent vegetative state that my doctors reasonably feel to be irreversible or incurable, I DO want the medical treatment necessary to provide care that would keep me comfortable, but I do NOT want the following **(Initial your choices, if desired):**

       [   ] (a) Cardiopulmonary resuscitation, for example, the use of drugs, electric shock, and artificial breathing.
       [   ] (b) Artificially-administered food and fluids.
       [   ] (c) To be taken to a hospital if at all avoidable.

[   ]   3. Notwithstanding my other directions, if I am known to be pregnant, I do NOT want life-sustaining treatment withheld or withdrawn if it is possible that the embryo/fetus will develop to the point of live birth with the continued application of life-sustaining treatment.

[   ]   4. Notwithstanding my other directions, I DO want the use of all medical care necessary to treat my condition until my doctors reasonably conclude that my condition is terminal or is irreversible and incurable or I am in a persistent vegetative state.

[   ]   5. I want my life to be prolonged to the greatest extent possible.

Other or Additional Statements of Desires **(add other statements, if any. If none, state "none"):**

Selection of Health Care Agent (Health Care Power of Attorney)

I designate _____ (name),
of _____ (address), as
my agent for all matters relating to my health care, including, without limitation, full power to give or refuse consent to all medical, surgical, hospital, and related health care. This power of attorney is effective on my inability to make or communicate health care decisions. All of my agent's actions under this power during any period when I am unable to make or communicate health care decisions or when there is uncertainty whether I am dead or alive have the same effect on my heirs, devisees and personal representatives as if I were alive, competent, and acting for myself
(Initial your choice):

I have [   ] **OR**   I have NOT [   ] completed and attached a living will for purposes of providing specific direction to my agent in situations that may occur during any period when I am unable to make or communicate health care decisions or after my death. My agent is directed to implement those choices I have initialed in the living will.

This health care directive is made under Section 36-3221, Arizona Revised Statutes, and continues in effect for all who may rely on it except those to whom I have given notice of its revocation.

Designation of Primary Physician

I designate the following physician as my primary physician: _____ (name)
_____ (address)
_____ (phone).

OPTIONAL- DESIGNATION OF ALTERNATE PRIMARY PHYSICIAN: If the physician I have designated above is not willing, able, or reasonably available to act as my primary physician, I designate the following physician as my primary physician:
_____ (name)
_____ (address)
_____ (phone).

Organ Donation

Under Arizona law, you may make a gift of all or part of your body to a bank or storage facility or a hospital, physician or medical or dental school for transplantation, therapy, medical or dental evaluation or research or for the advancement of medical or dental science. You may also authorize your agent to do so or a member of your family may make a gift unless you give them notice that you do not want a gift made. In the space below you may make a gift yourself or state that you do not want to make a gift. If you do not complete this section, your agent will have the authority to make a gift of a part of your body pursuant to law. Note: The donation elections you make in this health care power of attorney survive your death. If any of the statements below reflects your desire, initial on the line next to that statement. You do not have to initial any of the statements. If you do not check any of the statements, your agent and your family will have the authority to make a gift of all or part of your body under Arizona law. **(Initial your choice, if desired):**

_____ I do not want to make an organ or tissue donation and I do not want my agent or family to do so.

_____ I have already signed a written agreement or donor card regarding organ and tissue donation with the following individual or institution: _____

_____ Pursuant to Arizona law, in the event of my death, I have placed my initials next to the following part(s) of my body that I wish donated for the purposes **that I have initialed below:**

[   ] any organs or parts **OR**
[   ] eyes   [   ] bone and connective tissue   [   ] skin
[   ] heart   [   ] kidney(s)   [   ] liver
[   ] lung(s)   [   ] pancreas   [   ]other _____

for the purposes of:
[   ] any purpose authorized by law **OR**
[   ] transplantation   [   ] research   [   ] therapy
[   ] medical education   [   ] other limitations _____

Signature

I sign this Advance Health Care Directive, consisting of the following sections, **which I have initialed below and have elected to adopt:**

[   ]   Living Will
[   ]   Selection of Health Care Agent (Health Care Power of Attorney)
[   ]   Designation of Primary Physician
[   ]   Organ Donation

BY SIGNING HERE I INDICATE THAT I UNDERSTAND THE PURPOSE AND EFFECT OF THIS DOCUMENT.

Signature _____   Date _____

City, County, and State of Residence _____

Notary Acknowledgment

State of _____

County of _____

On _____ , _____ came before me personally and, under oath, stated that he or she is the person described in the above document and he or she signed the above document in my presence. I declare under penalty of perjury that the person whose name is subscribed to this instrument appears to be of sound mind and under no duress, fraud, or undue influence.

_____
Notary Public
My commission expires _____

Witness Acknowledgment

The declarant has been personally known to me and I believe him or her to be of sound mind. I did not sign the declarant's signature above for or at the direction of the declarant and I am not appointed as the health care proxy or attorney-in-fact therein. I am at least eighteen (18) years of age and I am not related to the declarant by blood, adoption, or marriage, entitled to any portion of the estate of the declarant according to the laws of intestate succession or under any will of declarant or codicil thereto, or directly financially responsible for declarant's medical care.

Witness Signature _____ Date _____

Printed Name of Witness _____

Second Witness Signature _____ Date _____

Printed Name of Second Witness _____

Acceptance of Health Care Agent and Attorney-in-Fact for Health Care

I accept my appointment as Health Care Agent and Attorney-in-Fact for Health Care.

Signature _____ Date _____

Arkansas Advance Health Care Directive

On this date of _____ , I, _____ , do hereby sign, execute, and adopt the following as my Advance Health Care Directive. I direct any and all persons or entities involved with my health care in any manner that these decisions are my wishes and were adopted without duress or force and of my own free will.

I have placed my initials next to the sections of this Directive that I have adopted:

[   ] Living Will Declaration
[   ] Selection of Health Care Agent (Durable Power of Attorney for Health Care)
[   ] Designation of Primary Physician
[   ] Organ Donation

Living Will Declaration

If I should have an incurable or irreversible condition that will cause my death within a relatively short time, and I am no longer able to make decisions regarding my medical treatment, **OR** if I should become permanently unconscious, I direct my attending physician, pursuant to the Arkansas Rights of the Terminally Ill or Permanently Unconscious Act **(initial your choices):**

[   ] to withhold or withdraw treatment that only prolongs the process of dying and is not necessary to my comfort or to alleviate pain.

     [   ] It is my specific directive that nutrition may be withheld after consultation with my attending physician. OR

     [   ] It is my specific directive that nutrition may not be withheld.

     [   ] It is my specific directive that hydration may be withheld after consultation with my attending physician. OR

     [   ] It is my specific directive that hydration may not be withheld.

Other directions **(add any additional directions)**

I direct my attending physician, pursuant to the Arkansas Rights of the Terminally Ill or Permanently Unconscious Act **(initial if chosen):**

[   ] to follow the instructions of _____ (name), whom I appoint below as my Health Care Attorney-in-Fact to decide whether life-sustaining treatment should be withheld or withdrawn.

Pursuant to state law: A physician or other health care provider who is furnished a copy of the declaration shall make it a part of the declarant's medical record and, if unwilling to comply with the declaration, promptly so advise the declarant. In the case of a qualified patient, the patient's health care attorney-in-fact, in consultation with the attending physician, shall have the authority to make treatment decisions for the patient including the withholding or withdrawal of life-sustaining procedures.

Selection of Health Care Agent
(Durable Power of Attorney for Health Care)

I hereby appoint _____ (name), of _____ (address), as my health care agent to make any and all health care decisions for me, except to the extent that I state otherwise. This Durable Power of Attorney for Health Care shall take effect in the event I become unable to make my own health care decisions. My health care agent and any alternate health care agent shall have the authority to make all health care decisions regarding any care, treatment, service, or procedure to maintain, diagnose, treat, or provide for my physical or mental health or personal care. My health care agent and any alternate agent shall also have the authority to make decisions regarding the providing, withholding, or withdrawing of life-sustaining treatment pursuant to the Arkansas Rights of the Terminally Ill or Permanently Unconscious Act.

Optional Instructions **(insert any additional instructions):**

Designation of Primary Physician

I designate the following physician as my primary physician: _____ (name)
_____ (address)
_____ (phone).

OPTIONAL- DESIGNATION OF ALTERNATE PRIMARY PHYSICIAN: If the physician I have designated above is not willing, able, or reasonably available to act as my primary physician, I designate the following physician as my primary physician:
_____ (name)
_____ (address)
_____ (phone).

Organ Donation

In the event of my death, I have placed my initials next to the following part(s) of my body that I wish donated for the purposes **that I have initialed below**:

[   ] any organs or parts **OR**

[   ] eyes   [   ] bone and connective tissue   [   ] skin

[   ] heart   [   ] kidney(s)   [   ] liver

[   ] lung(s)   [   ] pancreas   [   ] other _____

for the purposes of:

[   ] any purpose authorized by law **OR**

[   ] transplantation   [   ] research   [   ] therapy

[   ] medical education   [   ] other limitations _____

Signature

I sign this Advance Health Care Directive, consisting of the following sections, **which I have initialed below and have elected to adopt**:

[   ]   Living Will Declaration

[   ]   Selection of Health Care Agent (Durable Power of Attorney for Health Care)

[   ]   Designation of Primary Physician

[   ]   Organ Donation

BY SIGNING HERE I INDICATE THAT I UNDERSTAND THE PURPOSE AND EFFECT OF THIS DOCUMENT.

Signature _____ Date _____

City, County, and State of Residence _____

Notary Acknowledgment

State of _____

County of _____

On _____ , _____ came before me personally and, under oath, stated that he or she is the person described in the above document and he or she signed the above document in my presence. I declare under penalty of perjury that the person whose name is subscribed to this instrument appears to be of sound mind and under no duress, fraud, or undue influence.

_____

Notary Public

My commission expires _____

Witness Acknowledgment

The declarant is personally known to me and I believe him or her to be of sound mind and under no duress, fraud, or undue influence. I did not sign the declarant's signature above and I am not appointed as the health care agent or attorney-in-fact herein. I am at least eighteen (18) years of age and I am not related to the declarant by blood, adoption, or marriage, entitled to any portion of the estate of the declarant, or directly financially responsible for declarant's medical care. I am not a health care provider of the declarant or an employee of the health facility in which the declarant is a patient.

Witness Signature _____ Date _____

Printed Name of Witness _____

Second Witness Signature _____ Date _____

Printed Name of Second Witness _____

Acceptance of Health Care Agent and Attorney-in-Fact for Health Care

I accept my appointment as Health Care Agent and Attorney-in-Fact for Health Care.

Signature _____ Date _____

California Advance Health Care Directive

On this date of _____ , I, _____ , do hereby sign, execute, and adopt the following as my Advance Health Care Directive. I direct any and all persons or entities involved with my health care in any manner that these decisions are my wishes and were adopted without duress or force and of my own free will.

I have placed my initials next to the sections of this Directive that I have adopted:

[   ]   Living Will (Instructions for Health Care)
[   ]   Selection of Health Care Agent (Power of Attorney for Health Care)
[   ]   Designation of Primary Physician
[   ]   Organ Donation

You have the right to give instructions about your own health care. You also have the right to name someone else to make health care decisions for you. This form lets you do either or both of these things. It also lets you express your wishes regarding donation of organs and the designation of your primary physician. If you use this form, you may complete or modify all or any part of it. You are free to use a different form.

PART 1 of this form lets you give specific instructions about any aspect of your health care, whether or not you appoint an agent. Choices are provided for you to express your wishes regarding the provision, withholding, or withdrawal of treatment to keep you alive, as well as the provision of pain relief. Space is provided for you to add to the choices you have made or for you to write out any additional wishes.

PART 2 of this form is a Power of Attorney for Health Care. Part 2 lets you name another individual as agent to make health care decisions for you if you become incapable of making your own decisions or if you want someone else to make those decisions for you now even though you are still capable. (Your agent may not be an operator or employee of a community care facility or a residential care facility where you are receiving care, or your supervising health care provider or employee of the health care institution where you are receiving care, unless your agent is related to you or is a co-worker.) Unless the form you sign limits the authority of your agent, your agent may make all health care decisions for you. This form has a place for you to limit the authority of your agent. You need not limit the authority of your agent if you wish to rely on your agent for all health care decisions that may have to be made. If you choose not to limit the authority of your agent, your agent will have the right to:

> (1) Consent or refuse consent to any care, treatment, service, or procedure to maintain, diagnose, or otherwise affect a physical or mental condition;
> (2) Select or discharge health care providers and institutions;
> (3) Approve or disapprove diagnostic tests, surgical procedures, and programs of medication;
> (4) Direct the provision, withholding, or withdrawal of artificial nutrition and hydration and all other forms of health care, including cardiopulmonary resuscitation; and
> (5) Make anatomical gifts, authorize an autopsy, and direct the disposition of your remains.

PART 3 of this form lets you designate a physician to have primary responsibility for your health care.

PART 4 of this form lets you express an intention to donate your bodily organs and tissues following your death.

After completing this form, sign and date the form at the end. The form must be signed by two (2) qualified witnesses or acknowledged before a notary public. Give a copy of the signed and completed form to your physician, any other health care providers you may have, any health care institution at which you are receiving care, and any health care agents you have named. You should talk to the person you have named as agent to make sure that he or she understands your wishes and is willing to take the responsibility. You have the right to revoke this advance health care directive or replace this form at any time.

Part 1: Living Will (Instructions for Health Care)

If you fill out this part of the form, you may strike any wording you do not want.

END-OF-LIFE DECISIONS: I direct that my health care providers and others involved in my care provide, withhold, or withdraw treatment in accordance with the choice I have marked below **(initial only one of the following two boxes):**

[   ] **Choice NOT To Prolong Life**. I do NOT want my life to be prolonged if:
(i) I have an incurable and irreversible condition that will result in my death within a relatively short time,
(ii) I become unconscious and, to a reasonable degree of medical certainty, I will not regain consciousness, **OR**
(iii) the likely risks and burdens of treatment would outweigh the expected benefits, **OR**

[   ] **Choice TO Prolong Life.** I DO want my life to be prolonged as long as possible within the limits of generally-accepted health care standards.

RELIEF FROM PAIN **(initial below if this is your choice):**

[   ] Except as I state in the following space, I direct that treatment for alleviation of pain or discomfort should be provided at all times even if it hastens my death.
(add exceptions and additional sheets as needed):

OTHER WISHES: (If you do not agree with any of the optional choices above and wish to write your own, or if you wish to add to the instructions you have given above, you may do so here. Add additional sheets if needed.)

I direct that:

Part 2: Selection of Health Care Agent
(Power of Attorney for Health Care)

DESIGNATION OF AGENT: I designate the following individual as my agent to make health care decisions for me: _____ (name) of _____ (address).

AGENT'S AUTHORITY: My agent is authorized to make all health care decisions for me, including decisions to provide, withhold, or withdraw artificial nutrition and hydration, and all other forms of healthcare to keep me alive, except as I state here **(add additional sheets if needed):**

WHEN AGENT'S AUTHORITY BECOMES EFFECTIVE: My agent's authority becomes effective when my primary physician determines that I am unable to make my own health care decisions unless I *initial* the following box. **If I initial this box** [   ], my agent's authority to make health care decisions for me takes effect immediately.

AGENT'S OBLIGATION: My agent shall make health care decisions for me in accordance with this power of attorney for health care, any instructions I give in Part 1 of this form, and my other wishes to the extent known to my agent. To the extent my wishes are unknown, my agent shall make health care decisions for me in accordance with what my agent determines to be in my best interest. In determining my best interest, my agent shall consider my personal values to the extent known to my agent.

AGENT'S POSTDEATH AUTHORITY: My agent is authorized to make anatomical gifts, authorize an autopsy, and direct disposition of my remains, except as I state here or in Part 4 of this form **(insert exceptions and additional sheets if needed):**

NOMINATION OF CONSERVATOR: If a conservator of my person needs to be appointed for me by a court, I nominate the agent designated in this form.

Part 3: Designation of Primary Physician

I designate the following physician as my primary physician: _____ (name)

_____ (address)

_____ (phone).

OPTIONAL- DESIGNATION OF ALTERNATE PRIMARY PHYSICIAN: If the physician I have designated above is not willing, able, or reasonably available to act as my primary physician, I designate the following physician as my primary physician:

_____ (name)

_____ (address)

_____ (phone).

Part 4: Organ Donation

In the event of my death, I have placed my initials next to the following part(s) of my body that I wish donated for the purposes **that I have initialed below:**

[   ] any organs or parts **OR**

[ ] eyes	[ ] bone and connective tissue	[ ] skin
[ ] heart	[ ] kidney(s)	[ ] liver
[ ] lung(s)	[ ] pancreas	[ ] other _____

for the purposes of:

[   ] any purpose authorized by law **OR**

[ ] transplantation	[ ] research	[ ] therapy
[ ] medical education	[ ] other limitations _____	

Signature

I sign this Advance Health Care Directive, consisting of the following sections, **which I have initialed below and have elected to adopt:**

[   ]   Living Will (Instructions for Health Care)

[   ]   Selection of Health Care Agent (Power of Attorney for Health Care)

[   ]   Designation of Primary Physician

[   ]   Organ Donation

BY SIGNING HERE I INDICATE THAT I UNDERSTAND THE PURPOSE AND EFFECT OF THIS DOCUMENT.

Signature _____   Date _____

City, County, and State of Residence _____

Notary Acknowledgment

State of _____

County of _____

On _____ , _____ came before me personally and, under oath, stated that he or she is the person described in the above document and he or she signed the above document in my presence. I declare under penalty of perjury that the person whose name is subscribed to this instrument appears to be of sound mind and under no duress, fraud, or undue influence.

_____
Notary Public
My commission expires _____

Witness Acknowledgment

Witness #1 Statement: I declare under penalty of perjury under the laws of California that:
(1) the individual who signed or acknowledged this advance health care directive is personally known to me, or that the individual's identity was proven to me by convincing evidence;
(2) the individual signed or acknowledged this advance directive in my presence;
(3) the individual appears to be of sound mind and under no duress, fraud, or undue influence;
(4) I am not a person appointed as an agent by this advance directive; and
(5) I am at least eighteen (18) years of age and I am not the individual's health care provider, an employee of the individual's health care provider, the operator of a community care facility, an employee of an operator of a community care facility, the operator of a residential care facility for the elderly, or an employee of an operator of a residential care facility for the elderly.

Signature of Witness _____ Date _____

Printed Name of Witness _____

Witness #2 Statement: I declare under penalty of perjury under the laws of California that:
(1) the individual who signed or acknowledged this advance health care directive is personally known to me, or that the individual's identity was proven to me by convincing evidence;
(2) the individual signed or acknowledged this advance directive in my presence;
(3) the individual appears to be of sound mind and under no duress, fraud, or undue influence;
(4) I am not a person appointed as an agent by this advance directive; and
(5) I am not the individual's health care provider, an employee of the individual's health care provider, the operator of a community care facility, an employee of an operator of a community care facility, the operator of a residential care facility for the elderly, nor an employee of an operator of a residential care facility for the elderly.
I further declare under penalty of perjury under the laws of California that I am at least eighteen (18) years of age and I am not related to the individual executing this advance health care directive

by blood, marriage, or adoption, and, to the best of my knowledge, am not entitled to any part of the individual's estate upon his or her death under a will now existing or by operation of law.

Second Witness Signature _____ Date _____

Printed Name of Second Witness _____

Special Witness Requirement: The following statement is required only if you are a patient in a skilled nursing facility--a health care facility that provides the following basic services: skilled nursing care and supportive care to patients whose primary need is for availability of skilled nursing care on an extended basis. The patient advocate or ombudsman must sign the following statement:

Statement of Patient Advocate or Ombudsman: I declare under penalty of perjury under the laws of California that I am a patient advocate or ombudsman as designated by the State Department of Aging and that I am serving as a witness as required by Section 4675 of the Probate Code.

Special Witness Signature _____ Date _____

Printed Name and Title of Special Witness _____

Acceptance of Health Care Agent and Attorney-in-Fact for Health Care

I accept my appointment as Health Care Agent and Attorney-in-Fact for Health Care.

Signature _____ Date _____

Colorado Advance Health Care Directive

On this date of _____ , I, _____ , do hereby sign, execute, and adopt the following as my Advance Health Care Directive. I direct any and all persons or entities involved with my health care in any manner that these decisions are my wishes and were adopted without duress or force and of my own free will.

I have placed my signature next to the sections of this Directive that I have adopted:

[   ] Living Will (Declaration as to Medical or Surgical Treatment)
[   ] Selection of Health Care Agent (Medical Durable Power of Attorney for Health Care)
[   ] Designation of Primary Physician
[   ] Organ Donation

Living Will (Declaration as to Medical or Surgical Treatment)

I, being of sound mind and at least eighteen (18) years of age, direct that my life shall not be artificially-prolonged under the circumstances set forth below and hereby declare that:

(1) If at any time my attending physician and one (1) other qualified physician certify in writing that:

> (a) I have an injury, disease, or illness which is not curable or reversible and which, in their judgment, is a terminal condition, and
>
> (b) For a period of seven (7) consecutive days or more, I have been unconscious, comatose, or otherwise incompetent so as to be unable to make or communicate responsible decisions concerning my person, then:

I direct that, in accordance with Colorado law, life-sustaining procedures shall be withdrawn and withheld pursuant to the terms of this declaration, it being understood that life-sustaining procedures shall not include any medical procedure or intervention for nourishment considered necessary by the attending physician to provide comfort or alleviate pain. However, I may specifically direct, in accordance with Colorado law, that artificial nourishment be withdrawn or withheld pursuant to the terms of this declaration.

(2) In the event that the only procedure I am being provided is artificial nourishment, I direct that one of the following actions be taken (**initial your choice**):

[   ] (a) Artificial nourishment SHALL NOT be continued when it is the only procedure being provided; **OR**

[   ] (b) Artificial nourishment SHALL be continued for _____ days when it is the only procedure being provided; **OR**

[   ] (c) Artificial nourishment SHALL be continued when it is the only procedure being provided.

Selection of Health Care Agent
(Medical Durable Power of Attorney for Health Care)

I hereby appoint _____ (name),
of _____ (address),
as my agent to make health care decisions for me if and when I am unable to make my own health care decisions. This gives my agent the power to consent to giving, withholding, or stopping any health care, treatment, service, or diagnostic procedure. My agent also has the authority to talk with health care personnel, get information, and sign forms necessary to carry out those decisions.

By this document I intend to create a Medical Durable Power of Attorney which shall take effect upon my incapacity to make my own health care decisions and shall continue during that incapacity. My agent shall make health care decisions as I may direct below or as I make known to him or her in some other way. If I have not expressed a choice about the health care in question, my agent shall base his or her decisions on what he or she believes to be in my best interest.

(1) Statement of desires concerning life-prolonging care, treatment, services, and procedures **(insert your wishes. Attach additional sheets if necessary)**:

(2) Special provisions and limitations **(add any provisions and limitations):**

Designation of Primary Physician

I designate the following physician as my primary physician: _____ (name)
_____ (address)
_____ (phone).

OPTIONAL- DESIGNATION OF ALTERNATE PRIMARY PHYSICIAN: If the physician I have designated above is not willing, able, or reasonably available to act as my primary physician, I designate the following physician as my primary physician:
_____ (name)
_____ (address)
_____ (phone).

Organ Donation

In the event of my death, I have placed my initials next to the following part(s) of my body that I wish donated for the purposes **that I have initialed below:**

[   ] any organs or parts **OR**

[   ] eyes   [   ] bone and connective tissue   [   ] skin

[   ] heart   [   ] kidney(s)   [   ] liver

[   ] lung(s)   [   ] pancreas   [   ] other _____

for the purposes of:

[   ] any purpose authorized by law **OR**

[   ] transplantation   [   ] research   [   ] therapy

[   ] medical education   [   ] other limitations _____

Signature

I sign this Advance Health Care Directive, consisting of the following sections, **which I have initialed below and have elected to adopt:**

[   ] Living Will (Declaration as to Medical or Surgical Treatment)

[   ] Selection of Health Care Agent (Medical Durable Power of Attorney for Health Care)

[   ] Designation of Primary Physician

[   ] Organ Donation

BY SIGNING HERE I INDICATE THAT I UNDERSTAND THE PURPOSE AND EFFECT OF THIS DOCUMENT.

Signature _____   Date _____

City, County, and State of Residence _____

Notary Acknowledgment

State of _____

County of _____

On _____ , _____ came before me personally and, under oath, stated that he or she is the person described in the above document and he or she signed the above document in my presence. I declare under penalty of perjury that the person whose name is subscribed to this instrument appears to be of sound mind and under no duress, fraud, or undue influence.

_____

Notary Public

My commission expires _____

Witness Acknowledgment

The declarant is personally known to me and I believe him or her to be of sound mind and under no duress, fraud, or undue influence. I did not sign the declarant's signature above for or at the direction of the declarant and I am not appointed as the health care agent or attorney-in-fact herein. I am at least eighteen (18) years of age and I am not related to the declarant by blood, adoption, or marriage, entitled to any portion of the estate of the declarant according to the laws of intestate succession or under any will of declarant or codicil thereto, or directly financially responsible for declarant's medical care. I am not a health care provider of the declarant or an employee of the health facility in which the declarant is a patient.

Witness Signature _____ Date _____

Printed Name of Witness _____

Second Witness Signature _____ Date _____

Printed Name of Second Witness _____

Acceptance of Health Care Agent and Attorney-in-Fact for Health Care

I accept my appointment as Health Care Agent and Attorney-in-Fact for Health Care

Signature _____ Date _____

Connecticut Advance Health Care Directive

On this date of _____ , I, _____ , do hereby sign, execute, and adopt the following as my Advance Health Care Directive. I direct any and all persons or entities involved with my health care in any manner that these decisions are my wishes and were adopted without duress or force and of my own free will.

I have placed my initials next to the sections of this Directive that I have adopted:

[   ] Living Will (Document Concerning Withholding or Withdrawal of Life Support Systems)
[   ] Selection of My Health Care Agent (Attorney-in-Fact for Health Care Decisions)
[   ] Designation of Primary Physician
[   ] Organ Donation

NOTICE TO ANY ATTENDING PHYSICIAN: These are my health care instructions including those concerning the withholding or withdrawal of life support systems, together with the appointment of my health care agent and my attorney-in-fact for health care decisions, the designation of my conservator of the person for future incapacity and my document of anatomical gift. As my physician, you may rely on any decision made by my health care agent, attorney-in-fact for health care decisions or conservator of my person, if I am unable to make a decision for myself.

Living Will (Document Concerning Withholding or Withdrawal of Life Support Systems)

If the time comes when I am incapacitated to the point when I can no longer actively take part in decisions for my own life, and am unable to direct my physician as to my own medical care, I wish this statement to stand as a testament of my wishes.

I, the author of this document, request that, if my condition is deemed terminal or if I am determined to be permanently unconscious, I be allowed to die and not be kept alive through life support systems.

By terminal condition, I mean that I have an incurable or irreversible medical condition which, without the administration of life support systems, will, in the opinion of my attending physician, result in death within a relatively short time.

By permanently unconscious I mean that I am in a permanent coma or persistent vegetative state which is an irreversible condition in which I am at no time aware of myself or the environment and show no behavioral response to the environment.

The life support systems which I do not want include, but are not limited to: Artificial respiration, cardiopulmonary resuscitation, and artificial means of providing nutrition and hydration. I do want sufficient pain medication to maintain my physical comfort. I do not intend any direct taking of my life, but only that my dying not be unreasonably prolonged.

Selection of My Health Care Agent (Attorney-in-Fact for Health Care Decisions)

I appoint _____ (name),
of _____ (address),
to be my health care agent and attorney-in-fact for health care decisions. If my attending physician determines that I am unable to understand and appreciate the nature and consequences of health care decisions and am unable to reach and communicate an informed decision regarding treatment, my health care agent and attorney-in-fact for health care decisions is authorized to:

(1) Convey to my physician my wishes concerning the withholding or removal of life support systems;
(2) Take whatever actions are necessary to ensure that any wishes are given effect;
(3) Consent, refuse, or withdraw consent to any medical treatment as long as such action is consistent with my wishes concerning the withholding or removal of life support systems; and
(4) Consent to any medical treatment designed solely for the purpose of maintaining physical comfort.

If the above-appointed person is unable or unwilling to serve, I appoint the following person as my alternative health care agent and attorney-in-fact for health care decisions:
_____ (name)
_____ (address)

If a conservator of my person should need to be appointed, I designate that the person above whom I have designated as my initial health care agent and attorney-in-fact for health care decisions also be appointed my conservator. If that person is unwilling or unable to serve, I designate the person appointed as my alternative health care agent and attorney-in-fact for health care decisions.

Designation of Primary Physician

I designate the following physician as my primary physician: _____ (name)
_____ (address)
_____ (phone).

OPTIONAL- DESIGNATION OF ALTERNATE PRIMARY PHYSICIAN: If the physician I have designated above is not willing, able, or reasonably available to act as my primary physician, I designate the following physician as my primary physician:
_____ (name)
_____ (address)
_____ (phone).

Organ Donation

In the event of my death, I have placed my initials next to the following part(s) of my body that I wish donated for the purposes **that I have initialed below**:

[   ] any organs or parts **OR**

[   ] eyes   [   ] bone and connective tissue   [   ] skin

[   ] heart   [   ] kidney(s)   [   ] liver

[   ] lung(s)   [   ] pancreas   [   ] other _____

for the purposes of:

[   ] any purpose authorized by law **OR**

[   ] transplantation   [   ] research   [   ] therapy

[   ] medical education   [   ] other limitations _____

Signature

I sign this Advance Health Care Directive, consisting of the following sections, **which I have initialed below and have elected to adopt:**

[   ] Living Will (Document Concerning Withholding or Withdrawal of Life Support Systems)

[   ] Selection of My Health Care Agent (Attorney-in-Fact for Health Care Decisions)

[   ] Designation of Primary Physician

[   ] Organ Donation

BY SIGNING HERE I INDICATE THAT I UNDERSTAND THE PURPOSE AND EFFECT OF THIS DOCUMENT.

Signature _____   Date _____

City, County, and State of Residence _____

Witness Acknowledgment

We, the subscribing witnesses, being duly sworn, say that we witnessed the execution of these health care instructions, the appointments of a health care agent and an attorney-in-fact, the designation of a conservator for future incapacity, the designation of a primary physician, and a document of anatomical gift by the author of this document; that the author subscribed, published, and declared the same to be the author's instructions, appointments, and designation in our presence; that we thereafter subscribed the document as witnesses in the author's presence, at the author's request, and in the presence of each other; that at the time of the execution of said document the author appeared to us to be eighteen (18) years of age or older, of sound mind, able to understand the nature and consequences of said document, and under no improper influence, and we make this affidavit at the author's request. The author has been personally known to us and we believe him or her to be of sound mind. We did not sign the author's signature above for or at the direction of the author and we are not appointed as the health care agent or attorney-in-fact therein. We are not related to the author by blood, adoption, or marriage, entitled to any portion of the estate of the author according to the laws of intestate succession or under any will of author or codicil thereto, or directly financially responsible for author's medical care.

Witness Signature _____ Date _____

Printed Name of Witness _____

Second Witness Signature _____ Date _____

Printed Name of Second Witness _____

Notary Acknowledgment

State of _____

County of _____

On _____ , _____ came before me personally and, under oath, stated that he or she is the person described in the above document and he or she signed the above document in my presence. I declare under penalty of perjury that the person whose name is subscribed to this instrument appears to be of sound mind and under no duress, fraud, or undue influence.

Additionally, on the same date and time, the following persons as witnesses subscribed and were sworn to the above witness acknowledgement.

_____ , witness

_____ , witness

_____
Notary Public
My commission expires _____

Acceptance of Health Care Agent and Attorney-in-Fact For Health Care Decisions

I accept my appointment as Health Care Agent and Attorney-in-Fact for Health Care Decisions:

Signature _____ Date _____

Delaware Advance Health Care Directive

On this date of _____ , I, _____ , do hereby sign, execute, and adopt the following as my Advance Health Care Directive. I direct any and all persons or entities involved with my health care in any manner that these decisions are my wishes and were adopted without duress or force and of my own free will.

I have placed my initials next to the sections of this Directive that I have adopted:

[   ] Living Will (Instructions for Health Care)
[   ] Selection of Health Care Agent (Power of Attorney for Health Care)
[   ] Designation of Primary Physician
[   ] Organ Donation

You have the right to give instructions about your own health care. You also have the right to name someone else to make health-care decisions for you. This form lets you do either or both of these things. It also lets you express your wishes regarding anatomical gifts and the designation of your primary physician. If you use this form, you may complete or modify all or any part of it. You are free to use a different form.

Part 1 of this form lets you give specific instructions about any aspect of your health care. Choices are provided for you to express your wishes regarding the provision, withholding or withdrawal of treatment to keep you alive, including the provision of artificial nutrition and hydration as well as the provision of pain relief. Space is also provided for you to add to the choices you have made or for you to write out any additional instructions for other than end of life decisions.

Part 2 of this form is a power of attorney for health care. Part 2 lets you name another individual as agent to make health-care decisions for you if you become incapable of making your own decisions. You may also name an alternate agent to act for you if your first choice is not willing, able or reasonably available to make decisions for you. Unless related to you, an agent may not have a controlling interest in or be an operator or employee of a residential long-term health-care institution at which you are receiving care. If you do not have a qualifying condition (terminal illness/injury or permanent unconsciousness), your agent may make all health-care decisions for you except for decisions providing, withholding or withdrawing of a life sustaining procedure. Unless you limit the agent's authority, your agent will have the right to:

(a) Consent or refuse consent to any care, treatment, service or procedure to maintain, diagnose or otherwise affect a physical or mental condition unless it's a life-sustaining procedure or otherwise required by law.

(b) Select or discharge health-care providers and health-care institutions;
If you have a qualifying condition, your agent may make all health-care decisions for you, including, but not limited to:

(c) The decisions listed in (a) and (b).

(d) Consent or refuse consent to life sustaining procedures, such as, but not limited to, cardiopulmonary resuscitation and orders not to resuscitate.

(e) Direct the providing, withholding or withdrawal of artificial nutrition and hydration and all other forms of health care.

Part 3 of this form lets you designate a physician to have primary responsibility for your health care.

Part 4 of this form lets you express an intention to donate your bodily organs and tissues following your death.

After completing this form, sign and date the form at the end. It is required that 2 other individuals sign as witnesses. Give a copy of the signed and completed form to your physician, to any other health-care providers you may have, to any health-care institution at which you are receiving care and to any health-care agents you have named. You should talk to the person you have named as agent to make sure that the person understands your wishes and is willing to take the responsibility. You have the right to revoke this advance health-care directive or replace this form at any time.

Living Will (Instructions for Health Care)

If you are satisfied to allow your agent to determine what is best for you in making end-of-life decisions, you need not fill out this part of the form. If you do fill out this part of the form, you may strike any wording you do not want.

END-OF-LIFE DECISIONS: If I am in a qualifying condition, I direct that my health care providers and others involved in my care provide, withhold, or withdraw treatment in accordance with the choice I have marked below:

Choice NOT To Prolong Life. I do NOT want my life to be prolonged if **(initial all that apply)**:
[   ] (1) I have a terminal condition (an incurable condition caused by injury, disease, or illness which, to a reasonable degree of medical certainty, makes death imminent and from which, despite the application of life-sustaining procedures, there can be no recovery) and regarding artificial nutrition and hydration, I make the following specific directions **(please initial your choices):**
Artificial nutrition through a conduit:
           [   ] YES, I want it used, **OR**
           [   ] NO, I do NOT want it used

Hydration through a conduit:
           [   ] YES, I want it used, **OR**
           [   ] NO, I do NOT want it used

[   ] (2) I become permanently unconscious (a medical condition that has been diagnosed in accordance with currently-accepted medical standards that has lasted at least four (4) weeks and with reasonable medical certainty as total and irreversible loss of consciousness and capacity for interaction with the environment. The term includes, without limitation, a persistent vegetative state

or irreversible coma) and regarding artificial nutrition and hydration, I make the following specific directions (**please initial your choices**):

Artificial nutrition through a conduit:

[   ] YES, I want it used, **OR**

[   ] NO, I do NOT want it used

Hydration through a conduit:

[   ] YES, I want it used, **OR**

[   ] NO, I do NOT want it used

Choice TO Prolong Life. (Please initial if you choose):

[   ] I want my life TO be prolonged as long as possible within the limits of generally-accepted health care standards.

RELIEF FROM PAIN: Except as I state in the following space, I direct treatment for alleviation of pain or discomfort be provided at all times, even if it hastens my death (**insert exceptions and additional sheets if needed**):

OTHER MEDICAL INSTRUCTIONS: (**If you do not agree with any of the optional choices above and wish to write your own, or if you wish to add to the instructions you have given above, you may do so here. Add additional sheets if necessary.**) I direct that:

Selection of Health Care Agent
(Power of Attorney for Health Care)

DESIGNATION OF AGENT: I designate the following individual as my agent to make health care decisions for me _____ (name), of _____ (address).

OPTIONAL - DESIGNATION OF ALTERNATE AGENT: If I revoke my agent's authority or if my agent is not willing, able, or reasonably available to make a health care decision for me, I designate as my first alternate agent:

_____ (name of individual you choose as first alternate agent)

_____ (address)

AGENT'S AUTHORITY: If I am not in a qualifying condition, my agent is authorized to make all health care decisions for me, except decisions about life-sustaining procedures and as I state here; and if I am in a qualifying condition, my agent is authorized to make all health care decisions for me, except as I state here (**add additional sheets if necessary**):

WHEN AGENT'S AUTHORITY BECOMES EFFECTIVE: My agent's authority becomes effective when my primary physician determines I lack the capacity to make my own health care decisions. As to decisions concerning the providing, withholding, and withdrawal of life-sustaining procedures, my agent's authority becomes effective when my primary physician determines I lack the capacity to make my own health care decisions and my primary physician and another physician determine I am in a terminal condition or permanently unconscious.

AGENT'S OBLIGATION: My agent shall make health care decisions for me in accordance with this power of attorney for health care, any instructions I give in this form, and my other wishes to the extent known to my agent. To the extent my wishes are unknown, my agent shall make health care decisions for me in accordance with what my agent determines to be in my best interest. In determining my best interest, my agent shall consider my personal values to the extent known to my agent.

NOMINATION OF GUARDIAN: If a guardian of my person needs to be appointed for me by a court **(please initial one)**:
[   ] I nominate the agent whom I named in this form to act as guardian.
[   ] I nominate the following to be my guardian **(insert name and address)**:

_____ (name),
of _____ (address)

[   ] I do NOT nominate anyone to be my guardian.

Designation of Primary Physician

I designate the following physician as my primary physician: _____ (name)
_____ (address)
_____ (phone).

OPTIONAL- DESIGNATION OF ALTERNATE PRIMARY PHYSICIAN: If the physician I have designated above is not willing, able, or reasonably available to act as my primary physician, I designate the following physician as my primary physician:

_____ (name)
_____ (address)
_____ (phone).

Organ Donation

In the event of my death, I have placed my initials next to the following part(s) of my body that I wish donated for the purposes **that I have initialed below**:

[   ] any organs or parts **OR**

[ ] eyes	[ ] bone and connective tissue	[ ] skin
[ ] heart	[ ] kidney(s)	[ ] liver
[ ] lung(s)	[ ] pancreas	[ ] other _____

for the purposes of:

[   ] any purpose authorized by law **OR**
[   ] transplantation   [   ] research   [   ] therapy
[   ] medical education   [   ] other limitations _____

Signature

I sign this Advance Health Care Directive, consisting of the following sections, **which I have initialed below and have elected to adopt:**

[   ] Living Will (Instructions for Health Care)
[   ] Selection of Health Care Agent (Power of Attorney for Health Care)
[   ] Designation of Primary Physician
[   ] Organ Donation

BY SIGNING HERE I INDICATE THAT I UNDERSTAND THE PURPOSE AND EFFECT OF THIS DOCUMENT.

Signature _____ Date _____

City, County, and State of Residence _____

Notary Acknowledgment

State of _____
County of _____
On _____ , _____ came before me personally and, under oath, stated that he or she is the person described in the above document and he or she signed the above document in my presence. I declare under penalty of perjury that the person whose name is subscribed to this instrument appears to be of sound mind and under no duress, fraud, or undue influence.

_____
Notary Public
My commission expires _____

Witness Acknowledgment

STATEMENTS OF WITNESSES: SIGNED AND DECLARED by the above-named declarant as and for his or her written declaration under 16 Del. C. §§ 2502 and 2503, in our presence, who in his or her presence, at his or her request, and in the presence of each other, have hereunto subscribed our names as witnesses, and state that:

(1) The Declarant is mentally competent.

(2) Neither of the witnesses:
   (a) Is related to the declarant by blood, marriage, or adoption;
   (b) Is entitled to any portion of the estate of the declarant under any will of the declarant or codicil thereto then existing nor, at the time of the executing of the advance health care directive, is so entitled by operation of law then existing;
   (c) Has, at the time of the execution of the advance health care directive, a present or inchoate claim against any portion of the estate of the declarant;
   (d) Has a direct financial responsibility for the declarant's medical care;
   (e) Has a controlling interest in or is an operator or an employee of a residential long-term health care institution in which the declarant is a resident; **OR**
   (f) Is under eighteen (18) years of age.

(3) If the declarant is a resident of a sanitarium, rest home, nursing home, boarding home, or related institution, one of the witnesses, _____(name), is, at the time of the execution of the advance health care directive, a patient advocate or ombudsman designated by the Division of Services for Aging and Adults with Physical Disabilities, or the Public Guardian.

(4) Neither witness is prohibited by the above-noted requirements of Section 2503 of Title 16 of the Delaware Code from being a witness.

Witness Signature _____ Date _____

Printed Name of Witness _____

Second Witness Signature _____ Date _____

Printed Name of Second Witness _____

Acceptance of Health Care Agent and Attorney-in-Fact for Health Care

I accept my appointment as Health Care Agent and Attorney-in-Fact for Health Care.

Signature _____ Date _____

I accept my appointment as Alternative Health Care Agent and Attorney-in-Fact for Health Care.

Signature _____ Date _____

District of Columbia (Washington D.C.) Advance Health Care Directive

On this date of _____ , I, _____ , do hereby sign, execute, and adopt the following as my Advance Health Care Directive. I direct any and all persons or entities involved with my health care in any manner that these decisions are my wishes and were adopted without duress or force and of my own free will.

I have placed my initials next to the sections of this Directive that I have adopted:
[   ]   Living Will (Declaration)
[   ]   Selection of Health Care Agent (Power of Attorney for Health Care)
[   ]   Designation of Primary Physician
[   ]   Organ Donation

Living Will (Declaration)

I, being of sound mind, willfully and voluntarily make known my desires that my dying shall not be artificially prolonged under the circumstances set forth below and do declare: If at any time I should have an incurable injury, disease, or illness certified to be a terminal condition by two (2) physicians who have personally examined me, one (1) of whom shall be my attending physician, and the physicians have determined that my death will occur whether or not life-sustaining procedures are utilized and where the application of life-sustaining procedures would serve only to artificially prolong the dying process, I direct that such procedures be withheld or withdrawn, and that I be permitted to die naturally with only the administration of medication or the performance of any medical procedure deemed necessary to provide me with comfort care or to alleviate pain.
Other directions **(insert other instructions if desired)**:

In the absence of my ability to give directions regarding the use of such life-sustaining procedures, it is my intention that this declaration shall be honored by my family and physician(s) as the final expression of my legal right to refuse medical or surgical treatment and to accept the consequences from such refusal.

I understand the full import of this declaration and I am emotionally and mentally competent to make this declaration.

Selection of Health Care Agent (Power of Attorney for Health Care)

INFORMATION ABOUT THIS DOCUMENT: This is an important legal document. Before signing this document, it is vital for you to know and understand these facts: This document gives the person you name as your attorney-in-fact the power to make health care decisions for you if you cannot make the decisions for yourself. After you have signed this document, you have the right to make health care decisions for yourself if you are mentally competent to do so. In addition, after you have signed this document, no treatment may be given to you or stopped over your objection if you are mentally competent to make that decision. You may state in this document any type of treatment that you do not desire and any that you want to make sure you receive. You have the right to take away the authority of your attorney-in-fact, unless you have been adjudicated incompetent, by notifying your attorney-in-fact or health care provider either orally or in writing. Should you revoke the authority of your attorney-in-fact, it is advisable to revoke in writing and to place copies of the revocation wherever this document is located. If there is anything in this document that you do not understand, you should ask a social worker, lawyer, or other person to explain it to you. You should keep a copy of this document after you have signed it. Give a copy to the person you name as your attorney-in-fact. If you are in a health care facility, a copy of this document should be included in your medical record.

I hereby appoint _____ (name),
of _____(address),
as my attorney-in-fact to make health care decisions for me if I become unable to make my own health care decisions. This gives my attorney-in-fact the power to grant, refuse, or withdraw consent on my behalf for any health care service, treatment, or procedure. My attorney-in-fact also has the authority to talk to health care personnel, get information, and sign forms necessary to carry out these decisions.

OPTIONAL - DESIGNATION OF ALTERNATE ATTORNEY-IN FACT FOR HEALTH CARE:
If I revoke my attorney-in-fact's authority or if my attorney-in-fact is not willing, able, or reasonably available to make a health care decision for me, I designate as my first alternate attorney-in-fact for health care.

_____ (name of individual you choose as first alternate agent)
_____ (address)

With this document, I intend to create a power of attorney for health care, which shall take effect if I become incapable of making my own health care decisions and shall continue during that incapacity. My attorney-in-fact shall make health care decisions as I direct below or as I make known to my attorney-in-fact in some other way.
Statement of directives concerning life-prolonging care, treatment, services and procedures (insert statement. Attach additional sheets if necessary):

Special provisions and limitations (add any provisions and limitations):

Designation of Primary Physician

I designate the following physician as my primary physician: _____ (name)
_____ (address)
_____ (phone).

OPTIONAL- DESIGNATION OF ALTERNATE PRIMARY PHYSICIAN: If the physician I have designated above is not willing, able, or reasonably available to act as my primary physician, I designate the following physician as my primary physician:
_____ (name)
_____ (address)
_____ (phone).

Organ Donation

In the event of my death, I have placed my initials next to the following part(s) of my body that I wish donated for the purposes **that I have initialed below**:

[   ] any organs or parts **OR**
[   ] eyes   [   ] bone and connective tissue   [   ] skin
[   ] heart   [   ] kidney(s)   [   ] liver
[   ] lung(s)   [   ] pancreas   [   ] other _____

for the purposes of:

[   ] any purpose authorized by law **OR**
[   ] transplantation   [   ] research   [   ] therapy
[   ] medical education   [   ] other limitations _____

Signature

I sign this Advance Health Care Directive, consisting of the following sections, **which I have initialed below and have elected to adopt:**
[   ]   Living Will (Declaration)
[   ]   Selection of Health Care Agent (Power of Attorney for Health Care)
[   ]   Designation of Primary Physician
[   ]   Organ Donation

BY SIGNING HERE I INDICATE THAT I UNDERSTAND THE PURPOSE AND EFFECT OF THIS DOCUMENT.

Signature _____   Date _____

City, County, and State of Residence _____

Notary Acknowledgment

State of _____
County of _____
On _____ , _____ came before me personally
and, under oath, stated that he or she is the person described in the above document and he or she
signed the above document in my presence. I declare under penalty of perjury that the person whose
name is subscribed to this instrument appears to be of sound mind and under no duress, fraud, or
undue influence.

_____
Notary Public
My commission expires _____

Witness Acknowledgment

The declarant is personally known to me and I believe him or her to be of sound mind and under
no duress, fraud, or undue influence. I did not sign the declarant's signature above for or at the
direction of the declarant and I am not appointed as the health care agent or attorney-in-fact herein.
I am at least eighteen (18) years of age and I am not related to the declarant by blood, adoption,
or marriage, entitled to any portion of the estate of the declarant according to the laws of intestate
succession or under any will of declarant or codicil thereto, or directly financially responsible for
declarant's medical care. I am not a health care provider of the declarant or an employee of the
health facility in which the declarant is a patient.

Witness Signature _____ Date _____

Printed Name of Witness _____

Second Witness Signature _____ Date _____

Printed Name of Witness _____

Acceptance of Health Care Agent and Attorney-in-Fact for Health Care

I accept my appointment as Health Care Agent and Attorney-in-Fact for Health Care:

Signature _____ Date _____

Signature of Alternate_____ Date _____

Florida Advance Health Care Directive

On this date of _____ , I, _____ , do hereby sign, execute, and adopt the following as my Advance Health Care Directive. I direct any and all persons or entities involved with my health care in any manner that these decisions are my wishes and were adopted without duress or force and of my own free will.

I have placed my initials next to the sections of this Directive that I have adopted:

[   ] Living Will
[   ] Selection of Health Care Agent (Designation of Health Care Surrogate)
[   ] Designation of Primary Physician
[   ] Organ Donation

Living Will

I willfully and voluntarily make known my desire that my dying not be artificially prolonged under the circumstances set forth below, and I do hereby declare that, if at any time I am incapacitated and **(initial your choices)**:

[   ] I have a terminal condition, **OR**
[   ] I have an end-stage condition, **OR**
[   ] I am in a persistent vegetative state,

and if my attending or treating physician and another consulting physician have determined that there is no reasonable medical probability of my recovery from such condition, I direct that life-prolonging procedures be withheld or withdrawn when the application of such procedures would serve only to prolong artificially the process of dying, and that I be permitted to die naturally with only the administration of medication or the performance of any medical procedure deemed necessary to provide me with comfort care or to alleviate pain.

It is my intention that this declaration be honored by my family and physician as the final expression of my legal right to refuse medical or surgical treatment and to accept the consequences for such refusal.

Additional Instructions **(optional)**:

Selection of Health Care Agent (Designation of Health Care Surrogate)

In the event that I have been determined to be incapacitated to provide express and informed consent to withholding, withdrawal, or continuation of life-prolonging procedures or to provide informed consent for medical treatment and surgical and diagnostic procedures, I wish to designate as my surrogate for health care decisions and to carry out the provisions of my living will (if I have adopted one) _____ (name), of _____ (address).

OPTIONAL - DESIGNATION OF ALTERNATE AGENT: If I revoke my agent's authority or if my agent is not willing, able, or reasonably available to make a health care decision for me, I designate as my first alternate agent

_____ (name of individual you choose as first alternate agent)
_____ (address)

I fully understand that this designation will permit my designee to make health care decisions, except for anatomical gifts, unless I have executed an anatomical gift declaration pursuant to law, and to provide, withhold, or withdraw consent on my behalf; to apply for public benefits to defray the cost of health care; and to authorize my admission to or transfer from a health care facility. Additional instructions (optional):

I further affirm that this designation is not being made as a condition of treatment or admission to a health care facility. I will notify and send a copy of this document to my primary physician. My failure to designate a surrogate shall not invalidate my living will.

Designation of Primary Physician

I designate the following physician as my primary physician: _____ (name)
_____ (address)
_____ (phone).

OPTIONAL- DESIGNATION OF ALTERNATE PRIMARY PHYSICIAN: If the physician I have designated above is not willing, able, or reasonably available to act as my primary physician, I designate the following physician as my primary physician:
_____ (name)
_____ (address)
_____ (phone).

Organ Donation

In the event of my death, I have placed my initials next to the following part(s) of my body that I wish donated for the purposes **that I have initialed below:**

[   ] any organs or parts **OR**

[   ] eyes   [   ] bone and connective tissue   [   ] skin

[   ] heart   [   ] kidney(s)   [   ] liver

[   ] lung(s)   [   ] pancreas   [   ] other _____

for the purposes of:

[   ] any purpose authorized by law **OR**

[   ] transplantation   [   ] research   [   ] therapy

[   ] medical education   [   ] other limitations _____

Signature

I sign this Advance Health Care Directive, consisting of the following sections, **which I have initialed below and have elected to adopt:**

[   ] Living Will

[   ] Selection of Health Care Agent (Designation of Health Care Surrogate)

[   ] Designation of Primary Physician

[   ] Organ Donation

BY SIGNING HERE I INDICATE THAT I UNDERSTAND THE PURPOSE AND EFFECT OF THIS DOCUMENT.

Signature _____ Date _____

City, County, and State of Residence _____

Notary Acknowledgment

State of _____

County of _____

On _____ , _____ came before me personally and, under oath, stated that he or she is the person described in the above document and he or she signed the above document in my presence. I declare under penalty of perjury that the person whose name is subscribed to this instrument appears to be of sound mind and under no duress, fraud, or undue influence.

_____

Notary Public

My commission expires _____

Witness Acknowledgment

The declarant is personally known to me and I believe him or her to be of sound mind and under no duress, fraud, or undue influence. I did not sign the declarant's signature above for or at the direction of the declarant and I am not appointed as the health care agent or attorney-in-fact herein. I am at least eighteen (18) years of age and I am not related to the declarant by blood, adoption, or marriage, entitled to any portion of the estate of the declarant according to the laws of intestate succession or under any will of declarant or codicil thereto, or directly financially responsible for declarant's medical care. I am not a health care provider of the declarant or an employee of the health facility in which the declarant is a patient.

Witness Signature _____ Date _____

Printed Name of Witness _____

Second Witness Signature _____ Date _____

Printed Name of Second Witness _____

Acceptance of Health Care Agent (Surrogate)

I accept my appointment as Health Care Agent (Surrogate).

Signature _____ Date _____

I accept my appointment as Alternate Health Care Agent (Surrogate).

Signature _____ Date _____

Georgia Advance Health Care Directive

On this date of _____ , I, _____ , do hereby sign, execute, and adopt the following as my Advance Health Care Directive. I direct any and all persons or entities involved with my health care in any manner that these decisions are my wishes and were adopted without duress or force and of my own free will.

I have placed my initials next to the sections of this Directive that I have adopted:

[   ] Living Will
[   ] Selection of Health Care Agent (Durable Power of Attorney for Health Care)
[   ] Designation of Primary Physician
[   ] Organ Donation

Living Will

I, being of sound mind, willfully and voluntarily make known my desire that my life shall not be prolonged under the circumstances set forth below and do declare that if at any time I should **(Initial each option desired)**:

[   ] have a terminal condition,
[   ] be in a coma with no reasonable expectation of regaining consciousness, **OR**
[   ] be in a persistent vegetative state with no reasonable expectation of regaining significant cognitive function, as defined in and established in accordance with the procedures set forth in paragraphs (2), (9), and (13) of Code Section 31-32-2 of the Official Code of Georgia Annotated,

Then, I direct that the application of life-sustaining procedures to my body **(Initial one option):**

[   ] including nourishment and hydration
[   ] including nourishment, but not hydration
[   ] excluding nourishment and hydration
be withheld or withdrawn and that I be permitted to die.

In the absence of my ability to give directions regarding the use of such life-sustaining procedures, it is my intention that this living will shall be honored by my family and physician(s) as the final expression of my legal right to refuse medical or surgical treatment and accept the consequences from such refusal. I understand that I may revoke this living will at any time. I understand the full import of this living will, and I am at least 18 years of age and am emotionally and mentally competent to make this living will.

If I am a female and I have been diagnosed as pregnant, this living will shall have no force and effect unless the fetus is not viable and I indicate by initialing after this sentence that I want this living will to be carried out. **(Initial if desired):**   [   ]
Other directions **(insert any other instructions):**

Selection of Health Care Agent
(Durable Power of Attorney for Health Care)

Notice: the purpose of this power of attorney is to give the person you designate (your agent) broad powers to make health care decisions for you, including power to require, consent to, or withdraw any type of personal care or medical treatment for any physical or mental condition and to admit you to or discharge you from any hospital, home, or other institution; but not including psychosurgery, sterilization, or involuntary hospitalization or treatment covered by title 37 of the official Code of Georgia Annotated. This form does not impose a duty on your agent to exercise granted powers; but, when a power is exercised, your agent will have to use due care to act for your benefit and in accordance with this form. A court can take away the powers of your agent if it finds the agent is not acting properly. You may name co-agents and successor agents under this form, but you may not name a health care provider who may be directly or indirectly involved in rendering health care to you under this power. Unless you expressly limit the duration of this power in the manner provided below or until you revoke this power or a court acting on your behalf terminates it, your agent may exercise the powers given in this power throughout your lifetime, even after you become disabled, incapacitated, or incompetent. The powers you give your agent, your right to revoke those powers, and the penalties for violating the law are explained more fully in code sections 31-36-6, 31-36-9, And 31-36-10 of the Georgia 'Durable Power of Attorney for Health Care Act' of which this form is a part. That act expressly permits the use of any different form of power of attorney you may desire. If there is anything about this form that you do not understand, you should ask a lawyer to explain it to you.

I hereby appoint _____ (name), of
_____ (address),
as my attorney-in-fact (my agent) to act for me and in my name in any way I could act in person to make any and all decisions for me concerning my personal care, medical treatment, hospitalization, and health care and to require, withhold, or withdraw any type of medical treatment or procedure, even though my death may ensue. My agent shall have the same access to my medical records that I have, including the right to disclose the contents to others. My agent shall also have full power to make a disposition of any part or all of my body for medical purposes, authorize an autopsy of my body, and direct the disposition of my remains.

The above grant of power is intended to be as broad as possible so that your agent will have authority to make any decision you could make to obtain or terminate any type of health care, including withdrawal of nourishment and fluids and other life-sustaining or death-delaying measures, if your agent believes such action would be consistent with your intent and desires. If you wish to limit the scope of your agent's powers or prescribe special rules to limit the power to make an anatomical gift, authorize autopsy, or dispose of remains, you may do so in the following paragraphs.

The powers granted above shall not include the following powers or shall be subject to the following rules or limitations (**here you may include any specific limitations you deem appropriate, such as your own definition of when life-sustaining or death-delaying measures should be withheld; a direction to continue nourishment and fluids or other life-sustaining or death-delaying treatment in all events; or instructions to refuse any specific types of treatment that are inconsistent with your religious beliefs or unacceptable to you for any other reason, such as blood transfusion, electroconvulsive therapy, or amputation**):

The subject of life-sustaining or death-delaying treatment is of particular importance. For your convenience in dealing with that subject, some general statements concerning the withholding or removal of life-sustaining or death-delaying treatment are set forth below. (**If you agree with one of these statements, you may initial that statement, but do not initial more than one**):

[   ] I do NOT want my life to be prolonged nor do I want life-sustaining or death-delaying treatment to be provided or continued if my agent believes the burdens of the treatment outweigh the expected benefits. I want my agent to consider the relief of suffering, the expense involved, and the quality as well as the possible extension of my life in making decisions concerning life-sustaining or death-delaying treatment.

[   ] I DO want my life to be prolonged and I want life-sustaining or death-delaying treatment to be provided or continued unless I am in a coma, including a persistent vegetative state, which my attending physician believes to be irreversible, in accordance with reasonable medical standards at the time of reference. If and when I have suffered such an irreversible coma, I want life-sustaining or death-delaying treatment to be withheld or discontinued.

[   ] I DO want my life to be prolonged to the greatest extent possible without regard to my condition, the chances I have for recovery, or the cost of the procedures.

This power of attorney may be amended or revoked by you at any time and in any manner while you are able to do so. In the absence of an amendment or revocation, the authority granted in this power of attorney will become effective at the time this power is signed and will continue until your death and will continue beyond your death if anatomical gift, autopsy, or disposition of remains is authorized, unless a limitation on the beginning date or duration is made by initialing and completing either or both of the following:

[   ] This power of attorney shall become effective on _____
(**Insert a future date or event during your lifetime, such as court determination of your disability, incapacity, or incompetency, when you want this power to first take effect**).

[   ] This power of attorney shall terminate on_____
(**Insert a future date or event during your lifetime, such as court determination of your disability, incapacity, or incompetency, when you want this power to terminate prior to your death**).

If you wish to name an alternate agent, insert the names and addresses of such successors in the following paragraph:

If I revoke my agent's authority or if my agent is not willing, able, or reasonably available to make a health care decision for me, I designate as my first alternate agent

_____ (name of individual you choose as first alternate agent)

_____ (address)

If you wish to name a guardian of your person in the event a court decides that one should be appointed, you may, but are not required to, do so by inserting the name of such guardian in the following paragraph. The court will appoint the person nominated by you if the court finds that such appointment will serve your best interests and welfare. You may, but are not required to, nominate as your guardian the same person named in this form as your agent.

If a guardian of my person is to be appointed, I nominate the following to serve as such guardian:

_____ (name of individual you choose as guardian)

_____ (address)

I am fully informed as to all the contents of this form and understand the full import of this grant of powers to my agent.

Designation of Primary Physician

I designate the following physician as my primary physician: _____ (name)

_____ (address)

_____ (phone).

OPTIONAL- DESIGNATION OF ALTERNATE PRIMARY PHYSICIAN: If the physician I have designated above is not willing, able, or reasonably available to act as my primary physician, I designate the following physician as my primary physician:

_____ (name)

_____ (address)

_____ (phone).

Organ Donation

In the event of my death, I have placed my initials next to the following part(s) of my body that I wish donated for the purposes **that I have initialed below:**

[   ] any organs or parts **OR**

[   ] eyes   [   ] bone and connective tissue   [   ] skin

[   ] heart   [   ] kidney(s)   [   ] liver

[   ] lung(s)   [   ] pancreas   [   ] other _____

for the purposes of:

[   ] any purpose authorized by law **OR**

[   ] transplantation   [   ] research   [   ] therapy

[   ] medical education   [   ] other limitations _____

Signature

I sign this Advance Health Care Directive, consisting of the following sections, **which I have initialed below and have elected to adopt:**

[   ] Living Will

[   ] Selection of Health Care Agent (Durable Power of Attorney for Health Care)

[   ] Designation of Primary Physician

[   ] Organ Donation

BY SIGNING HERE I INDICATE THAT I UNDERSTAND THE PURPOSE AND EFFECT OF THIS DOCUMENT.

Signature _____ Date _____

City, County, and State of Residence _____

Notary Acknowledgment

State of _____

County of _____

On _____ , _____ came before me personally and, under oath, stated that he or she is the person described in the above document and he or she signed the above document in my presence. I declare under penalty of perjury that the person whose name is subscribed to this instrument appears to be of sound mind and under no duress, fraud, or undue influence.

_____

Notary Public

My commission expires _____

Witness Acknowledgment

The declarant is personally known to me and I believe him or her to be of sound mind and under no duress, fraud, or undue influence. I did not sign the declarant's signature above for or at the direction of the declarant and I am not appointed as the health care agent or attorney-in-fact herein. I am at least eighteen (18) years of age and I am not related to the declarant by blood, adoption, or marriage, entitled to any portion of the estate of the declarant according to the laws of intestate succession or under any will of declarant or codicil thereto, or directly financially responsible for declarant's medical care. I am not a health care provider of the declarant or an employee of the health facility in which the declarant is a patient.

Witness Signature _____ Date _____

Printed Name of Witness _____

Second Witness Signature _____ Date _____

Printed Name of Second Witness _____

An additional witness is required when this document is signed by a patient in a hospital or skilled nursing facility. I hereby witness this living will and attest that I believe the declarant to be of sound mind and to have made this living will willingly and voluntarily.

Additional Witness Signature _____ Date _____

Printed Name of Witness _____
(Medical director of skilled nursing facility or staff physician not participating in care of the patient, or chief of the hospital medical staff, staff physician, or hospital designee not participating in care of the patient.)

Acceptance of Health Care Agent and Attorney-in-Fact for Health Care

I accept my appointment as Health Care Agent and Attorney-in-Fact for Health Care:

Signature _____ Date _____

I accept my appointment as Alternate Health Care Agent and Attorney-in-Fact for Health Care:

Signature _____ Date _____

Hawaii Advance Health Care Directive

On this date of _____ , I, _____ , do hereby sign, execute, and adopt the following as my Advance Health Care Directive. I direct any and all persons or entities involved with my health care in any manner that these decisions are my wishes and were adopted without duress or force and of my own free will.

I have placed my initials next to the sections of this Directive that I have adopted:

[   ]   Living Will (Instructions for Health Care)
[   ]   Selection of Health Care Agent (Power of Attorney for Health Care)
[   ]   Designation of Primary Physician
[   ]   Organ Donation

You have the right to give instructions about your own health care. You also have the right to name someone else to make health care decisions for you. This form lets you do either or both of these things. It also lets you express your wishes regarding donation of organs and the designation of your primary physician. If you use this form, you may complete or modify all or any part of it. You are free to use a different form.

PART 1 of this form lets you give specific instructions about any aspect of your health care, whether or not you appoint an agent. Choices are provided for you to express your wishes regarding the provision, withholding, or withdrawal of treatment to keep you alive, as well as the provision of pain relief. Space is provided for you to add to the choices you have made or for you to write out any additional wishes. If you are satisfied to allow your agent to determine what is best for you in making end-of-life decisions, you need not fill out Part 1 of this form.

PART 2 of this form is a Power of Attorney for Health Care. Part 2 lets you name another individual as your agent to make health care decisions for you if you become incapable of making your own decisions or if you want someone else to make those decisions for you now even though you are still capable. Your agent may not be an operator or employee of a community care facility or a residential care facility where you are receiving care, or your supervising health care provider or employee of the health care institution where you are receiving care, unless your agent is related to you or is a co-worker. Unless the form you sign limits the authority of your agent, your agent may make all health care decisions for you. This form has a place for you to limit the authority of your agent. You need not limit the authority of your agent if you wish to rely on your agent for all health care decisions that may have to be made. If you choose not to limit the authority of your agent, your agent will have the right to:

> (a) Consent or refuse consent to any care, treatment, service, or procedure to maintain, diagnose, or otherwise affect a physical or mental condition;
> (b) Select or discharge health care providers and institutions;
> (c) Approve or disapprove diagnostic tests, surgical procedures, and programs of medication;
> (d) Direct the provision, withholding, or withdrawal of artificial nutrition and hydration and all other forms of health care, including cardiopulmonary resuscitation; and
> (e) Make anatomical gifts, authorize an autopsy, and direct the disposition of your remains.

PART 3 of this form lets you designate a physician to have primary responsibility for your health care.

PART 4 of this form lets you express an intention to donate your bodily organs and tissues following your death.

After completing this form, sign and date the form at the end. The form must be signed by two (2) qualified witnesses or acknowledged before a notary public. Give a copy of the signed and completed form to your physician, any other health care providers you may have, any health care institution at which you are receiving care, and any health care agents you have named. You should talk to the person you have named as agent to make sure that he or she understands your wishes and is willing to take the responsibility. You have the right to revoke this advance health care directive or replace this form at any time.

Part 1: Living Will (Instructions for Health Care)

END-OF-LIFE DECISIONS: I direct that my health care providers and others involved in my care provide, withhold, or withdraw treatment in accordance with the choice I have marked below **(initial only one box)**:

[   ] **Choice NOT To Prolong Life**. I do not want my life to be prolonged if:

(a) I have an incurable and irreversible condition that will result in my death within a relatively short time;

(b) I become unconscious and, to a reasonable degree of medical certainty, I will not regain consciousness; **OR**

(c) the likely risks and burdens of treatment would outweigh the expected benefits; **OR**

[   ] **Choice TO Prolong Life**. I want my life to be prolonged as long as possible within the limits of generally accepted health care standards.

RELIEF FROM PAIN: Except as I state in the following space, I direct that treatment for alleviation of pain or discomfort should be provided at all times even if it hastens my death **(insert exceptions):**

OTHER WISHES: **(If you do not agree with any of the optional choices above and wish to write your own, or if you wish to add to the instructions you have given above, you may do so here.) (Add additional sheets if needed)**
I direct that :

Part 2: Selection of Health Care Agent
(Power of Attorney for Health Care)

DESIGNATION OF AGENT: I designate the following individual as my agent to make health care decisions for me _____ (name), of _____ (address).

OPTIONAL - DESIGNATION OF ALTERNATE AGENT: If I revoke my agent's authority or if my agent is not willing, able, or reasonably available to make a health care decision for me, I designate as my first alternate agent

_____ (name of individual you choose as first alternate agent)
_____ (address)

AGENT'S AUTHORITY: My agent is authorized to make all health care decisions for me, including decisions to provide, withhold, or withdraw artificial nutrition and hydration, and all other forms of healthcare to keep me alive, except as I state here **(add additional sheets if needed)**:

WHEN AGENT'S AUTHORITY BECOMES EFFECTIVE: My agent's authority becomes effective when my primary physician determines that I am unable to make my own health care decisions unless I mark the following box. **If I initial this box** [　], my agent's authority to make health care decisions for me takes effect immediately.

AGENT'S OBLIGATION: My agent shall make health care decisions for me in accordance with this power of attorney for health care, any instructions I give in Part 2 of this form, and my other wishes to the extent known to my agent. To the extent my wishes are unknown, my agent shall make health care decisions for me in accordance with what my agent determines to be in my best interest. In determining my best interest, my agent shall consider my personal values to the extent known to my agent.

AGENT'S POSTDEATH AUTHORITY: My agent is authorized to make anatomical gifts, authorize an autopsy, and direct disposition of my remains, except as I state here or in Part 4 of this form **(insert any exceptions)**:

NOMINATION OF CONSERVATOR: If a conservator of my person needs to be appointed for me by a court, I nominate the agent designated in this form. If that agent is unable or unwilling to serve then I nominate the person designated as alternate agent in this form.

Part 3: Designation of Primary Physician

I designate the following physician as my primary physician: _____ (name)
_____ (address)
_____ (phone).

OPTIONAL- DESIGNATION OF ALTERNATE PRIMARY PHYSICIAN: If the physician I have designated above is not willing, able, or reasonably available to act as my primary physician, I designate the following physician as my primary physician:
_____ (name)
_____ (address)
_____ (phone).

Part 4: Organ Donation

In the event of my death, I have placed my initials next to the following part(s) of my body that I wish donated for the purposes **that I have initialed below:**

[   ] any organs or parts **OR**
[   ] eyes   [   ] bone and connective tissue   [   ] skin
[   ] heart   [   ] kidney(s)   [   ] liver
[   ] lung(s)   [   ] pancreas   [   ] other _____

for the purposes of:

[   ] any purpose authorized by law **OR**
[   ] transplantation   [   ] research   [   ] therapy
[   ] medical education   [   ] other limitations _____

Signature

I sign this Advance Health Care Directive, consisting of the following sections, **which I have initialed below and have elected to adopt:**
[   ] Living Will (Instructions for Health Care)
[   ] Selection of Health Care Agent (Power of Attorney for Health Care)
[   ] Designation of Primary Physician
[   ] Organ Donation

BY SIGNING HERE I INDICATE THAT I UNDERSTAND THE PURPOSE AND EFFECT OF THIS DOCUMENT.

Signature _____ Date _____

City, County, and State of Residence _____

Notary Acknowledgment

State of _____

County of _____

On _____ , _____ came before me personally and, under oath, stated that he or she is the person described in the above document and he or she signed the above document in my presence. I declare under penalty of perjury that the person whose name is subscribed to this instrument appears to be of sound mind and under no duress, fraud, or undue influence.

Notary Public

My commission expires _____

Witness Acknowledgment

I declare under penalty of false swearing pursuant to section 710-1062, Hawaii Revised Statutes, that the principal is personally known to me, that the principal signed or acknowledged this power of attorney in my presence, that the principal appears to be of sound mind and under no duress, fraud, or undue influence, that I am not the person appointed as agent by this document, and that I am not a health-care provider, nor an employee of a health-care provider or facility. I am not related to the principal by blood, marriage, or adoption, and to the best of my knowledge, I am not entitled to any part of the estate of the principal upon the death of the principal under a will now existing or by operation of law.

Witness Signature _____ Date _____

Printed Name of Witness _____

Second Witness Signature _____ Date _____

Printed Name of Second Witness _____

Acceptance of Health Care Agent and Attorney-in-Fact for Health Care

I accept my appointment as Health Care Agent and Attorney-in-Fact for Health Care.

Signature _____ Date _____

I accept my appointment as Alternate Health Care Agent and Attorney-in-Fact for Health Care.

Signature _____ Date _____

Idaho Advance Health Care Directive

On this date of _____ , I, _____ , do hereby sign, execute, and adopt the following as my Advance Health Care Directive. I direct any and all persons or entities involved with my health care in any manner that these decisions are my wishes and were adopted without duress or force and of my own free will.

I have placed my initials next to the sections of this Directive that I have adopted:

[   ] Living Will (Directive to Withhold or to Provide Treatment)

[   ] Selection of Health Care Agent (Durable Power of Attorney for Health Care)

[   ] Designation of Primary Physician

[   ] Organ Donation

Living Will (Directive to Withhold or to Provide Treatment)

This Directive shall only be effective if I am unable to communicate my instructions and

      1.) I have an incurable or irreversible injury, disease, illness or condition, and a medical doctor who has examined me has certified: A. That such injury, disease, illness or condition is terminal; and B. That the application of artificial life-sustaining procedures would serve only to prolong artificially my life; and C. That my death is imminent, whether or not artificial life-sustaining procedures are utilized; **OR**

      2.) I have been diagnosed as being in a persistent vegetative state.

In such event, I direct that the following initialed expression of my intent be followed, and that I receive any medical treatment or care that may be required to keep me free of pain or distress.

(Initial one of the following three boxes next to the left-hand margin):

[   ] I direct that all medical treatment, care, nutrition, and hydration necessary to restore my health, sustain my life, and abolish or alleviate pain or distress be provided to me. Nutrition and hydration shall not be withheld or withdrawn from me if I would die from malnutrition or dehydration rather than from my injury, disease, illness, or condition.

[   ] I direct that all medical treatment, care and procedures, including artificial life-sustaining procedures, be withheld or withdrawn, except that nutrition and hydration, whether artificial or non-artificial shall not be withheld or withdrawn from me if, as a result, I would likely die primarily from malnutrition or dehydration rather than from my injury, disease, illness or condition, as follows: *(If none of the following three indented boxes are initialed, then both nutrition and hydration, of any nature, whether artificial or non-artificial, shall be administered.)* **(Initial one of the following three indented boxes if desired)**

      [   ] Only hydration of any nature, whether artificial or non-artificial, shall be administered;

      [   ] Only nutrition, of any nature, whether artificial or non-artificial, shall be administered;

      [   ] Both nutrition and hydration, of any nature, whether artificial or non-artificial shall be administered.

[   ] I direct that all medical treatment, care and procedures be withheld or withdrawn, including withdrawal of the administration of artificial nutrition and hydration.

If I have been diagnosed as pregnant, this Directive shall have no force during the course of my pregnancy. I understand the full importance of this Directive and am mentally competent to make this Directive. No participant in the making of this Directive or in its being carried into effect shall be held responsible in any way for complying with my directions.

PHYSICIAN'S ORDERS FOR SCOPE OF TREATMENT: **Initial one of the following boxes:**

[   ] I have discussed these decisions with my physician and have also completed a Physician Orders for Scope of Treatment (POST) form that contains directions that may be more specific than, but are compatible with, this Directive. I hereby approve of those orders and incorporate them herein as if fully set forth. OR

[   ] I have not completed a Physician Orders for Scope of Treatment (POST) form. If a POST form is later signed by my physician, then this living will shall be deemed modified to be compatible with the terms of the POST form.

Selection of Health Care Agent
(Durable Power of Attorney for Health Care)

DESIGNATION OF HEALTH CARE AGENT.: None of the following may be designated as your agent: (1) your treating health care provider; (2) a nonrelative employee of your treating health care provider; (3) an operator of a community care facility; or (4) a nonrelative employee of an operator of a community care facility. If the agent or an alternate agent designated in this Directive is your spouse, and our marriage is thereafter dissolved, such designation shall be thereupon revoked.

I do hereby designate and appoint _____ (name), of _____ (address), as my attorney-in-fact (agent) to make health care decisions for me as authorized in this document. For the purposes of this document, "health care decision" means consent, refusal of consent, or withdrawal of consent to any care, treatment, service, or procedure to maintain, diagnose, or treat an individual's physical condition.

OPTIONAL - DESIGNATION OF ALTERNATE AGENT: If I revoke my agent's authority or if my agent is not willing, able, or reasonably available to make a health care decision for me, I designate as my first alternate agent
_____ (name of individual you choose as first alternate agent)
_____ (address)

CREATION OF DURABLE POWER OF ATTORNEY FOR HEALTH CARE. By this document I intend to create a durable power of attorney for health care. This power of attorney shall not be affected by my subsequent incapacity. This power shall be effective only when I am unable to communicate rationally.

GENERAL STATEMENT OF AUTHORITY GRANTED. Subject to any limitations in this document, I hereby grant to my agent full power and authority to make health care decisions for me to the same extent that I could make such decisions for myself if I had the capacity to do so. In exercising this authority, my agent shall make health care decisions that are consistent with my desires as stated in this document or otherwise made known to my agent, including, but not limited to, my desires concerning obtaining or refusing or withdrawing artificial life-sustaining care, treatment, services, and procedures including such desires set forth in a living will, Physician Orders for Scope of Treatment (POST) form, or similar document executed by me, if any. **(If you want to limit the authority of your agent to make health care decisions for you, you can state the limitations in next paragraph "Statement of Desires, Special Provisions, and Limitations" below. You can indicate your desires by including a statement of your desires in the same paragraph.)**

STATEMENT OF DESIRES, SPECIAL PROVISIONS, AND LIMITATIONS. **(Your agent must make health care decisions that are consistent with your known desires. You can, but are not required to, state your desires in the space provided below. You should consider whether you want to include a statement of your desires concerning artificial life-sustaining care, treatment, services and procedures. You can also include a statement of your desires concerning other matters relating to your health care, including a list of one or more persons whom you designate to be able to receive medical information about you and/or to be allowed to visit you in a medical institution. You can also make your desires known to your agent by discussing your desires with your agent or by some other means. If there are any types of treatment that you do not want to be used, you should state them in the space below. If you want to limit in any other way the authority given your agent by this Directive, you should state the limits in the space below. If you do not state any limits, your agent will have broad powers to make health care decisions for you, except to the extent that there are limits provided by law.)**

In exercising the authority under this durable power of attorney for health care, my agent shall act consistently with my desires as stated below and is subject to the special provisions and limitations stated in my Physician Orders for Scope of Treatment (POST) form, a living will, or similar document executed by me, if any. **(You may attach additional pages or documents if you need more space to complete your statement.)**

INSPECTION AND DISCLOSURE OF INFORMATION RELATING TO MY PHYSICAL OR MENTAL HEALTH. Subject to any limitations in this document, my agent has the power and authority to do all of the following: (a) Request, review, and receive any information, verbal or written, regarding my physical or mental health, including, but not limited to, medical and hospital records; (b) Execute on my behalf any releases or other documents that may be required in order to obtain this information; (c) Consent to the disclosure of this information; and (d) Consent to the donation of any of my organs for medical purposes.
(If you want to limit the authority of your agent to receive and disclose information relating to your health, you must state the limitations in "Statement of Desires, Special Provisions, and Limitations" above.)

HIPAA RELEASE AUTHORITY. My agent shall be treated as I would be with respect to my rights regarding the use and disclosure of my individually identifiable health information or other medical records. This release authority applies to any information governed by the Health Insurance Portability and Accountability Act of 1996 (HIPAA), 42 U.S.C. 1320d and 45 CFR 160 through 164. I authorize any physician, health care professional, dentist, health plan, hospital, clinic, laboratory, pharmacy, or other covered health care provider, any insurance company, and the Medical Information Bureau, Inc. or other health care clearinghouse that has provided treatment or services to me, or that has paid for or is seeking payment from me for such services, to give, disclose and release to my agent, without restriction, all of my individually identifiable health information and medical records regarding any past, present or future medical or mental health condition, including all information relating to the diagnosis of HIV/AIDS, sexually transmitted diseases, mental illness, and drug or alcohol abuse. The authority given my agent shall supersede any other agreement that I may have made with my health care providers to restrict access to or disclosure of my individually identifiable health information. The authority given my agent has no expiration date and shall expire only in the event that I revoke the authority in writing and deliver it to my health care provider.

SIGNING DOCUMENTS, WAIVERS, AND RELEASES. Where necessary to implement the health care decisions that my agent is authorized by this document to make, my agent has the power and authority to execute on my behalf all of the following: (a) Documents titled or purporting to be a "Refusal to Permit Treatment" and "Leaving Hospital Against Medical Advice;" and (b) Any necessary waiver or release from liability required by a hospital or physician.

PRIOR DESIGNATIONS REVOKED. I revoke any prior durable power of attorney for health care.

Designation of Primary Physician

I designate the following physician as my primary physician: _____ (name)
_____ (address)
_____(phone).

OPTIONAL- DESIGNATION OF ALTERNATE PRIMARY PHYSICIAN: If the physician I have designated above is not willing, able, or reasonably available to act as my primary physician, I designate the following physician as my primary physician:
_____ (name)
_____ (address)
_____ (phone).

Organ Donation

In the event of my death, I have placed my initials next to the following part(s) of my body that I wish donated for the purposes **that I have initialed below:**

[　　] any organs or parts **OR**

[　　] eyes　　　　　　[　　] bone and connective tissue　　　[　　] skin

[　　] heart　　　　　　[　　] kidney(s)　　　　　　　　　　　[　　] liver

[　　] lung(s)　　　　　[　　] pancreas　　　　　　　　　　　[　　] other _____

for the purposes of:

[　　] any purpose authorized by law **OR**

[　　] transplantation　　　　　[　　] research　　　　　[　　] therapy

[　　] medical education　　　　[　　] other limitations _____

Signature

I sign this Advance Health Care Directive, consisting of the following sections, **which I have initialed below and have elected to adopt:**

[　　] Living Will (Directive to Withhold or to Provide Treatment)

[　　] Selection of Health Care Agent (Durable Power of Attorney for Health Care)

[　　] Designation of Primary Physician

[　　] Organ Donation

BY SIGNING HERE I INDICATE THAT I UNDERSTAND THE PURPOSE AND EFFECT OF THIS DOCUMENT.

Signature _____　　Date _____

City, County, and State of Residence _____

Notary Acknowledgment

State of _____

County of _____

On _____ , _____ came before me personally and, under oath, stated that he or she is the person described in the above document and he or she signed the above document in my presence. I declare under penalty of perjury that the person whose name is subscribed to this instrument appears to be of sound mind and under no duress, fraud, or undue influence.

_____

Notary Public

My commission expires _____

Witness Acknowledgment

The declarant is personally known to me and I believe him or her to be of sound mind and under no duress, fraud, or undue influence. I did not sign the declarant's signature above for or at the direction of the declarant and I am not appointed as the health care agent or attorney-in-fact herein. I am at least eighteen (18) years of age and I am not related to the declarant by blood, adoption, or marriage, entitled to any portion of the estate of the declarant according to the laws of intestate succession or under any will of declarant or codicil thereto, or directly financially responsible for declarant's medical care. I am not a health care provider of the declarant or an employee of the health facility in which the declarant is a patient.

Witness Signature _____   Date _____

Printed Name of Witness _____

Second Witness Signature _____   Date _____

Printed Name of Second Witness _____

Acceptance of Health Care Agent and Attorney-in-Fact for Health Care

I accept my appointment as Health Care Agent and Attorney-in-Fact for Health Care.

Signature _____   Date _____

I accept my appointment as Alternate Health Care Agent and Attorney-in-Fact for Health Care.

Signature _____   Date _____

Illinois Advance Health Care Directive

On this date of _____ , I, _____ , do hereby sign, execute, and adopt the following as my Advance Health Care Directive. I direct any and all persons or entities involved with my health care in any manner that these decisions are my wishes and were adopted without duress or force and of my own free will.

I have placed my initials next to the sections of this Directive that I have adopted:

[   ] Living Will Declaration
[   ] Selection of Health Care Agent (Power of Attorney for Health Care)
[   ] Designation of Primary Physician
[   ] Organ Donation

Living Will Declaration

If at any time I should have an incurable and irreversible injury, disease, or illness judged to be a terminal condition by my attending physician who has personally examined me and has determined that my death is imminent except for death-delaying procedures, I direct that such procedures which would only prolong the dying process be withheld or withdrawn, and that I be permitted to die naturally with only the administration of medication, sustenance, or the performance of any medical procedure deemed necessary by my attending physician to provide me with comfort care.

In the absence of my ability to give directions regarding the use of such death-delaying procedures, it is my intention that this declaration shall be honored by my family and physician as the final expression of my legal right to refuse medical or surgical treatment and accept the consequences from such refusal.

Selection of Health Care Agent (Power of Attorney for Health Care)

NOTICE: The purpose of this power of attorney is to give the person you designate (your "agent") broad powers to make health care decisions for you, including power to require, consent to, or withdraw any type of personal care or medical treatment for any physical or mental condition, and to admit you to or discharge you from any hospital, home, or other institution. This form does not impose a duty on your agent to exercise granted powers; but when powers are exercised, your agent will have to use due care to act for your benefit and in accordance with this form and keep a record of receipts, disbursements, and significant actions taken as agent. A court can take away the powers of your agent if it finds the agent is not acting properly. Unless you expressly limit the duration of this power in the manner provided below, until you revoke this power or a court acting on your behalf terminates it, your agent may exercise the powers given here throughout your lifetime, even after you become disabled. The powers you give your agent, your right to revoke those powers, and the penalties for violating the law are explained more fully in Sections 4-5, 4-6, 4-9, and 4-10[b] of the Illinois "Powers of Attorney for Health Care Law" of which this form is a part. That law expressly permits the use of any different form of power of attorney you may desire. If there is anything about this form that you do not understand, you should ask a lawyer to explain it to you.

I hereby appoint _____ (name),
of _____ (address), as
my attorney-in-fact (my "agent") to act for me and in my name (in any way I could act in person) to make any and all decisions for me concerning my personal care, medical treatment, hospitalization, and health care and to require, withhold, or withdraw any type of medical treatment or procedure, even though my death may ensue. My agent shall have the same access to my medical records that I have, including the right to disclose the contents to others. My agent shall also have full power to authorize an autopsy and direct the disposition of my remains. Effective upon my death, my agent has the full power to make an anatomical gift of the following:

[   ] Any organ, tissues, or eyes suitable for transplantation or used for research or education
[   ] Specific organs (*list the specific organs*).

(The above grant of power is intended to be as broad as possible so that your agent will have authority to make any decision you could make to obtain or terminate any type of health care, including withdrawal of food and water and other life-sustaining measures, if your agent believes such action would be consistent with your intent and desires. If you wish to limit the scope of your agent's powers or prescribe special rules or limit the power to make an anatomical gift, authorize autopsy or dispose of remains, you may do so in the following paragraphs.)

The powers granted above shall not include the following powers or shall be subject to the following rules or limitations (**Here you may include any specific limitations you deem appropriate, such as: your own definition of when life-sustaining measures should be withheld; a direction to continue food and fluids or life-sustaining treatment in all events; or instructions to refuse any specific types of treatment that are inconsistent with your religious beliefs or unacceptable to you for any other reason, such as blood transfusion, electro-convulsive therapy, amputation, psychosurgery, voluntary admission to a mental institution, etc.):**

The subject of life-sustaining treatment is of particular importance. For your convenience in dealing with that subject, some general statements concerning the withholding or removal of life-sustaining treatment are set forth on the following pages. If you agree with one of these statements, you may initial that statement; but do not initial more than one.

[   ] I do NOT want my life to be prolonged nor do I want life-sustaining treatment to be provided or continued if my agent believes the burdens of the treatment outweigh the expected benefits. I want my agent to consider the relief of suffering, the expense involved, and the quality as well as the possible extension of my life in making decisions concerning life-sustaining treatment.

[   ] I DO want my life to be prolonged and I want life-sustaining treatment to be provided or continued unless I am in a coma which my attending physician believes to be irreversible, in accordance with reasonable medical standards at the time of reference. If and when I have suffered irreversible coma, I want life-sustaining treatment to be withheld or discontinued.

[   ] I DO want my life to be prolonged to the greatest extent possible without regard to my condition, the chances I have for recovery, or the cost of the procedures.

This power of attorney may be amended or revoked by you at any time and in any manner while you are able to do so. In the absence of an amendment or revocation, the authority granted in this power of attorney will become effective at the time this power is signed and will continue until your death and will continue beyond your death if anatomical gift, autopsy, or disposition of remains is authorized, unless a limitation on the beginning date or duration is made by initialing and completing either or both of the following:

[   ] This power of attorney shall become effective on _____
(Insert a future date or event during your lifetime, such as court determination of your disability, incapacity, or incompetency, when you want this power to first take effect).

[   ] This power of attorney shall terminate on _____
(Insert a future date or event during your lifetime, such as court determination of your disability, incapacity, or incompetency, when you want this power to terminate prior to your death).

If you wish to name an alternate agent, insert the name and address of such successor in the following paragraph:

If I revoke my agent's authority or if my agent is not willing, able, or reasonably available to make a health care decision for me, I designate as my first alternate agent
_____ (name of individual you choose as first alternate agent)
_____ (address)

If you wish to name a guardian of your person in the event a court decides that one should be appointed, you may, but are not required to, do so by inserting the name of such guardian in the following paragraph. The court will appoint the person nominated by you if the court finds that such appointment will serve your best interests and welfare. You may, but are not required to, nominate as your guardian the same person named in this form as your agent.

If a guardian of my person is to be appointed, I nominate the following to serve as such guardian:
_____ (name of individual you choose as guardian)
_____ (address)

I am fully informed as to all the contents of this form and understand the full import of this grant of powers to my agent.

Designation of Primary Physician

I designate the following physician as my primary physician: _____ (name)
_____ (address)
_____(phone).

OPTIONAL- DESIGNATION OF ALTERNATE PRIMARY PHYSICIAN: If the physician I have designated above is not willing, able, or reasonably available to act as my primary physician, I designate the following physician as my primary physician:
_____ (name)
_____ (address)
_____(phone).

Organ Donation

In the event of my death, I have placed my initials next to the following part(s) of my body that I wish donated for the purposes **that I have initialed below**:

[   ] any organs or parts **OR**
[   ] eyes   [   ] bone and connective tissue   [   ] skin
[   ] heart   [   ] kidney(s)   [   ] liver
[   ] lung(s)   [   ] pancreas   [   ] other _____
for the purposes of:

[   ] any purpose authorized by law **OR**
[   ] transplantation   [   ] research   [   ] therapy
[   ] medical education   [   ] other limitations _____

Signature

I sign this Advance Health Care Directive, consisting of the following sections, **which I have initialed below and have elected to adopt:**
[   ] Living Will Declaration
[   ] Selection of Health Care Agent (Power of Attorney for Health Care)
[   ] Designation of Primary Physician
[   ] Organ Donation

BY SIGNING HERE I INDICATE THAT I UNDERSTAND THE PURPOSE AND EFFECT OF THIS DOCUMENT.

Signature _____   Date _____

City, County, and State of Residence _____

Notary Acknowledgment

State of _____

County of _____

On _____ , _____ came before me personally and, under oath, stated that he or she is the person described in the above document and he or she signed the above document in my presence. I declare under penalty of perjury that the person whose name is subscribed to this instrument appears to be of sound mind and under no duress, fraud, or undue influence.

_____

Notary Public

My commission expires _____

Witness Acknowledgment

The declarant is personally known to me and I believe him or her to be of sound mind. I saw the declarant sign the declaration in my presence (or the declarant acknowledged in my presence that he or she had signed the declaration) and I signed the declaration as a witness in the presence of the declarant. I did not sign the declarant's signature above for or at the direction of the declarant. At the date of this instrument, I am not entitled to any portion of the estate of the declarant according to the laws of intestate succession or, to the best of my knowledge and belief, under any will of declarant or other instrument taking effect at declarant's death, or directly financially responsible for declarant's medical care.

Witness Signature _____ Date _____

Printed Name of Witness _____

Second Witness Signature _____ Date _____

Printed Name of Second Witness _____

Acceptance of Health Care Agent and Attorney-in-Fact for Health Care

I accept my appointment as Health Care Agent and Attorney-in-Fact for Health Care.

Signature _____ Date _____

I accept my appointment as Alternate Health Care Agent and Attorney-in-Fact for Health Care.

Signature _____ Date _____

Indiana Advance Health Care Directive

On this date of _____ , I, _____ , do hereby sign, execute, and adopt the following as my Advance Health Care Directive. I direct any and all persons or entities involved with my health care in any manner that these decisions are my wishes and were adopted without duress or force and of my own free will.

I have placed my initials next to the sections of this Directive that I have adopted:

[   ] Living Will Declaration or Life-Prolonging Procedures Declaration
[   ] Selection of Health Care Agent (Health Care Representative and Attorney-in-Fact for Health Care)
[   ] Designation of Primary Physician
[   ] Organ Donation

Living Will Declaration or Life-Prolonging Procedures Declaration

You may select either a Living Will Declaration OR a Life-Prolonging Procedures Declaration (on next page), but not both.

Living Will Declaration [   ] (Initial if you choose this option.)

I, being of sound mind and at least 18 years of age, willfully and voluntarily make known my desires that my dying shall not be artificially prolonged under the circumstances set forth below, and I declare that:

If at any time my attending physician certifies in writing that:

> (1) I have an incurable injury, disease, or illness,
> (2) my death will occur within a short time, and
> (3) the use of life-prolonging procedures would serve only to artificially prolong the dying process,

I direct that such procedures be withheld or withdrawn, and that I be permitted to die naturally with only the performance or provision of any medical procedure or medication necessary to provide me with comfort care or to alleviate pain, and, if I have so indicated below, the provision of artificially-supplied nutrition and hydration **(indicate your choice by initialing only one of the following):**

[   ] I DO wish to receive artificially-supplied nutrition and hydration, even if the effort to sustain life is futile or excessively burdensome to me.

[   ] I do NOT wish to receive artificially-supplied nutrition and hydration, if the effort to sustain life is futile or excessively burdensome to me.

[   ] I intentionally make no decision concerning artificially-supplied nutrition and hydration, leaving the decision to my health care representative appointed under IC 16-36-1-7 or my attorney-in-fact with health care powers under IC 30-5-5.

In the absence of my ability to give directions regarding the use of life-prolonging procedures, it is my intention that this declaration be honored by my family and physician as the final expression of my legal right to refuse medical or surgical treatment and accept the consequences of the refusal. I understand the full import of this declaration.

OR

Life-prolonging Procedures Declaration [   ] **(Initial if you choose this option.)**

I, being of sound mind and at least 18 years of age, willfully and voluntarily make know my desire that if at any time I have an incurable injury, disease, or illness determined to be a terminal condition, I request the use of life-prolonging procedures that would extend my life. This includes appropriate nutrition and hydration, the administration of medication, and the performance of all other medical procedures necessary to extend my life, to provide comfort care, or to alleviate pain.

In the absence of my ability to give directions regarding the use of life-prolonging procedures, it is my intention that this declaration be honored by my family and physician as the final expression of my legal right to request medical or surgical treatment and accept the consequences of the request. I understand the full import of this declaration.

Selection of Health Care Agent (Health Care Representative and Attorney-in-Fact for Health Care)

Under the terms of Indiana Code, Sections 30-5-5 and 16-36-1-7, I hereby appoint:

_____(name),

of _____ (address),

as both my health care representative and my attorney-in-fact for health care to make health care decisions on my behalf whenever I am incapable of making my own health care decisions. I grant my attorney-in-fact the following powers in matters affecting my health care to: (1) employ or contract with servants, companions, or health care providers involved in my health care, (2) admit or release me from a hospital or health care facility, (3) have access to my records, including medical records, (4) make anatomical gifts on my behalf, (5) request an autopsy, and (6) make plans for the disposition of my body.

APPOINTMENT OF MY ATTORNEY-IN-FACT AS MY HEALTH CARE REPRESENTATIVE: In addition to the powers granted above, I appoint my attorney-in-fact as my health care representative to make decisions in my best interest concerning the consent, withdrawal, or withholding of health care. I understand health care to include any medical care, treatment, service, or procedure to maintain, diagnose, treat, or provide for my physical or mental well-being. Health care also includes the providing of nutrition and hydration. If at any time, based on my previously-expressed preferences and the diagnosis and prognosis, my health care representative is satisfied that certain health care is not or would not be beneficial, or that such health care is or would be excessively burdensome, then my health care representative may express my will that such health care be withheld or withdrawn and may consent on my behalf that any or all health care be discontinued or not instituted, even if death may result. My health care representative must try to discuss this decision with me. However, if I am unable to communicate, my health care representative may make such a decision for me, after consultation with my physician or physicians and other relevant health care givers. To the extent appropriate, my health care representative may also discuss this decision with my family and others, to the extent they are available.

Designation of Primary Physician

I designate the following physician as my primary physician: _____ (name)

_____ (address)

_____(phone).

OPTIONAL- DESIGNATION OF ALTERNATE PRIMARY PHYSICIAN: If the physician I have designated above is not willing, able, or reasonably available to act as my primary physician, I designate the following physician as my primary physician:

_____ (name)

_____ (address)

_____(phone).

Organ Donation

In the event of my death, I have placed my initials next to the following part(s) of my body that I wish donated for the purposes **that I have initialed below:**

[   ] any organs or parts **OR**

[   ] eyes   [   ] bone and connective tissue   [   ] skin

[   ] heart   [   ] kidney(s)   [   ] liver

[   ] lung(s)   [   ] pancreas   [   ] other _____

for the purposes of:

[   ] any purpose authorized by law **OR**

[   ] transplantation   [   ] research   [   ] therapy

[   ] medical education   [   ] other limitations _____

Signature

I sign this Advance Health Care Directive, consisting of the following sections, **which I have initialed below and have elected to adopt:**

[   ] Living Will Declaration or Life-Prolonging Procedures Declaration

[   ] Selection of Health Care Agent (Health Care Representative and Attorney-in-Fact for Health Care)

[   ] Designation of Primary Physician

[   ] Organ Donation

BY SIGNING HERE I INDICATE THAT I UNDERSTAND THE PURPOSE AND EFFECT OF THIS DOCUMENT.

Signature _____ Date _____

City, County, and State of Residence _____

Notary Acknowledgment

State of _____
County of _____

On _____ , _____ came before me personally and, under oath, stated that he or she is the person described in the above document and he or she signed the above document in my presence. I declare under penalty of perjury that the person whose name is subscribed to this instrument appears to be of sound mind and under no duress, fraud, or undue influence.

_____

Notary Public
My commission expires _____

Witness Acknowledgment

The declarant is personally known to me and I believe him or her to be of sound mind and under no duress, fraud, or undue influence. I did not sign the declarant's signature above for or at the direction of the declarant and I am not appointed as the health care agent or attorney-in-fact herein. I am at least eighteen (18) years of age and I am not related to the declarant by blood, adoption, or marriage, entitled to any portion of the estate of the declarant according to the laws of intestate succession or under any will of declarant or codicil thereto, or directly financially responsible for declarant's medical care. I am not a health care provider of the declarant or an employee of the health facility in which the declarant is a patient.

Witness Signature _____ Date _____

Printed Name of Witness _____

Second Witness Signature _____ Date _____

Printed Name of Second Witness _____

Acceptance of Health Care Representative and Attorney-in-Fact for Health Care

I accept my appointment as Health Care Representative and Attorney-in-Fact for Health Care

Signature _____ Date _____

Iowa Advance Health Care Directive

On this date of _____ , I, _____ , do hereby sign, execute, and adopt the following as my Advance Health Care Directive. I direct any and all persons or entities involved with my health care in any manner that these decisions are my wishes and were adopted without duress or force and of my own free will.

I have placed my initials next to the sections of this Directive that I have adopted:

[   ] Living Will Declaration
[   ] Selection of Health Care Agent (Durable Power of Attorney for Health Care)
[   ] Designation of Primary Physician
[   ] Organ Donation

Living Will Declaration

If I should have an incurable or irreversible condition that will result either in death within a relatively short period of time or a state of permanent unconsciousness from which, to a reasonable degree of medical certainty, there can be no recovery, it is my desire that my life not be prolonged by the administration of life-sustaining procedures. If I am unable to participate in my health care decisions, I direct my attending physician to withhold or withdraw life-sustaining procedures that merely prolong the dying process and are not necessary to my comfort or freedom from pain.

Selection of Health Care Agent (Durable Power of Attorney for Health Care)

I hereby appoint _____ (name), of _____ (address), as my attorney-in-fact (my agent) and give to my agent the power to make health care decisions for me. This power exists only when I am unable, in the judgment of my attending physician, to make those health care decisions. The attorney-in-fact must act consistently with my desires as stated in this document or otherwise made known.

Except as otherwise specified in this document, this document gives my agent the power, where otherwise consistent with the law of this state, to consent to my physician not giving health care or stopping health care which is necessary to keep me alive. This document gives my agent power to make health care decisions on my behalf, including the power to consent, refuse to consent, or withdraw consent to the provision of any care, treatment, service, or procedure to maintain, diagnose, or treat a physical or mental condition. This power is subject to any statement of my desires and any limitations included in this document. My agent has the right to examine my medical records and to consent to disclosure of such records.

Optional instructions **(include additional instructions, if any)**:

Designation of Primary Physician

I designate the following physician as my primary physician: _____ (name)

_____ (address)

_____ (phone).

OPTIONAL- DESIGNATION OF ALTERNATE PRIMARY PHYSICIAN: If the physician I have designated above is not willing, able, or reasonably available to act as my primary physician, I designate the following physician as my primary physician:

_____ (name)

_____ (address)

_____ (phone).

Organ Donation

In the event of my death, I have placed my initials next to the following part(s) of my body that I wish donated for the purposes **that I have initialed below:**

[   ] any organs or parts **OR**

[   ] eyes   [   ] bone and connective tissue   [   ] skin

[   ] heart   [   ] kidney(s)   [   ] liver

[   ] lung(s)   [   ] pancreas   [   ] other _____

for the purposes of:

[   ] any purpose authorized by law **OR**

[   ] transplantation   [   ] research   [   ] therapy

[   ] medical education   [   ] other limitations _____

Signature

I sign this Advance Health Care Directive, consisting of the following sections, **which I have initialed below and have elected to adopt:**

[   ] Living Will Declaration

[   ] Selection of Health Care Agent (Durable Power of Attorney for Health Care)

[   ] Designation of Primary Physician

[   ] Organ Donation

BY SIGNING HERE I INDICATE THAT I UNDERSTAND THE PURPOSE AND EFFECT OF THIS DOCUMENT.

Signature _____ Date _____

City, County, and State of Residence _____

Notary Acknowledgment

State of _____

County of _____

On _____ , _____ came before me personally and, under oath, stated that he or she is the person described in the above document and he or she signed the above document in my presence. I declare under penalty of perjury that the person whose name is subscribed to this instrument appears to be of sound mind and under no duress, fraud, or undue influence.

_____
Notary Public
My commission expires _____

Witness Acknowledgment

The declarant is personally known to me and I believe him or her to be of sound mind and under no duress, fraud, or undue influence. I did not sign the declarant's signature above for or at the direction of the declarant and I am not appointed as the health care agent or attorney-in-fact herein. I am at least eighteen (18) years of age and I am not related to the declarant by blood, adoption, or marriage, entitled to any portion of the estate of the declarant according to the laws of intestate succession or under any will of declarant or codicil thereto, or directly financially responsible for declarant's medical care. I am not a health care provider of the declarant or an employee of the health facility in which the declarant is a patient.

Witness Signature _____ Date _____

Printed Name of Witness _____

Second Witness Signature _____ Date _____

Printed Name of Second Witness _____

Acceptance of Health Care Agent
(Attorney-in-Fact for Health Care)

I accept my appointment as Health Care Agent and Attorney-in-Fact for Health Care.

Signature _____ Date _____

Kansas Advance Health Care Directive

On this date of _____ , I, _____ , do hereby sign, execute, and adopt the following as my Advance Health Care Directive. I direct any and all persons or entities involved with my health care in any manner that these decisions are my wishes and were adopted without duress or force and of my own free will.

I have placed my initials next to the sections of this Directive that I have adopted:

[   ]   Living Will Declaration
[   ]   Selection of Health Care Agent (Durable Power of Attorney for Health Care)
[   ]   Designation of Primary Physician
[   ]   Organ Donation

Living Will Declaration

I, being of sound mind, willfully and voluntarily make known my desire that my dying shall not be artificially prolonged under the circumstances set forth below, and do hereby declare: If at any time I should have an incurable injury, disease, or illness certified to be a terminal condition by two physicians who have personally examined me, one of whom shall be my attending physician, and the physicians have determined that my death will occur whether or not life-sustaining procedures are utilized and where the application of life-sustaining procedures would serve only to artificially prolong the dying process, I direct that such procedures be withheld or withdrawn, and that I be permitted to die naturally with only the administration of medication or the performance of any medical procedure deemed necessary to provide me with comfort care. In the absence of my ability to give directions regarding the use of such life-sustaining procedures, it is my intention that this declaration shall be honored by my family and physician(s) as the final expression of my legal right to refuse medical or surgical treatment and accept the consequences from such refusal. I understand the full import of this declaration and I am emotionally and mentally competent to make this declaration.

OTHER DIRECTIONS **(attach additional sheets if needed)**:

Selection of Health Care Agent
(Durable Power of Attorney for Health Care)

I designate and appoint _____ (name),
of _____ (address), to be my agent for health care decisions and pursuant to the language stated below, on my behalf to:

> (1) Consent, refuse consent, or withdraw consent to any care, treatment, service, or procedure to maintain, diagnose, or treat a physical or mental condition, and to make decisions about organ donation, autopsy, and disposition of the body;

(2) Make all necessary arrangements at any hospital, psychiatric hospital, psychiatric treatment facility, hospice, nursing home, or similar institution;

(3) Employ or discharge health care personnel to include physicians, psychiatrists, psychologists, dentists, nurses, therapists, or any other person who is licensed, certified, or otherwise authorized or permitted by the laws of this state to administer health care as the agent shall deem necessary for my physical, mental, and emotional well-being; and

(4) Request, receive, and review any information, verbal or written, regarding my personal affairs or physical or mental health including medical and hospital records and to execute any releases of other documents that may be required in order to obtain such information.

In exercising the grant of authority set forth above, my agent for health care decisions shall **(Here may be inserted any special instructions or statement of the principal's desires to be followed by the agent in exercising the authority granted)**:

The powers of the agent herein shall be limited to the extent set out in writing in this durable power of attorney for health care decisions and shall not include the power to revoke or invalidate any previously existing declaration made in accordance with the natural death act.

The agent shall be prohibited from authorizing consent for the following items **(Insert any prohibitions on agent's authority to give consent)**:

This durable power of attorney for health care decisions shall be subject to the additional following limitations **(Insert any limitations on the agent's authority)**:

This power of attorney for health care decisions shall become effective immediately and shall not be affected by my subsequent disability or incapacity or upon the occurrence of my disability or incapacity. Any durable power of attorney for health care decisions I have previously made is hereby revoked. This durable power of attorney for health care decisions shall be revoked by an instrument in writing executed, witnessed, or acknowledged in the same manner as required herein.

Designation of Primary Physician

I designate the following physician as my primary physician: _____ (name)

_____ (address)

_____ (phone).

OPTIONAL- DESIGNATION OF ALTERNATE PRIMARY PHYSICIAN: If the physician I have designated above is not willing, able, or reasonably available to act as my primary physician, I designate the following physician as my primary physician:

_____ (name)

_____ (address)

_____ (phone).

Organ Donation

In the event of my death, I have placed my initials next to the following part(s) of my body that I wish donated for the purposes **that I have initialed below:**

[   ] any organs or parts **OR**

[   ] eyes   [   ] bone and connective tissue   [   ] skin

[   ] heart   [   ] kidney(s)   [   ] liver

[   ] lung(s)   [   ] pancreas   [   ] other _____

for the purposes of:

[   ] any purpose authorized by law **OR**

[   ] transplantation   [   ] research   [   ] therapy

[   ] medical education   [   ] other limitations _____

Signature

I sign this Advance Health Care Directive, consisting of the following sections, **which I have initialed below and have elected to adopt:**

[   ] Living Will Declaration

[   ] Selection of Health Care Agent (Durable Power of Attorney for Health Care)

[   ] Designation of Primary Physician

[   ] Organ Donation

BY SIGNING HERE I INDICATE THAT I UNDERSTAND THE PURPOSE AND EFFECT OF THIS DOCUMENT.

Signature _____   Date _____

City, County, and State of Residence _____

Notary Acknowledgment

State of _____

County of _____

On _____ , _____ came before me personally and, under oath, stated that he or she is the person described in the above document and he or she signed the above document in my presence. I declare under penalty of perjury that the person whose name is subscribed to this instrument appears to be of sound mind and under no duress, fraud, or undue influence.

_____

Notary Public

My commission expires _____

Witness Acknowledgment

The declarant is personally known to me and I believe him or her to be of sound mind and under no duress, fraud, or undue influence. I did not sign the declarant's signature above for or at the direction of the declarant and I am not appointed as the health care agent or attorney-in-fact herein. I am at least eighteen (18) years of age and I am not related to the declarant by blood, adoption, or marriage, entitled to any portion of the estate of the declarant according to the laws of intestate succession or under any will of declarant or codicil thereto, or directly financially responsible for declarant's medical care. I am not a health care provider of the declarant or an employee of the health facility in which the declarant is a patient.

Witness Signature _____ Date _____

Printed Name of Witness _____

Second Witness Signature _____ Date _____

Printed Name of Second Witness _____

Acceptance of Health Care Agent and Attorney-in-Fact for Health Care

I accept my appointment as Health Care Agent and Attorney-in-Fact for Health Care:

Signature _____ Date _____

Kentucky Advance Health Care Directive

On this date of _____, I, _____, do hereby sign, execute, and adopt the following as my Advance Health Care Directive. I direct any and all persons or entities involved with my health care in any manner that these decisions are my wishes and were adopted without duress or force and of my own free will.

I have placed my initials next to the sections of this Directive that I have adopted:

[   ] Living Will Directive
[   ] Selection of Health Care Agent (Health Care Surrogate)
[   ] Designation of Primary Physician
[   ] Organ Donation

Living Will Directive

My wishes regarding life-prolonging treatment and artificially-provided nutrition and hydration to be provided to me if I no longer have decisional capacity, have a terminal condition, or become permanently unconscious have been indicated by initialing the appropriate lines below. By *initialing* the appropriate lines, I specifically provide the following directions to my attending physician:
(Initial one)

[   ] I direct that treatment be withheld or withdrawn, and that I be permitted to die naturally with only the administration of medication or the performance of any medical treatment deemed necessary to alleviate pain.

[   ] I Do NOT authorize that life-prolonging treatment be withheld or withdrawn.

(Initial one)

[   ] I authorize the withholding or withdrawal of artificially-provided food, water, or other artificially-provided nourishment or fluids.

[   ] I Do NOT authorize the withholding or withdrawal of artificially-provided food, water, or other artificially-provided nourishment or fluids.

[   ] I authorize my health care surrogate, designated on the following page, to withhold or withdraw artificially-provided nourishment or fluids, or other treatment if the surrogate determines that withholding or withdrawing is in my best interest; but I do not mandate that withholding or withdrawing.

In the absence of my ability to give directions regarding the use of life-prolonging treatment and artificially-provided nutrition and hydration, it is my intention that this directive shall be honored by my attending physician, my family, and any surrogate designated pursuant to this directive as the final expression of my legal right to refuse medical or surgical treatment and I accept the consequences of the refusal. If I have been diagnosed as pregnant and that diagnosis is known to my attending physician, this directive shall have no force or effect during the course of my pregnancy.

Selection of Health Care Agent (Health Care Surrogate)

I designate _____ (name), of
_____ (address), as
my health care surrogate to make health care decisions for me in accordance with this directive
when I no longer have decisional capacity.

OPTIONAL - DESIGNATION OF ALTERNATE SURROGATE: If I revoke my surrogate's authority or if my surrogate is not willing, able, or reasonably available to make a health care decision for me, I designate as my first alternate health care surrogate
_____ (name of individual you choose as alternate surrogate)
_____ (address)

Any prior designation is revoked. If I do not designate a surrogate, the above instructions indicated in my living will are my directions to my attending physician. If I have designated a surrogate, my surrogate shall comply with my wishes as indicated above in my living will.

Designation of Primary Physician

I designate the following physician as my primary physician: _____ (name)
_____ (address)
_____ (phone).

OPTIONAL- DESIGNATION OF ALTERNATE PRIMARY PHYSICIAN: If the physician I have designated above is not willing, able, or reasonably available to act as my primary physician, I designate the following physician as my primary physician:
_____ (name)
_____ (address)
_____ (phone).

Organ Donation

In the event of my death, I have placed my initials next to the following part(s) of my body that I wish donated for the purposes **that I have initialed below**:

[   ] any organs or parts **OR**
[   ] eyes   [   ] bone and connective tissue   [   ] skin
[   ] heart   [   ] kidney(s)   [   ] liver
[   ] lung(s)   [   ] pancreas   [   ] other _____
for the purposes of:
[   ] any purpose authorized by law **OR**
[   ] transplantation   [   ] research   [   ] therapy
[   ] medical education   [   ] other limitations _____

Signature

I sign this Advance Health Care Directive, consisting of the following sections, **which I have initialed below and have elected to adopt:**

[   ] Living Will Directive
[   ] Selection of Health Care Agent (Health Care Surrogate)
[   ] Designation of Primary Physician
[   ] Organ Donation

BY SIGNING HERE I INDICATE THAT I UNDERSTAND THE PURPOSE AND EFFECT OF THIS DOCUMENT.

Signature _____ Date _____

City, County, and State of Residence _____

Notary Acknowledgment
State of _____
County of _____

On _____ , _____ came before me personally and, under oath, stated that he or she is the person described in the above document and he or she signed the above document in my presence. I declare under penalty of perjury that the person whose name is subscribed to this instrument appears to be of sound mind and under no duress, fraud, or undue influence.

_____
Notary Public
My commission expires _____

Witness Acknowledgment

The declarant is personally known to me and I believe him or her to be of sound mind and under no duress, fraud, or undue influence. I did not sign the declarant's signature above for or at the direction of the declarant and I am not appointed as the health care agent or attorney-in-fact herein. I am at least eighteen (18) years of age and I am not related to the declarant by blood, adoption, or marriage, entitled to any portion of the estate of the declarant according to the laws of intestate succession or under any will of declarant or codicil thereto, or directly financially responsible for declarant's medical care. I am not a health care provider of the declarant or an employee of the health facility in which the declarant is a patient.

Witness Signature _____ Date _____

Printed Name of Witness _____

Second Witness Signature _____ Date _____

Printed Name of Second Witness _____

Acceptance of Health Care Agent (Health Care Surrogate)

I accept my appointment as Health Care Agent (Health Care Surrogate):

Signature _____ Date _____

I accept my appointment as Alternate Health Care Agent (Health Care Surrogate):

Signature _____ Date _____

Louisiana Advance Health Care Directive

On this date of _____ , I, _____ , do hereby sign, execute, and adopt the following as my Advance Health Care Directive. I direct any and all persons or entities involved with my health care in any manner that these decisions are my wishes and were adopted without duress or force and of my own free will.

I have placed my initials next to the sections of this Directive that I have adopted:

[   ] Living Will (Declaration)
[   ] Selection of Health Care Agent
[   ] Designation of Primary Physician
[   ] Organ Donation

Living Will (Declaration)

If at any time I should have an incurable injury, disease or illness, be in a continual profound comatose state with no reasonable chance of recovery, or am certified to be in a terminal and irreversible condition by two (2) physicians who have personally examined me, one (1) of whom shall be my attending physician, and the physicians have determined that my death will occur whether or not life-sustaining procedures are utilized and where the application of life-sustaining procedures would serve only to prolong artificially the dying process, I direct **(initial one only)**:

[   ] That all life-sustaining procedures, including nutrition and hydration, be withheld or withdrawn so that food and water will not be administered invasively.

[   ] That life-sustaining procedures, except nutrition and hydration, be withheld or withdrawn so that food and water can be administered invasively.

I further direct that I be permitted to die naturally with only the administration of medication or the performance of any medical procedure deemed necessary to provide me with comfort care. In the absence of my ability to give directions regarding the use of such life-sustaining procedures, it is my intention that this declaration shall be honored by my family and physician(s) as the final expression of my legal right to refuse medical or surgical treatment and accept the consequences from such refusal.

Selection of Health Care Agent

I authorize _____ (name), of _____ (address), to make all medical treatment decisions for me, including decisions to withhold or withdraw any form of life-sustaining procedure on my behalf should I be: (1) diagnosed as suffering from a terminal and irreversible condition, and (2) comatose, incompetent, or otherwise mentally or physically incapable of communication. I have discussed my desires concerning terminal care with my agent named previously, and I trust his or her judgment on my behalf. I understand that if I have not filled in any name in this clause or if the agent I have chosen is unavailable or unwilling to act on my behalf, my living will declaration will nevertheless be given effect should the above-discussed circumstance arise.

Designation of Primary Physician

I designate the following physician as my primary physician: _____ (name)
_____ (address)
_____ (phone).

OPTIONAL- DESIGNATION OF ALTERNATE PRIMARY PHYSICIAN: If the physician I have designated above is not willing, able, or reasonably available to act as my primary physician, I designate the following physician as my primary physician:
_____ (name)
_____ (address)
_____ (phone).

Organ Donation

In the event of my death, I have placed my initials next to the following part(s) of my body that I wish donated for the purposes **that I have initialed below:**

[   ] any organs or parts **OR**
[   ] eyes   [   ] bone and connective tissue   [   ] skin
[   ] heart   [   ] kidney(s)   [   ] liver
[   ] lung(s)   [   ] pancreas   [   ] other _____
for the purposes of:
[   ] any purpose authorized by law **OR**
[   ] transplantation   [   ] research   [   ] therapy
[   ] medical education   [   ] other limitations _____

Signature

I sign this Advance Health Care Directive, consisting of the following sections, **which I have initialed below and have elected to adopt:**
[   ] Living Will (Declaration)
[   ] Selection of Health Care Agent
[   ] Designation of Primary Physician
[   ] Organ Donation
BY SIGNING HERE I INDICATE THAT I UNDERSTAND THE PURPOSE AND EFFECT OF THIS DOCUMENT.

Signature _____   Date _____

City, Parish, and State of Residence _____

Notary Acknowledgment

State of _____
Parish of _____

On _____ , _____ came before me personally and, under oath, stated that he or she is the person described in the above document and he or she signed the above document in my presence. I declare under penalty of perjury that the person whose name is subscribed to this instrument appears to be of sound mind and under no duress, fraud, or undue influence.

_____
Notary Public
My commission expires _____

Witness Acknowledgment

The declarant is personally known to me and I believe him or her to be of sound mind and under no duress, fraud, or undue influence. I did not sign the declarant's signature above for or at the direction of the declarant and I am not appointed as the health care agent or attorney-in-fact herein. I am at least eighteen (18) years of age and I am not related to the declarant by blood, adoption, or marriage, entitled to any portion of the estate of the declarant according to the laws of intestate succession or under any will of declarant or codicil thereto, or directly financially responsible for declarant's medical care. I am not a health care provider of the declarant or an employee of the health facility in which the declarant is a patient.

Witness Signature _____ Date _____

Printed Name of Witness _____

Second Witness Signature _____ Date _____

Printed Name of Second Witness _____

Acceptance of Health Care Agent

I accept my appointment as Health Care Agent:

Signature _____ Date _____

Maine Advance Health Care Directive

On this date of _____ , I, _____ , do hereby sign, execute, and adopt the following as my Advance Health Care Directive. I direct any and all persons or entities involved with my health care in any manner that these decisions are my wishes and were adopted without duress or force and of my own free will.

I have placed my initials next to the sections of this Directive that I have adopted:

[   ] Living Will (Instructions for Health Care)
[   ] Selection of Health Care Agent (Power of Attorney for Health Care)
[   ] Designation of Primary Physician
[   ] Organ Donation

You have the right to give instructions about your own health care. You also have the right to name someone else to make health-care decisions for you. This form lets you do either or both of these things. It also lets you express your wishes regarding donation of organs and the designation of your primary physician. If you use this form, you may complete or modify all or any part of it. You are free to use a different form.

Part 1 of this form lets you give specific instructions about any aspect of your health care. Choices are provided for you to express your wishes regarding the provision, withholding or withdrawal of treatment to keep you alive, including the provision of artificial nutrition and hydration, as well as the provision of pain relief. Space is also provided for you to add to the choices you have made or for you to write out any additional wishes.

Part 2 of this form is a power of attorney for health care. Part 2 lets you name another individual as agent to make health-care decisions for you if you become incapable of making your own decisions or if you want someone else to make those decisions for you now even though you are still capable. You may also name an alternate agent to act for you if your first choice is not willing, able or reasonably available to make decisions for you. Unless related to you, your agent may not be an owner, operator or employee of a residential long-term health-care institution at which you are receiving care.

Unless the form you sign limits the authority of your agent, your agent may make all health-care decisions for you. This form has a place for you to limit the authority of your agent. You need not limit the authority of your agent if you wish to rely on your agent for all health-care decisions that may have to be made. If you choose not to limit the authority of your agent, your agent will have the right to: (a) Consent or refuse consent to any care, treatment, service or procedure to maintain, diagnose or otherwise affect a physical or mental condition; (b) Select or discharge health-care providers and institutions; (c) Approve or disapprove diagnostic tests, surgical procedures, programs of medication and orders not to resuscitate; and (d) Direct the provision, withholding or withdrawal of artificial nutrition and hydration and all other forms of health care, including life-sustaining treatment.

Part 3 of this form lets you designate a physician to have primary responsibility for your health care.

Part 4 of this form lets you express an intention to donate your bodily organs and tissues following your death.

After completing this form, sign and date the form at the end. You must have 2 other individuals sign as witnesses. Give a copy of the signed and completed form to your physician, to any other health-care providers you may have, to any health-care institution at which you are receiving care and to any health-care agents you have named. You should talk to the person you have named as agent to make sure that he or she understands your wishes and is willing to take the responsibility. You have the right to revoke this advance health-care directive or replace this form at any time.

Living Will Declaration (Instructions for Health Care)

(If you are satisfied to allow your agent to determine what is best for you in making end-of-life decisions, you need not fill out this part of the form. If you do fill out this part of the form, you may strike any wording you do not want.)

END-OF-LIFE DECISIONS: I direct that my health care providers and others involved in my care provide, withhold, or withdraw treatment in accordance **with the choice I have initialed below**:

[   ] **Choice NOT To Prolong Life:** I do NOT want my life to be prolonged if:
    (a) I have an incurable and irreversible condition that will result in my death within a relatively short time;
    (b) I become unconscious and, to a reasonable degree of medical certainty, I will not regain consciousness; **OR**
    (c) the likely risks and burdens of treatment would outweigh the expected benefits.
           OR
[   ] **Choice TO Prolong Life**: I DO want my life to be prolonged as long as possible within the limits of generally-accepted health care standards.

ARTIFICIAL NUTRITION AND HYDRATION: Artificial nutrition and hydration must be provided, withheld, or withdrawn in accordance with the choice I have made in paragraph (6) unless I mark the following box:
If I initial this box[   ], artificial nutrition and hydration must be provided regardless of my condition and regardless of the choice I have made in paragraph (6).

RELIEF FROM PAIN: Except as I state in the following space, I direct that treatment for alleviation of pain or discomfort be provided at all times, even if it hastens my death **(list any exceptions)**:

OTHER WISHES: **(If you do not agree with any of the optional choices above and wish to write your own, or if you wish to add to the instructions you have given above, you may do so here.) (Add additional sheets if needed)**
 I direct that :

Selection of Health Care Agent
(Power of Attorney for Health Care)

DESIGNATION OF AGENT: I designate the following individual as my agent to make health care decisions for me _____ (name), of _____ (address).

OPTIONAL - DESIGNATION OF ALTERNATE AGENT: If I revoke my agent's authority or if my agent is not willing, able, or reasonably available to make a health care decision for me, I designate as my first alternate agent

_____ (name of individual you choose as first alternate agent)

_____ (address)

AGENT'S AUTHORITY: My agent is authorized to make all health care decisions for me, including decisions to provide, withhold, or withdraw artificial nutrition and hydration and all other forms of health care to keep me alive, except as I state here **(add additional sheets if needed)**:

WHEN AGENT'S AUTHORITY BECOMES EFFECTIVE: My agent's authority becomes effective when my primary physician determines that I am unable to make my own health care decisions unless I mark the following box:
If I initial this box [   ], my agent's authority to make health care decisions for me takes effect immediately.

AGENT'S OBLIGATION: My agent shall make health care decisions for me in accordance with this power of attorney for health care, any instructions I give in this form, and my other wishes to the extent known to my agent. To the extent my wishes are unknown, my agent shall make health care decisions for me in accordance with what my agent determines to be in my best interest. In determining my best interest, my agent shall consider my personal values to the extent known to my agent.

NOMINATION OF GUARDIAN: If a guardian of my person needs to be appointed for me by a court, I nominate the agent (or alternate agent if then serving) designated in this form.

Designation of Primary Physician

I designate the following physician as my primary physician: _____ (name)

_____ (address)

_____ (phone).

OPTIONAL- DESIGNATION OF ALTERNATE PRIMARY PHYSICIAN: If the physician I have designated above is not willing, able, or reasonably available to act as my primary physician, I designate the following physician as my primary physician:

_____ (name)

_____ (address)

_____ (phone).

Organ Donation

In the event of my death, I have placed my initials next to the following part(s) of my body that I wish donated for the purposes **that I have initialed below:**

[   ] any organs or parts **OR**

[   ] eyes   [   ] bone and connective tissue   [   ] skin
[   ] heart   [   ] kidney(s)   [   ] liver
[   ] lung(s)   [   ] pancreas   [   ] other _____

for the purposes of:

[   ] any purpose authorized by law **OR**

[   ] transplantation   [   ] research   [   ] therapy
[   ] medical education   [   ] other limitations _____

Signature

I sign this Advance Health Care Directive, consisting of the following sections, **which I have initialed below and have elected to adopt:**

[   ]   Living Will (Instructions for Health Care)
[   ]   Selection of Health Care Agent (Power of Attorney for Health Care)
[   ]   Designation of Primary Physician
[   ]   Organ Donation

BY SIGNING HERE I INDICATE THAT I UNDERSTAND THE PURPOSE AND EFFECT OF THIS DOCUMENT.

Signature _____   Date _____

City, County, and State of Residence _____

Notary Acknowledgment

State of _____

County of _____

On _____ , _____ came before me personally and, under oath, stated that he or she is the person described in the above document and he or she signed the above document in my presence. I declare under penalty of perjury that the person whose name is subscribed to this instrument appears to be of sound mind and under no duress, fraud, or undue influence.

_____
Notary Public
My commission expires _____

Witness Acknowledgment

The declarant is personally known to me and I believe him or her to be of sound mind and under no duress, fraud, or undue influence. I did not sign the declarant's signature above for or at the direction of the declarant and I am not appointed as the health care agent or attorney-in-fact herein. I am at least eighteen (18) years of age and I am not related to the declarant by blood, adoption, or marriage, entitled to any portion of the estate of the declarant according to the laws of intestate succession or under any will of declarant or codicil thereto, or directly financially responsible for declarant's medical care. I am not a health care provider of the declarant or an employee of the health facility in which the declarant is a patient.

Witness Signature _____ Date _____

Printed Name of Witness _____

Second Witness Signature _____ Date _____

Printed Name of Second Witness _____

Acceptance of Health Care Agent and Attorney-in-Fact for Health Care

I accept my appointment as Health Care Agent and Attorney-in-Fact for Health Care.

Signature _____ Date _____

I accept my appointment as Alternate Health Care Agent and Attorney-in-Fact for Health Care:

Signature _____ Date _____

Maryland Advance Health Care Directive

On this date of _____ , I, _____ , do hereby sign, execute, and adopt the following as my Advance Health Care Directive. I direct any and all persons or entities involved with my health care in any manner that these decisions are my wishes and were adopted without duress or force and of my own free will. **I have placed my initials next to the sections of this Directive that I have adopted:**

[   ] Living Will (Treatment Preferences)
[   ] Selection of Health Care Agent
[   ] Designation of Primary Physician
[   ] Organ Donation

Using this advance directive form to do health care planning is completely optional. Other forms are also valid in Maryland. No matter what form you use, talk to your family and others close to you about your wishes. Part I lets you write your preferences about efforts to extend your life in three situations: terminal condition, persistent vegetative state, and end-stage condition. Part II of this form lets you choose someone to make your health care decisions for you if you cannot make them. The person you pick is called your health care agent. Make sure you talk to your health care agent (and any back-up agents) about this important role. Part III allows you to designate your choice as your primary doctor. In Part IV, you can choose to become an organ donor after your death. You can fill out any or all parts of this form. Use the form to reflect your wishes, then sign in front of two witnesses and a notary public. If your wishes change, make a new advance directive. Make sure you give a copy of the completed form to your health care agent, your doctor, and others who might need it. Keep a copy at home in a place where someone can get it if needed. Review what you have written periodically.

Part I: Living Will (Treatment Preferences)

If I am not able to make an informed decision regarding my health care, I direct my health care providers to follow my instructions as set forth below:

PREFERENCE IN CASE OF TERMINAL CONDITION: **(If you want to state your preference, initial one statement only. If you do not want to state a preference here, cross through the whole section.)**

[   ] Keep me comfortable and allow natural death to occur. I do not want any medical interventions used to try to extend my life. I do not want to receive nutrition and fluids by tube or other medical means.

[   ] Keep me comfortable and allow natural death to occur. I do not want medical interventions used to try to extend my life. If I am unable to take enough nourishment by mouth, however, I want to receive nutrition and fluids by tube or other medical means.

[   ] Try to extend my life for as long as possible, using all available interventions that in reasonable medical judgment would prevent or delay my death. If I am unable to take enough nourishment by mouth, I want to receive nutrition and fluids by tube or other medical means.

PREFERENCE IN CASE OF PERSISTENT VEGETATIVE STATE: **(If you want to state your preference, initial one statement only. If you do not want to state a preference here, cross through the whole section.)**

If my doctors certify that I am in a persistent vegetative state, that is, if I am not conscious and am not aware of myself or my environment or able to interact with others, and there is no reasonable expectation that I will ever regain consciousness:

[   ] Keep me comfortable and allow natural death to occur. I do not want any medical interventions used to try to extend my life. I do not want to receive nutrition and fluids by tube or other medical means.

[   ] Keep me comfortable and allow natural death to occur. I do not want medical interventions used to try to extend my life. If I am unable to take enough nourishment by mouth, however, I want to receive nutrition and fluids by tube or other medical means.

[   ] Try to extend my life for as long as possible, using all available interventions that in reasonable medical judgment would prevent or delay my death. If I am unable to take enough nourishment by mouth, I want to receive nutrition and fluids by tube or other medical means.

PREFERENCE IN CASE OF END-STAGE CONDITION: **(If you want to state your preference, initial one statement only. If you do not want to state a preference here, cross through the whole section.)**

If my doctors certify that I am in an end-stage condition, that is, an incurable condition that will continue in its course until death and that has already resulted in loss of capacity and complete physical dependency:

[   ] Keep me comfortable and allow natural death to occur. I do not want any medical interventions used to try to extend my life. I do not want to receive nutrition and fluids by tube or other medical means.

[   ] Keep me comfortable and allow natural death to occur. I do not want medical interventions used to try to extend my life. If I am unable to take enough nourishment by mouth, however, I want to receive nutrition and fluids by tube or other medical means.

[   ] Try to extend my life for as long as possible, using all available interventions that in reasonable medical judgment would prevent or delay my death. If I am unable to take enough nourishment by mouth, I want to receive nutrition and fluids by tube or other medical means.

PAIN RELIEF: No matter what my condition, give me the medicine or other treatment I need to relieve pain.

IN CASE OF PREGNANCY: (Optional, for women of child-bearing years only): If I am pregnant, my decision concerning life-sustaining procedures shall be modified as follows:

EFFECT OF STATED PREFERENCES: (**Read both of these statements carefully. Then, initial one only.**)

[   ] I realize I cannot foresee everything that might happen after I can no longer decide for myself. My stated preferences are meant to guide whoever is making decisions on my behalf and my health care providers, but I authorize them to be flexible in applying these statements if they feel that doing so would be in my best interest.

[   ] I realize I cannot foresee everything that might happen after I can no longer decide for myself. Still, I want whoever is making decisions on my behalf and my health care providers to follow my stated preferences exactly as written, even if they think that some alternative is better.

OPTIONAL: STATEMENT OF GOALS AND VALUES: I want to say something about my goals and values, and especially what's most important to me during the last part of my life:

Part II: Selection of Health Care Agent

I appoint the following individual as my agent to make health care decisions for me:

_____ (name),

of _____ (address).

OPTIONAL - DESIGNATION OF ALTERNATE AGENT: If I revoke my agent's authority or if my agent is not willing, able, or reasonably available to make a health care decision for me, I designate as my first alternate agent

_____ (name of individual you choose as first alternate agent)

_____ (address)

POWERS AND RIGHTS OF HEALTH CARE AGENT: I want my agent to have full power to make health care decisions for me, including the power to: 1. Consent or not consent to medical procedures and treatments which my doctors offer, including things that are intended to keep me alive, like ventilators and feeding tubes; 2. Decide who my doctor and other health care providers should be; and 3. Decide where I should be treated, including whether I should be in a hospital, nursing home, other medical care facility, or hospice program. 4. I also want my agent to: a. Ride with me in an ambulance if ever I need to be rushed to the hospital; and b. Be able to visit me if I am in a hospital or any other health care facility.

This advance directive does not make my agent responsible for any of the costs of my care.

This power is subject to the following conditions or limitations:

HOW MY AGENT IS TO DECIDE SPECIFIC ISSUES: I trust my agent's judgment. My agent should look first to see if there is anything in Part II of this advance directive that helps decide the issue. Then, my agent should think about the conversations we have had, my religious or other beliefs and values, my personality, and how I handled medical and other important issues in the past. If what I would decide is still unclear, then my agent is to make decisions for me that my agent believes are in my best interest. In doing so, my agent should consider the benefits, burdens, and risks of the choices presented by my doctors.

OPTIONAL - PEOPLE MY AGENT SHOULD CONSULT: In making important decisions on my behalf, I encourage my agent to consult with the following people. By filling this in, I do not intend to limit the number of people with whom my agent might want to consult or my agent's power to make these decisions.

IN CASE OF PREGNANCY (OPTIONAL, for women of child-bearing years only)
If I am pregnant, my agent shall follow these specific instructions:

ACCESS TO MY HEALTH INFORMATION - Federal Privacy Law (HIPAA) Authorization
If, prior to the time the person selected as my agent has power to act under this document, my doctor wants to discuss with that person my capacity to make my own health care decisions, I authorize my doctor to disclose protected health information which relates to that issue. Once my agent has full power to act under this document, my agent may request, receive, and review any information, oral or written, regarding my physical or mental health, including, but not limited to, medical and hospital records and other protected health information, and consent to disclosure of this information. For all purposes related to this document, my agent is my personal representative under the Health Insurance Portability and Accountability Act (HIPAA). My agent may sign, as my personal representative, any release forms or other HIPAA-related materials.

EFFECTIVENESS OF THIS PART: My agent's power is in effect: **(Initial your choice)**

[   ] Immediately after I sign this document, subject to my right to make any decision about my health care if I want and am able to. **OR**

[   ] Whenever I am not able to make informed decisions about my health care, either because the doctor in charge of my care (attending physician) decides that I have lost this ability temporarily, or my attending physician and a consulting doctor agree that I have lost this ability permanently.

Part III: Designation of Primary Physician

I designate the following physician as my primary physician: _____ (name)
_____ (address)
_____ (phone).

OPTIONAL- DESIGNATION OF ALTERNATE PRIMARY PHYSICIAN: If the physician I have designated above is not willing, able, or reasonably available to act as my primary physician, I designate the following physician as my primary physician:

_____ (name)
_____ (address)
_____ (phone).

Part IV: Organ Donation

In the event of my death, I have placed my initials next to the following part(s) of my body that I wish donated for the purposes **that I have initialed below**:

[   ] any organs or parts **OR**
[   ] eyes   [   ] bone and connective tissue   [   ] skin
[   ] heart   [   ] kidney(s)   [   ] liver
[   ] lung(s)   [   ] pancreas   [   ] other _____

for the purposes of:
[   ] any purpose authorized by law **OR**
[   ] transplantation   [   ] research   [   ] therapy
[   ] medical education   [   ] other limitations _____

Signature

I sign this Advance Health Care Directive, consisting of the following sections, **which I have initialed below and have elected to adopt:**
[   ] Living Will (Treatment Preferences)
[   ] Selection of Health Care Agent
[   ] Designation of Primary Physician
[   ] Organ Donation

BY SIGNING HERE I INDICATE THAT I UNDERSTAND THE PURPOSE AND EFFECT OF THIS DOCUMENT.

Signature _____   Date _____

City, County, and State of Residence _____

Notary Acknowledgment

State of _____

County of _____

On _____ , _____ came before me personally and, under oath, stated that he or she is the person described in the above document and he or she signed the above document in my presence. I declare under penalty of perjury that the person whose name is subscribed to this instrument appears to be of sound mind and under no duress, fraud, or undue influence.

_____
Notary Public
My commission expires _____

Witness Acknowledgment

The declarant is personally known to me and I believe him or her to be of sound mind and under no duress, fraud, or undue influence. I did not sign the declarant's signature above for or at the direction of the declarant and I am not appointed as the health care agent or attorney-in-fact herein. I am at least eighteen (18) years of age and I am not related to the declarant by blood, adoption, or marriage, entitled to any portion of the estate of the declarant according to the laws of intestate succession or under any will of declarant or codicil thereto, or directly financially responsible for declarant's medical care. I am not a health care provider of the declarant or an employee of the health facility in which the declarant is a patient.

Witness Signature _____ Date _____

Printed Name of Witness _____

Second Witness Signature _____ Date _____

Printed Name of Second Witness _____

Acceptance of Health Care Agent

I accept my appointment as Health Care Agent:

Signature _____ Date _____

I accept my appointment as Alternate Health Care Agent:

Signature _____ Date _____

Massachusetts Advance Health Care Directive

On this date of _____ , I, _____ , do hereby sign, execute, and adopt the following as my Advance Health Care Directive. I direct any and all persons or entities involved with my health care in any manner that these decisions are my wishes and were adopted without duress or force and of my own free will.

I have placed my initials next to the sections of this Directive that I have adopted:

[   ] Living Will (Declaration and Directive to Physicians)
[   ] Selection of Health Care Agent (Health Care Proxy)
[   ] Designation of Primary Physician
[   ] Organ Donation

Living Will (Declaration and Directive to Physicians)

I, willfully and voluntarily, make known my desire that my life not be artificially prolonged under the circumstances set forth below, and, pursuant to any and all applicable laws in the State of Massachusetts, I declare that:

If at any time I should have an incurable injury, disease, or illness which has been certified as a terminal condition by my attending physician and one (1) additional physician, both of whom have personally examined me, and such physicians have determined that there can be no recovery from such condition and my death is imminent, and where the application of life-prolonging procedures would serve only to artificially prolong the dying process, I direct that such procedures be withheld or withdrawn, and that I be permitted to die naturally with only the administration of medication, the administration of nutrition, or the performance of any medical procedure deemed necessary to provide me with comfort, care, or to alleviate pain.

If at any time I should have been diagnosed as being in a persistent vegetative state which has been certified as incurable by my attending physician and one (1) additional physician, both of whom have personally examined me, and such physicians have determined that there can be no recovery from such condition, and where the application of life-prolonging procedures would serve only to artificially prolong the dying process, I direct that such procedures be withheld or withdrawn, and that I be permitted to die naturally with only the administration of medication, the administration of nutrition, or the performance of any medical procedure deemed necessary to provide me with comfort, care, or to alleviate pain.

In the absence of my ability to give directions regarding my treatment in the above situations, including directions regarding the use of such life-prolonging procedures, it is my intention that this declaration shall be honored by my family, my physician, and any court of law, as the final expression of my legal right to refuse medical and surgical treatment. I declare that I fully accept the consequences for such refusal. If I am diagnosed as pregnant, this document shall have no force and effect during my pregnancy.

I understand the full importance of this declaration and I am emotionally and mentally competent to make this declaration and Living Will. No person shall be in any way responsible for the making or placing into effect of this declaration and Living Will or for carrying out my express directions. I also understand that I may revoke this document at any time.

Selection of Health Care Agent (Health Care Proxy)

I hereby appoint _____(name), of _____ (address), as my health care agent to make any and all health care decisions for me, except to the extent that I state otherwise below. This Health Care Proxy shall take effect in the event I become unable to make or communicate my own health care decisions.

OPTIONAL - DESIGNATION OF ALTERNATE AGENT: If I revoke my agent's authority or if my agent is not willing, able, or reasonably available to make a health care decision for me, I designate as my first alternate agent

_____ (name of individual you choose as first alternate agent)

_____ (address)

I direct my agent to make health care decisions in accord with my wishes and limitations as may be stated below, and as stated in my living will directions, or as he or she otherwise knows. If my wishes are unknown, I direct my agent to make health care decisions in accord with what he or she determines to be my best interests.

Other directions (*optional, add additional pages if necessary*):

Designation of Primary Physician

I designate the following physician as my primary physician: _____ (name)
_____ (address)
_____ (phone).

OPTIONAL- DESIGNATION OF ALTERNATE PRIMARY PHYSICIAN: If the physician I have designated above is not willing, able, or reasonably available to act as my primary physician, I designate the following physician as my primary physician:
_____ (name)
_____ (address)
_____ (phone).

Organ Donation

In the event of my death, I have placed my initials next to the following part(s) of my body that I wish donated for the purposes **that I have initialed below:**

[　　] any organs or parts **OR**
[　　] eyes   [　　] bone and connective tissue   [　　] skin
[　　] heart   [　　] kidney(s)   [　　] liver
[　　] lung(s)   [　　] pancreas   [　　] other _____
for the purposes of:
[　　] any purpose authorized by law **OR**
[　　] transplantation   [　　] research   [　　] therapy
[　　] medical education   [　　] other limitations _____

Signature

I sign this Advance Health Care Directive, consisting of the following sections, **which I have initialed below and have elected to adopt:**
[　　] Living Will (Declaration and Directive to Physicians)
[　　] Selection of Health Care Agent (Health Care Proxy)
[　　] Designation of Primary Physician
[　　] Organ Donation

BY SIGNING HERE I INDICATE THAT I UNDERSTAND THE PURPOSE AND EFFECT OF THIS DOCUMENT.

Signature _____ Date _____

City, County, and State of Residence _____

Notary Acknowledgment

State of _____
County of _____

On _____ , _____ came before me personally and, under oath, stated that he or she is the person described in the above document and he or she signed the above document in my presence. I declare under penalty of perjury that the person whose name is subscribed to this instrument appears to be of sound mind and under no duress, fraud, or undue influence.

_____
Notary Public
My commission expires _____

Witness Acknowledgment

(1) The Declarant is personally known to me and, to the best of my knowledge, the Declarant signed this instrument freely, under no constraint or undue influence, and is of sound mind and memory and legal age, and fully aware of the possible consequences of this action.

(2) I am at least nineteen (19) years of age and I am not related to the Declarant in any manner by blood, marriage, or adoption.

(3) I am not the Declarant's attending physician, or a patient or employee of the Declarant's attending physician, or a patient, physician, or employee of the health care facility in which the Declarant is a patient, unless such person is required or allowed to witness the execution of this document by the laws of the state in which this document is executed.

(4) I am not entitled to any portion of the Declarant's estate on the Declarant's death under the laws of intestate succession of any state or country, nor under the Last Will and Testament of the Declarant or any Codicil to such Last Will and Testament.

(5) I have no claim against any portion of the Declarant's estate on the Declarant's death.

(6) I am not directly financially responsible for the Declarant's medical care.

(7) I did not sign the Declarant's signature for the Declarant or on the direction of the Declarant, nor have I been paid any fee for acting as a witness to the execution of this document.

Witness Signature _____   Date _____

Printed Name of Witness _____

Second Witness Signature _____   Date _____

Printed Name of Second Witness _____

Acceptance of Health Care Agent (Health Care Proxy)

I accept my appointment as Health Care Agent and Health Care Proxy:

Signature _____   Date _____

I accept my appointment as Alternate Health Care Agent and Health Care Proxy:

Signature _____   Date _____

Michigan Advance Health Care Directive

On this date of _____ , I, _____ , do hereby sign, execute, and adopt the following as my Advance Health Care Directive. I direct any and all persons or entities involved with my health care in any manner that these decisions are my wishes and were adopted without duress or force and of my own free will.

I have placed my initials next to the sections of this Directive that I have adopted:

[   ] Living Will (Declaration and Directive to Physicians)
[   ] Selection of Health Care Agent (Designation of Patient Advocate for Health Care)
[   ] Designation of Primary Physician
[   ] Organ Donation

Living Will (Declaration and Directive to Physicians)

I, willfully and voluntarily, make known my desire that my life not be artificially prolonged under the circumstances set forth below, and, pursuant to any and all applicable laws in the State of Michigan, I declare that:

If at any time I should have an incurable injury, disease, or illness which has been certified as a terminal condition by my attending physician and one (1) additional physician, both of whom have personally examined me, and such physicians have determined that there can be no recovery from such condition and my death is imminent, and where the application of life-prolonging procedures would serve only to artificially prolong the dying process, I direct that such procedures be withheld or withdrawn, and that I be permitted to die naturally with only the administration of medication, the administration of nutrition, or the performance of any medical procedure deemed necessary to provide me with comfort, care, or to alleviate pain.

If at any time I should have been diagnosed as being in a persistent vegetative state which has been certified as incurable by my attending physician and one (1) additional physician, both of whom have personally examined me, and such physicians have determined that there can be no recovery from such condition, and where the application of life-prolonging procedures would serve only to artificially prolong the dying process, I direct that such procedures be withheld or withdrawn, and that I be permitted to die naturally with only the administration of medication, the administration of nutrition, or the performance of any medical procedure deemed necessary to provide me with comfort, care, or to alleviate pain.

In the absence of my ability to give directions regarding my treatment in the above situations, including directions regarding the use of such life-prolonging procedures, it is my intention that this Declaration shall be honored by my family, my physician, and any court of law, as the final expression of my legal right to refuse medical and surgical treatment. I declare that I fully accept the consequences for such refusal. If I am diagnosed as pregnant, this document shall have no force and effect during my pregnancy.

I understand the full importance of this Declaration and I am emotionally and mentally competent to make this Declaration and Living Will. No person shall be in any way responsible for the making or placing into effect of this Declaration and Living Will or for carrying out my express directions. I also understand that I may revoke this document at any time.

Selection of Health Care Agent
(Designation of Patient Advocate for Health Care)

I am of sound mind, and I voluntarily make this designation. I designate :

_____ (name),

of _____ (address),

as my patient advocate to make care, custody, or medical treatment decisions for me only when I become unable to participate in medical treatment decisions. The determination of when I am unable to participate in medical treatment decisions shall be made by my attending physician and another physician or licensed psychologist.

OPTIONAL - DESIGNATION OF ALTERNATE PATIENT ADVOCATE: If I revoke my Patient Advocate's authority or if my agent is not willing, able, or reasonably available to make a health care decision for me, I designate as my alternate Patient Advocate:

_____ (name of individual you choose as alternate Patient Advocate)

_____ (address)

I authorize my patient advocate to decide to withhold or withdraw medical treatment which could or would allow me to die. I am fully aware that such a decision could or would lead to my death. In making decisions for me, my patient advocate shall be guided by my wishes, whether expressed orally, in a living will, or in this designation. If my wishes as to a particular situation have not been expressed, my patient advocate shall be guided by his or her best judgment of my probable decision, given the benefits, burdens, and consequences of the decision, even if my death, or the chance of my death, is one consequence.

My patient advocate shall have the same authority to make care, custody, and medical treatment decisions as I would if I had the capacity to make them EXCEPT **(here list the limitations, if any, you wish to place on your patient advocate's authority):**

This designation of patient advocate shall not be affected by my disability or incapacity. This designation of patient advocate is governed by Michigan law, although I request that it be honored in any state in which I may be found. I reserve the power to revoke this designation at any time by communicating my intent to revoke it in any manner in which I am able to communicate. Photostatic copies of this document, after it is signed and witnessed, shall have the same legal force as the original document. I voluntarily sign this designation of patient advocate after careful consideration. I accept its meaning and I accept its consequences.

Designation of Primary Physician

I designate the following physician as my primary physician: _____ (name)
_____ (address)
_____ (phone).

OPTIONAL- DESIGNATION OF ALTERNATE PRIMARY PHYSICIAN: If the physician I have designated above is not willing, able, or reasonably available to act as my primary physician, I designate the following physician as my primary physician:

_____ (name)
_____ (address)
_____ (phone).

Organ Donation

In the event of my death, I have placed my initials next to the following part(s) of my body that I wish donated for the purposes **that I have initialed below:**

[   ] any organs or parts **OR**
[   ] eyes   [   ] bone and connective tissue   [   ] skin
[   ] heart   [   ] kidney(s)   [   ] liver
[   ] lung(s)   [   ] pancreas   [   ] other _____

for the purposes of:

[   ] any purpose authorized by law **OR**
[   ] transplantation   [   ] research   [   ] therapy
[   ] medical education   [   ] other limitations _____

Signature

I sign this Advance Health Care Directive, consisting of the following sections, **which I have initialed below and have elected to adopt:**
[   ] Living Will (Declaration and Directive to Physicians)
[   ] Selection of Health Care Agent (Designation of Patient Advocate for Health Care)
[   ] Designation of Primary Physician
[   ] Organ Donation

BY SIGNING HERE I INDICATE THAT I UNDERSTAND THE PURPOSE AND EFFECT OF THIS DOCUMENT.

Signature _____ Date _____

City, County, and State of Residence _____

Notary Acknowledgment

State of _____

County of _____

On _____ , _____ came before me personally and, under oath, stated that he or she is the person described in the above document and he or she signed the above document in my presence. I declare under penalty of perjury that the person whose name is subscribed to this instrument appears to be of sound mind and under no duress, fraud, or undue influence.

_____
Notary Public
My commission expires _____

Witness Acknowledgment

On the date noted below next to our signatures, in the presence of all of us, the above-named Declarant published and signed this Living Will and Directive to Physicians, and then at the Declarant's request, and in the Declarant's presence, and in each other's presence, we all signed below as witnesses, and we each declare, under penalty of perjury, that, to the best of our knowledge:

(1) The Declarant is personally known to me and, to the best of my knowledge, the Declarant signed this instrument freely, under no constraint or undue influence, and is of sound mind and memory and legal age, and fully aware of the possible consequences of this action.

(2) I am at least nineteen (19) years of age and I am not related to the Declarant in any manner by blood, marriage, or adoption.

(3) I am not the Declarant's attending physician, or a patient or employee of the Declarant's attending physician, or a patient, physician, or employee of the health care facility in which the Declarant is a patient, unless such person is required or allowed to witness the execution of this document by the laws of the state in which this document is executed.

(4) I am not entitled to any portion of the Declarant's estate on the Declarant's death under the laws of intestate succession of any state or country, nor under the Last Will and Testament of the Declarant or any Codicil to such Last Will and Testament.

(5) I have no claim against any portion of the Declarant's estate on the Declarant's death.

(6) I am not directly financially responsible for the Declarant's medical care.

(7) I did not sign the Declarant's signature for the Declarant or on the direction of the Declarant, nor have I been paid any fee for acting as a witness to the execution of this document.

Witness Signature _____ Date _____

Printed Name of Witness _____

Second Witness Signature _____ Date _____

Printed Name of Second Witness _____

Acceptance of Health Care Agent and Patient Advocate

I accept my appointment as Health Care Agent and Patient Advocate:

Signature _____   Date _____

I accept my appointment as Alternate Health Care Agent and Patient Advocate:

Signature _____   Date _____

Minnesota Advance Health Care Directive

On this date of _____ , I, _____ , do hereby sign, execute, and adopt the following as my Advance Health Care Directive. I direct any and all persons or entities involved with my health care in any manner that these decisions are my wishes and were adopted without duress or force and of my own free will.

I have placed my initials next to the sections of this Directive that I have adopted:

[   ]   Living Will (Health Care Living Will)
[   ]   Selection of Health Care Agent (Proxy Designation)
[   ]   Designation of Primary Physician
[   ]   Organ Donation

Notice: This is an important legal document. Before signing this document, you should know these important facts:

(a) This document gives your health care providers or your designated proxy the power and guidance to make health care decisions according to your wishes when you are in a terminal condition and cannot do so. This document may include what kind of treatment you want or do not want and under what circumstances you want these decisions to be made. You may state where you want or do not want to receive any treatment.

(b) If you name a proxy in this document and that person agrees to serve as your proxy, that person has a duty to act consistently with your wishes. If the proxy does not know your wishes, the proxy has the duty to act in your best interests. If you do not name a proxy, your health care providers have a duty to act consistently with your instructions or tell you that they are unwilling to do so.

(c) This document will remain valid and in effect until and unless you amend or revoke it. Review this document periodically to make sure it continues to reflect your preferences. You may amend or revoke the living will at any time by notifying your health care providers.

d) Your named proxy has the same right as you have to examine your medical records and to consent to their disclosure for purposes related to your health care or insurance unless you limit this right in this document.

(e) If there is anything in this document that you do not understand, you should ask for professional help to have it explained to you.

Living Will (Health Care Living Will)

TO MY FAMILY, DOCTORS, AND ALL THOSE CONCERNED WITH MY CARE:

I, being an adult of sound mind, willfully and voluntarily make this statement as a directive to be followed if I am in a terminal condition and become unable to participate in decisions regarding my health care. I understand that my health care providers are legally bound to act consistently with my wishes, within the limits of reasonable medical practice and other applicable law. I also understand that I have the right to make medical and health care decisions for myself as long as I am able to do so and to revoke this living will at any time.

The following are my feelings and wishes regarding my health care (**You may state the circumstances under which this living will applies**):

I particularly DO want to have all appropriate health care that will help in the following ways (**You may give instructions for care you do want**):

I particularly do NOT want the following (**You may list specific treatment you do not want in certain circumstances**):

I particularly DO want to have the following kinds of life-sustaining treatment if I am diagnosed to have a terminal condition (**You may list the specific types of life-sustaining treatment that you do want if you have a terminal condition**):

I particularly do NOT want the following kinds of life-sustaining treatment if I am diagnosed to have a terminal condition (**You may list the specific types of life-sustaining treatment that you do not want if you have a terminal condition**):

I recognize that if I reject artificially-administered sustenance, then I may die of dehydration or malnutrition rather than from my illness or injury. The following are my feelings and wishes regarding artificially-administered sustenance should I have a terminal condition (**You may indicate whether you wish to receive food and fluids given to you in some other way than by mouth if you have a terminal condition**):

Thoughts I feel are relevant to my instructions (**You may, but need not, give your religious beliefs, philosophy, or other personal values that you feel are important. You may also state preferences concerning the location of your care**):

Selection of Health Care Agent (Proxy Designation)

(If you wish, you may name someone to see that your wishes are carried out, but you do not have to do this. You may also name a proxy without including specific instructions regarding your care. If you name a proxy, you should discuss your wishes with that person.)

If I become unable to communicate my instructions, I designate the following person(s) to act on my behalf consistently with my instructions, if any, as stated in this document.
_____ (name)
_____ (address)

OPTIONAL - DESIGNATION OF ALTERNATE PROXY: If I revoke my proxy's authority or if my proxy is not willing, able, or reasonably available to make a health care decision for me, I designate as my alternate proxy
_____ (name of individual you choose as alternate proxy)
_____ (address)

Unless I write instructions that limit my proxy's authority, my proxy has full power and authority to make health care decisions for me. If a guardian is to be appointed for me, I nominate my proxy (or alternate proxy, if then serving) named in this document to act as my guardian.

I understand that I have the right to revoke the appointment of the persons named above to act on my behalf at any time by communicating that decision to the proxy or my health care provider.

Designation of Primary Physician

I designate the following physician as my primary physician: _____ (name)
_____ (address)
_____ (phone).

OPTIONAL- DESIGNATION OF ALTERNATE PRIMARY PHYSICIAN: If the physician I have designated above is not willing, able, or reasonably available to act as my primary physician, I designate the following physician as my primary physician:
_____ (name)
_____ (address)
_____ (phone).

Organ Donation

In the event of my death, I have placed my initials next to the following part(s) of my body that I wish donated for the purposes **that I have initialed below:**

[   ] any organs or parts **OR**

[   ] eyes   [   ] bone and connective tissue   [   ] skin

[   ] heart   [   ] kidney(s)   [   ] liver

[   ] lung(s)   [   ] pancreas   [   ] other _____

for the purposes of:

[   ] any purpose authorized by law **OR**

[   ] transplantation   [   ] research   [   ] therapy

[   ] medical education   [   ] other limitations _____

Signature

I sign this Advance Health Care Directive, consisting of the following sections, **which I have initialed below and have elected to adopt:**

[   ] Living Will (Health Care Living Will)

[   ] Selection of Health Care Agent (Proxy Designation)

[   ] Designation of Primary Physician

[   ] Organ Donation

BY SIGNING HERE I INDICATE THAT I UNDERSTAND THE PURPOSE AND EFFECT OF THIS DOCUMENT.

Signature _____   Date _____

City, County, and State of Residence _____

Notary Acknowledgment

State of _____

County of _____

On _____ , _____ came before me personally and, under oath, stated that he or she is the person described in the above document and he or she signed the above document in my presence. I declare under penalty of perjury that the person whose name is subscribed to this instrument appears to be of sound mind and under no duress, fraud, or undue influence.

_____

Notary Public

My commission expires _____

Witness Acknowledgment

The declarant is personally known to me and I believe him or her to be of sound mind and under no duress, fraud, or undue influence. I did not sign the declarant's signature above for or at the direction of the declarant and I am not appointed as the health care agent or proxy herein. I am at least eighteen (18) years of age and I am not related to the declarant by blood, adoption, or marriage, entitled to any portion of the estate of the declarant according to the laws of intestate succession or under any will of declarant or codicil thereto, or directly financially responsible for declarant's medical care. I am not a health care provider of the declarant or an employee of the health facility in which the declarant is a patient.

Witness Signature _____ Date _____

Printed Name of Witness _____

Second Witness Signature _____ Date _____

Printed Name of Second Witness _____

Acceptance of Health Care Agent and Proxy

I accept my appointment as Health Care Agent and Proxy:

Signature _____ Date _____

I accept my appointment as Alternate Health Care Agent and Proxy:

Signature _____ Date _____

Mississippi Advance Health Care Directive

On this date of _____ , I, _____ , do hereby sign, execute, and adopt the following as my Advance Health Care Directive. I direct any and all persons or entities involved with my health care in any manner that these decisions are my wishes and were adopted without duress or force and of my own free will.

I have placed my initials next to the sections of this Directive that I have adopted:

[   ]   Living Will (Instructions for Health Care)
[   ]   Selection of Health Care Agent (Power of Attorney for Health Care)
[   ]   Designation of Primary Physician
[   ]   Organ Donation

You have the right to give instructions about your own health care. You also have the right to name someone else to make health care decisions for you. This form lets you do either or both of these things. It also lets you express your wishes regarding the designation of your primary physician and make an organ donation. If you use this form, you may complete or modify all or any part of it. You are free to use a different form.

PART 1 of this form lets you give specific instructions about any aspect of your health care. Choices are provided for you to express your wishes regarding the provision, withholding, or withdrawal of treatment to keep you alive, including the provision of artificial nutrition and hydration, as well as the provision of pain relief. Space is provided for you to add to the choices you have made or for you to write out any additional wishes.

PART 2 of this form is a Power of Attorney for Health Care. Part 2 lets you name another individual as agent to make health care decisions for you if you become incapable of making your own decisions or if you want someone else to make those decisions for you now even though you are still capable. Unless related to you, your agent may not be an owner, operator, or employee of a residential long-term health care institution at which you are receiving care. Unless the form you sign limits the authority of your agent, your agent may make all health care decisions for you. This form has a place for you to limit the authority of your agent. You need not limit the authority of your agent if you wish to rely on your agent for all health care decisions that may have to be made. If you choose not to limit the authority of your agent, your agent will have the right to: (1) Consent or refuse consent to any care, treatment, service, or procedure to maintain, diagnose, or otherwise affect a physical or mental condition, (2) Select or discharge health care providers and institutions, (3) Approve or disapprove diagnostic tests, surgical procedures, programs of medication, and orders not to resuscitate, and (4) Direct the provision, withholding, or withdrawal of artificial nutrition and hydration and all other forms of health care.

PART 3 of this form lets you designate a physician to have primary responsibility for your health care.

PART 4 of this form allows you to specify your desires concerning organ donation after death.

After completing this form, sign and date the form at the end in front of two (2) witnesses and a notary public. Give a copy of the signed and completed form to your physician, any other health care providers you may have, any health care institution at which you are receiving care, and any health care agents you have named. You should talk to the person you have named as agent to make sure that he or she understands your wishes and is willing to take the responsibility. You have the right to revoke this advance health care directive or replace this form at any time.

Part 1: Living Will (Instructions for Health Care)

If you are satisfied to allow your agent to determine what is best for you in making end-of-life decisions, you need not fill out this part of the form. If you do fill out this part of the form, you may strike any wording you do not want.

END-OF-LIFE DECISIONS: I direct that my health care providers and others involved in my care provide, withhold, or withdraw treatment in accordance with the choice **I have initialed below**:

[   ] **Choice NOT To Prolong Life**: I do NOT want my life to be prolonged if:
    (a) I have an incurable and irreversible condition that will result in my death within a relatively short time;
    (b) I become unconscious and, to a reasonable degree of medical certainty, I will not regain consciousness; **OR**
    (c) the likely risks and burdens of treatment would outweigh the expected benefits.

        OR

[   ] **Choice TO Prolong Life**: I DO want my life to be prolonged as long as possible within the limits of generally-accepted health care standards.

ARTIFICIAL NUTRITION AND HYDRATION: Artificial nutrition and hydration must be provided, withheld, or withdrawn in accordance with the choice I have made above **unless I initial the following box:**
If I initial this box[   ], artificial nutrition and hydration must be provided regardless of my condition and regardless of the choice I have made above.

RELIEF FROM PAIN: Except as I state in the following space, I direct that treatment for alleviation of pain or discomfort be provided at all times, even if it hastens my death **(list exceptions)**:

OTHER WISHES: **(If you do not agree with any of the optional choices above and wish to write your own, or if you wish to add to the instructions you have given above, you may do so here.) I direct that (add additional sheets if needed):**

Part 2: Selection of Health Care Agent
(Power of Attorney for Health Care)

DESIGNATION OF AGENT: I designate the following individual as my agent to make health care decisions for me _____ (name), of _____ (address).

OPTIONAL - DESIGNATION OF ALTERNATE AGENT: If I revoke my agent's authority or if my agent is not willing, able, or reasonably available to make a health care decision for me, I designate as my alternate agent

_____ (name of individual you choose as alternate agent)
_____ (address)

AGENT'S AUTHORITY: My agent is authorized to make all health care decisions for me, including decisions to provide, withhold, or withdraw artificial nutrition and hydration, and all other forms of health care to keep me alive, except as I state here (add additional sheets if needed):

WHEN AGENT'S AUTHORITY BECOMES EFFECTIVE: My agent's authority becomes effective when my primary physician determines that I am unable to make my own health care decisions unless I mark the following box:

If I initial this box[   ], my agent's authority to make health care decisions for me takes effect immediately.

AGENT'S OBLIGATION: My agent shall make health care decisions for me in accordance with this power of attorney for health care, any instructions I give in Part 1 of this form, and my other wishes to the extent known to my agent. To the extent my wishes are unknown, my agent shall make health care decisions for me in accordance with what my agent determines to be in my best interest. In determining my best interest, my agent shall consider my personal values to the extent known to my agent.

NOMINATION OF GUARDIAN: If a guardian of my person needs to be appointed for me by a court, I nominate the agent (or alternate agent if then serving) designated in this form.

Part 3: Designation of Primary Physician

I designate the following physician as my primary physician: _____ (name)

_____ (address)

_____ (phone).

OPTIONAL- DESIGNATION OF ALTERNATE PRIMARY PHYSICIAN: If the physician I have designated above is not willing, able, or reasonably available to act as my primary physician, I designate the following physician as my primary physician:

_____ (name)

_____ (address)

_____ (phone).

Part 4: Organ Donation

In the event of my death, I have placed my initials next to the following part(s) of my body that I wish donated for the purposes **that I have initialed below**:

[   ] any organs or parts **OR**

[ ] eyes	[ ] bone and connective tissue	[ ] skin
[ ] heart	[ ] kidney(s)	[ ] liver
[ ] lung(s)	[ ] pancreas	[ ] other _____

for the purposes of:

[   ] any purpose authorized by law **OR**

[ ] transplantation	[ ] research	[ ] therapy
[ ] medical education	[ ] other limitations _____	

Signature

I sign this Advance Health Care Directive, consisting of the following sections, **which I have initialed below and have elected to adopt:**

[   ] Living Will (Instructions for Health Care)
[   ] Selection of Health Care Agent (Power of Attorney for Health Care)
[   ] Designation of Primary Physician
[   ] Organ Donation

BY SIGNING HERE I INDICATE THAT I UNDERSTAND THE PURPOSE AND EFFECT OF THIS DOCUMENT.

Signature _____   Date _____

City, County, and State of Residence _____

Notary Acknowledgment

State of _____

County of _____

On _____ , _____ came before me personally and, under oath, stated that he or she is the person described in the above document and he or she signed the above document in my presence. I declare under penalty of perjury that the person whose name is subscribed to this instrument appears to be of sound mind and under no duress, fraud, or undue influence.

_____

Notary Public

My commission expires _____

Witness Acknowledgment

WITNESS #1

I declare under penalty of perjury pursuant to Section 97-9-61, Mississippi Code of 1972, that the principal is personally known to me, that the principal signed or acknowledged this power of attorney in my presence, that the principal appears to be of sound mind and under no duress, fraud, or undue influence, that I am not the person appointed as agent by this document, and that I am not a health care provider, or an employee of a health care provider or facility. I am at least eighteen (18) years of age and I am not related to the principal by blood, marriage, or adoption, and to the best of my knowledge, I am not entitled to any part of the estate of the principal upon the death of the principal under a will now existing or by operation of law.

Witness #1 Signature _____   Date _____

Printed Name of Witness _____

WITNESS #2

I declare under penalty of perjury pursuant to Section 97-9-61, Mississippi Code of 1972, that the principal is personally known to me, that the principal signed or acknowledged this power of attorney in my presence, that the principal appears to be of sound mind and under no duress, fraud, or undue influence, that I am not the person appointed as agent by this document, and that I am at least eighteen (18) years of age and I am not a health care provider, or an employee of a health care provider or facility.

Witness #2 Signature _____   Date _____

Printed Name of Witness _____

Acceptance of Health Care Agent and Attorney-in-Fact for Health Care

I accept my appointment as Health Care Agent and Attorney-in-Fact for Health Care:

Signature _____ Date _____

I accept my appointment as Alternate Health Care Agent and Attorney-in-Fact for Health Care:

Signature _____ Date _____

Missouri Advance Health Care Directive

On this date of _____ , I, _____ , do hereby sign, execute, and adopt the following as my Advance Health Care Directive. I direct any and all persons or entities involved with my health care in any manner that these decisions are my wishes and were adopted without duress or force and of my own free will.

I have placed my initials next to the sections of this Directive that I have adopted:

[   ] Living Will Declaration
[   ] Selection of Health Care Agent (Durable Power of Attorney for Health Care)
[   ] Designation of Primary Physician
[   ] Organ Donation

Living Will Declaration

I have the primary right to make my own decisions concerning treatment that might unduly prolong the dying process. By this declaration I express to my physician, family, and friends my intent. If I should have a terminal condition it is my desire that my dying not be prolonged by administration of death-prolonging procedures. If my condition is terminal and I am unable to participate in decisions regarding my medical treatment, I direct my attending physician to withhold or withdraw medical procedures that merely prolong the dying process and are not necessary to my comfort or to alleviate pain. It is not my intent to authorize affirmative or deliberate acts or omissions to shorten my life, rather, only to permit the natural process of dying.

Selection of Health Care Agent
(Durable Power of Attorney for Health Care)

I hereby designate _____ (name),
of _____ (address),
as my attorney-in-fact.

This is a durable power of attorney and the authority of my attorney-in-fact shall not terminate if I become disabled or incapacitated.

This power of attorney becomes effective upon certification by two (2) licensed physicians that I am incapacitated and can no longer make my own medical decisions. The powers and duties of my attorney-in-fact shall cease upon certification that I am no longer incapacitated. This determination of incapacity shall be periodically reviewed by my attending physician and my attorney-in-fact. I authorize my attorney-in-fact to make any and all health care decisions for me, including decisions to withhold or withdraw any form of life support.

I expressly authorize my attorney-in-fact to make all decisions regarding artificially-supplied nutrition and hydration in all medical circumstances.

Designation of Primary Physician

I designate the following physician as my primary physician: _____ (name)
_____ (address)
_____ (phone).

OPTIONAL- DESIGNATION OF ALTERNATE PRIMARY PHYSICIAN: If the physician I have designated above is not willing, able, or reasonably available to act as my primary physician, I designate the following physician as my primary physician:
_____ (name)
_____ (address)
_____ (phone).

Organ Donation

In the event of my death, I have placed my initials next to the following part(s) of my body that I wish donated for the purposes **that I have initialed below:**

[   ] any organs or parts **OR**

[   ] eyes   [   ] bone and connective tissue   [   ] skin
[   ] heart   [   ] kidney(s)   [   ] liver
[   ] lung(s)   [   ] pancreas   [   ] other _____

for the purposes of:

[   ] any purpose authorized by law **OR**

[   ] transplantation   [   ] research   [   ] therapy
[   ] medical education   [   ] other limitations _____

Signature

I sign this Advance Health Care Directive, consisting of the following sections, **which I have initialed below and have elected to adopt:**

[   ] Living Will Declaration
[   ] Selection of Health Care Agent (Durable Power of Attorney for Health Care)
[   ] Designation of Primary Physician
[   ] Organ Donation

BY SIGNING HERE I INDICATE THAT I UNDERSTAND THE PURPOSE AND EFFECT OF THIS DOCUMENT.

Signature _____   Date _____

City, County, and State of Residence _____

Notary Acknowledgment

State of _____
County of _____

On _____ , _____ came before me personally and, under oath, stated that he or she is the person described in the above document and he or she signed the above document in my presence. I declare under penalty of perjury that the person whose name is subscribed to this instrument appears to be of sound mind and under no duress, fraud, or undue influence.

_____
Notary Public
My commission expires _____

Witness Acknowledgment

The declarant is personally known to me and I believe him or her to be of sound mind and under no duress, fraud, or undue influence. I did not sign the declarant's signature above for or at the direction of the declarant and I am not appointed as the health care agent or attorney-in-fact herein. I am at least eighteen (18) years of age and I am not related to the declarant by blood, adoption, or marriage, entitled to any portion of the estate of the declarant according to the laws of intestate succession or under any will of declarant or codicil thereto, or directly financially responsible for declarant's medical care. I am not a health care provider of the declarant or an employee of the health facility in which the declarant is a patient.

Witness Signature _____ Date _____

Printed Name of Witness _____

Second Witness Signature _____ Date _____

Printed Name of Second Witness _____

Acceptance of Health Care Agent and Attorney-in-Fact for Health Care

I accept my appointment as Health Care Agent and Attorney-in-fact for Health Care:

Signature _____ Date _____

Montana Advance Health Care Directive

On this date of _____ , I, _____ , do hereby sign, execute, and adopt the following as my Advance Health Care Directive. I direct any and all persons or entities involved with my health care in any manner that these decisions are my wishes and were adopted without duress or force and of my own free will.

I have placed my initials next to the sections of this Directive that I have adopted:

[   ]   Living Will Declaration
[   ]   Selection of Health Care Agent
[   ]   Designation of Primary Physician
[   ]   Organ Donation

Living Will Declaration

If I should have an incurable or irreversible condition that, without the administration of life-sustaining treatment, will, in the opinion of my attending physician, cause my death within a relatively short time and I am no longer able to make decisions regarding my medical treatment, I direct my attending physician, pursuant to the Montana Rights of the Terminally Ill Act, to withhold or withdraw treatment that only prolongs the process of dying and is not necessary to my comfort or to alleviate pain.

Selection of Health Care Agent

If I should have an incurable and irreversible condition that, without the administration of life-sustaining treatment, will, in the opinion of my attending physician, cause my death within a relatively short time and I am no longer able to make decisions regarding my medical treatment, I appoint _____ (name), of
_____(address), to make decisions on my behalf regarding withholding or withdrawal of treatment that only prolongs the process of dying and is not necessary for my comfort or to alleviate pain, pursuant to the Montana Rights of the Terminally Ill Act.

OPTIONAL - DESIGNATION OF ALTERNATE AGENT: If I revoke my agent's authority or if my agent is not willing, able, or reasonably available to make a health care decision for me, I designate as my alternate agent
_____ (name of individual you choose as alternate agent)
_____ (address)

If the individuals I have appointed are not reasonably available or is unwilling to serve, I direct my attending physician, pursuant to the Montana Rights of the Terminally Ill Act, to withhold or withdraw treatment that only prolongs the process of dying and is not necessary for my comfort or to alleviate pain.

Designation of Primary Physician

I designate the following physician as my primary physician: _____ (name)

_____ (address)

_____ (phone).

OPTIONAL- DESIGNATION OF ALTERNATE PRIMARY PHYSICIAN: If the physician I have designated above is not willing, able, or reasonably available to act as my primary physician, I designate the following physician as my primary physician:

_____ (name)

_____ (address)

_____ (phone).

Organ Donation

In the event of my death, I have placed my initials next to the following part(s) of my body that I wish donated for the purposes **that I have initialed below**:

[   ] any organs or parts **OR**

[   ] eyes   [   ] bone and connective tissue   [   ] skin

[   ] heart   [   ] kidney(s)   [   ] liver

[   ] lung(s)   [   ] pancreas   [   ] other _____

for the purposes of:

[   ] any purpose authorized by law **OR**

[   ] transplantation   [   ] research   [   ] therapy

[   ] medical education   [   ] other limitations _____

Signature

I sign this Advance Health Care Directive, consisting of the following sections, **which I have initialed below and have elected to adopt**:

[   ] Living Will Declaration

[   ] Selection of Health Care Agent

[   ] Designation of Primary Physician

[   ] Organ Donation

BY SIGNING HERE I INDICATE THAT I UNDERSTAND THE PURPOSE AND EFFECT OF THIS DOCUMENT.

Signature _____ Date _____

City, County, and State of Residence _____

Notary Acknowledgment

State of _____

County of _____

On _____ , _____ came before me personally and, under oath, stated that he or she is the person described in the above document and he or she signed the above document in my presence. I declare under penalty of perjury that the person whose name is subscribed to this instrument appears to be of sound mind and under no duress, fraud, or undue influence.

_____
Notary Public
My commission expires _____

Witness Acknowledgment

The declarant is personally known to me and I believe him or her to be of sound mind and under no duress, fraud, or undue influence. I did not sign the declarant's signature above for or at the direction of the declarant and I am not appointed as the health care agent or attorney-in-fact herein. I am at least eighteen (18) years of age and I am not related to the declarant by blood, adoption, or marriage, entitled to any portion of the estate of the declarant according to the laws of intestate succession or under any will of declarant or codicil thereto, or directly financially responsible for declarant's medical care. I am not a health care provider of the declarant or an employee of the health facility in which the declarant is a patient.

Witness Signature _____ Date _____

Printed Name of Witness _____

Second Witness Signature _____ Date _____

Printed Name of Second Witness _____

Acceptance of Health Care Agent

I accept my appointment as Health Care Agent:

Signature _____ Date _____

I accept my appointment as Alternate Health Care Agent:

Signature _____ Date _____

Nebraska Advance Health Care Directive

On this date of _____ , I, _____ , do hereby sign, execute, and adopt the following as my Advance Health Care Directive. I direct any and all persons or entities involved with my health care in any manner that these decisions are my wishes and were adopted without duress or force and of my own free will.

I have placed my initials next to the sections of this Directive that I have adopted:

[   ] Living Will Declaration
[   ] Selection of Health Care Agent (Power of Attorney for Health Care)
[   ] Designation of Primary Physician
[   ] Organ Donation

Living Will Declaration

If I should lapse into a persistent vegetative state or have an incurable and irreversible condition that, without the administration of life-sustaining treatment, will, in the opinion of my attending physician, cause my death within a relatively short time and I am no longer able to make decisions regarding my medical treatment, I direct my attending physician, pursuant to the Rights of the Terminally Ill Act, to withhold or withdraw life sustaining treatment that is not necessary for my comfort or to alleviate pain.

Selection of Health Care Agent
(Power of Attorney for Health Care)

I appoint _____ (name),
of _____ (address),
as my attorney-in-fact for health care. I authorize my attorney-in-fact appointed by this document to make health care decisions for me when I am determined to be incapable of making my own health care decisions. I have read the warning which accompanies this document and understand the consequences of executing a power of attorney for health care.

(Optional) I direct that my attorney-in-fact comply with the following instructions or limitations on life-sustaining treatment:

(Optional) I direct that my attorney-in-fact comply with the following instructions on artificially-administered nutrition and hydration:

I have read this power of attorney for health care. I understand that it allows another person to make life and death decisions for me if I am incapable of making such decisions. I also understand that I can revoke this power of attorney for health care at any time by notifying my attorney-in-fact, my physician, or the facility in which I am a patient or resident. I also understand that I can require in this power of attorney for health care that the fact of my incapacity in the future be confirmed by a second physician.

Designation of Primary Physician

I designate the following physician as my primary physician: _____ (name)
_____ (address)
_____(phone).

OPTIONAL- DESIGNATION OF ALTERNATE PRIMARY PHYSICIAN: If the physician I have designated above is not willing, able, or reasonably available to act as my primary physician, I designate the following physician as my primary physician:
_____ (name)
_____ (address)
_____(phone).

Organ Donation

In the event of my death, I have placed my initials next to the following part(s) of my body that I wish donated for the purposes **that I have initialed below**:

[   ] any organs or parts **OR**

[   ] eyes   [   ] bone and connective tissue   [   ] skin
[   ] heart   [   ] kidney(s)   [   ] liver
[   ] lung(s)   [   ] pancreas   [   ] other _____

for the purposes of:

[   ] any purpose authorized by law **OR**

[   ] transplantation   [   ] research   [   ] therapy
[   ] medical education   [   ] other limitations _____

Signature

I sign this Advance Health Care Directive, consisting of the following sections, **which I have initialed below and have elected to adopt:**

[   ] Living Will Declaration
[   ] Selection of Health Care Agent (Power of Attorney for Health Care)
[   ] Designation of Primary Physician
[   ] Organ Donation

BY SIGNING HERE I INDICATE THAT I UNDERSTAND THE PURPOSE AND EFFECT OF THIS DOCUMENT.

Signature _____   Date _____

City, County, and State of Residence _____

Notary Acknowledgment

State of _____

County of _____

On _____ , _____ came before me personally and, under oath, stated that he or she is the person described in the above document and he or she signed the above document in my presence. I declare under penalty of perjury that the person whose name is subscribed to this instrument appears to be of sound mind and under no duress, fraud, or undue influence.

_____

Notary Public

My commission expires _____

Witness Acknowledgment

The declarant is personally known to me and I believe him or her to be of sound mind and under no duress, fraud, or undue influence. I did not sign the declarant's signature above for or at the direction of the declarant and I am not appointed as the health care agent or attorney-in-fact herein. I am at least eighteen (18) years of age and I am not related to the declarant by blood, adoption, or marriage, entitled to any portion of the estate of the declarant according to the laws of intestate succession or under any will of declarant or codicil thereto, or directly financially responsible for declarant's medical care. I am not a health care provider of the declarant or an employee of the health facility in which the declarant is a patient.

Witness Signature _____ Date _____

Printed Name of Witness _____

Second Witness Signature _____ Date _____

Printed Name of Second Witness _____

Acceptance of Health Care Agent and Attorney-in-Fact for Health Care

I accept my appointment as Health Care Agent and Attorney-in-Fact for Health Care:

Signature _____ Date _____

Nevada Advance Health Care Directive

On this date of _____, I, _____, do hereby sign, execute, and adopt the following as my Advance Health Care Directive. I direct any and all persons or entities involved with my health care in any manner that these decisions are my wishes and were adopted without duress or force and of my own free will.

I have placed my initials next to the sections of this Directive that I have adopted:

[   ] Living Will Declaration
[   ] Selection of Health Care Agent (Durable Power of Attorney for Health Care Decisions)
[   ] Designation of Primary Physician
[   ] Organ Donation

Living Will Declaration

If I should have an incurable and irreversible condition that, without the administration of life-sustaining treatment, will, in the opinion of my attending physician, cause my death within a relatively short time, and I am no longer able to make decisions regarding my medical treatment, I direct my attending physician, pursuant to NRS 449.535 to 449.690, inclusive, to withhold or withdraw treatment that only prolongs the process of dying and is not necessary for my comfort or to alleviate pain.

If you wish to include this statement in this declaration, you must initial the statement in the box provided:

[   ] Withholding or withdrawal of artificial nutrition and hydration may result in death by starvation or dehydration. *Initial* this box if you want to receive or continue receiving artificial nutrition and hydration by way of the gastro-intestinal tract after all other treatment is withheld pursuant to this declaration.

Selection of Health Care Agent
(Durable Power of Attorney for Health Care Decisions)

If I should have an incurable and irreversible condition that, without the administration of life-sustaining treatment, will, in the opinion of my attending physician, cause my death within a relatively short time, and I am no longer able to make decisions regarding my medical treatment, I appoint _____ (name), of _____ (address), to act as my attorney-in-fact for all health care decisions and to make all decisions on my behalf regarding withholding or withdrawal of treatment that only prolongs the process of dying and is not necessary for my comfort or to alleviate pain, pursuant to NRS 449.535 to 449.690, inclusive. If the person I have so appointed is not reasonably available or is unwilling to serve, I direct my attending physician, pursuant to those sections, to withhold or withdraw treatment that only prolongs the process of dying and is not necessary for my comfort or to alleviate pain.

If you wish to include this statement in this declaration, you must initial the statement in the box provided:

[   ] Withholding or withdrawal of artificial nutrition and hydration may result in death by starvation or dehydration. *Initial* this box if you want to receive or continue receiving artificial nutrition and hydration by way of the gastro-intestinal tract after all other treatment is withheld pursuant to this declaration.

I understand the consequences of executing a power of attorney for health care. I have read this power of attorney for health care. I understand that it allows another person to make life and death decisions for me if I am incapable of making such decisions. I also understand that I can revoke this power of attorney for health care at any time by notifying my attorney-in-fact, my physician, or the facility in which I am a patient or resident. I also understand that I can require in this power of attorney for health care that the fact of my incapacity in the future be confirmed by a second physician.

Designation of Primary Physician

I designate the following physician as my primary physician: _____ (name)
_____ (address)
_____ (phone).

OPTIONAL- DESIGNATION OF ALTERNATE PRIMARY PHYSICIAN: If the physician I have designated above is not willing, able, or reasonably available to act as my primary physician, I designate the following physician as my primary physician:
_____ (name)
_____ (address)
_____ (phone).

Organ Donation

In the event of my death, I have placed my initials next to the following part(s) of my body that I wish donated for the purposes **that I have initialed below**:

[   ] any organs or parts **OR**
[   ] eyes   [   ] bone and connective tissue   [   ] skin
[   ] heart   [   ] kidney(s)   [   ] liver
[   ] lung(s)   [   ] pancreas   [   ] other _____

for the purposes of:

[   ] any purpose authorized by law **OR**
[   ] transplantation   [   ] research   [   ] therapy
[   ] medical education   [   ] other limitations _____

Signature

I sign this Advance Health Care Directive, consisting of the following sections, **which I have initialed below and have elected to adopt:**

[   ]   Living Will Declaration
[   ]   Selection of Health Care Agent (Durable Power of Attorney for Health Care Decisions)
[   ]   Designation of Primary Physician
[   ]   Organ Donation

BY SIGNING HERE I INDICATE THAT I UNDERSTAND THE PURPOSE AND EFFECT OF THIS DOCUMENT.

Signature _____   Date _____

City, County, and State of Residence _____

Notary Acknowledgment

State of _____
County of _____

On _____ , _____ came before me personally and, under oath, stated that he or she is the person described in the above document and he or she signed the above document in my presence. I declare under penalty of perjury that the person whose name is subscribed to this instrument appears to be of sound mind and under no duress, fraud, or undue influence.

_____
Notary Public
My commission expires _____

Witness Acknowledgment

The declarant is personally known to me and I believe him or her to be of sound mind and under no duress, fraud, or undue influence. I did not sign the declarant's signature above for or at the direction of the declarant and I am not appointed as the health care agent or attorney-in-fact herein. I am at least eighteen (18) years of age and I am not related to the declarant by blood, adoption, or marriage, entitled to any portion of the estate of the declarant according to the laws of intestate succession or under any will of declarant or codicil thereto, or directly financially responsible for declarant's medical care. I am not a health care provider of the declarant or an employee of the health facility in which the declarant is a patient.

Witness Signature _____ Date _____

Printed Name of Witness _____

Second Witness Signature _____ Date _____

Printed Name of Second Witness _____

Acceptance of Health Care Agent and Attorney-in-Fact for Health Care

I accept my appointment as Health Care Agent and Attorney-in-Fact for Health Care:

Signature _____ Date _____

New Hampshire Advance Health Care Directive

On this date of _____ , I, _____ , do hereby sign, execute, and adopt the following as my Advance Health Care Directive. I direct any and all persons or entities involved with my health care in any manner that these decisions are my wishes and were adopted without duress or force and of my own free will.
I have placed my initials next to the sections of this Directive that I have adopted:

[   ] Living Will Declaration
[   ] Selection of Health Care Agent (Durable Power of Attorney for Health Care)
[   ] Designation of Primary Physician
[   ] Organ Donation

Living Will Declaration

I, being of sound mind, willfully and voluntarily make known my desire that my dying shall not be artificially prolonged under the circumstances set forth below, and do hereby declare:

If at any time I should have an incurable injury, disease, or illness certified to be a terminal condition or a permanently-unconscious condition by two (2) physicians who have personally examined me, one of whom shall be my attending physician, and the physicians have determined that my death will occur whether or not life-sustaining procedures are utilized or that I will remain in a permanently-unconscious condition and where the application of life-sustaining procedures would serve only to artificially prolong the dying process, I direct that such procedures be withheld or withdrawn, and that I be permitted to die naturally with only the administration of medication, sustenance, or the performance of any medical procedure deemed necessary to provide me with comfort care.

I realize that situations could arise in which the only way to allow me to die would be to discontinue artificial nutrition and hydration.

In carrying out any instruction I have given under this section, I authorize that:
(initial your choice):

[   ] Artificial nutrition and hydration should NOT be started or, if started, be discontinued.
[   ] Artificial nutrition and hydration SHOULD be provided and not be removed.

In the absence of my ability to give directions regarding the use of such life-sustaining procedures, it is my intention that this declaration shall be honored by my family and physicians as the final expression of my right to refuse medical or surgical treatment and to accept the consequences of such refusal. I understand the full import of this declaration and I am emotionally and mentally competent to make this declaration.

Selection of Health Care Agent
(Durable Power of Attorney for Health Care)

DISCLOSURE STATEMENT: THIS IS AN IMPORTANT LEGAL DOCUMENT. BEFORE SIGNING THIS DOCUMENT YOU SHOULD KNOW THESE IMPORTANT FACTS:

Except to the extent you state otherwise, this document gives the person you name as your agent the authority to make any and all health care decisions for you when you are no longer capable of making them yourself. ""Health care" means any treatment, service or procedure to maintain, diagnose or treat your physical or mental condition. Your agent, therefore, can have the power to make a broad range of health care decisions for you. Your agent may consent, refuse to consent, or withdraw consent to medical treatment and may make decisions about withdrawing or withholding life-sustaining treatment. Your agent cannot consent or direct any of the following: commitment to a state institution, sterilization, or termination of treatment if you are pregnant and if the withdrawal of that treatment is deemed likely to terminate the pregnancy unless the failure to withhold the treatment will be physically harmful to you or prolong severe pain which cannot be alleviated by medication.

You may state in this document any treatment you do not desire, except as stated above, or treatment you want to be sure you receive. Your agent's authority will begin when your doctor certifies that you lack the capacity to make health care decisions. If for moral or religious reasons you do not wish to be treated by a doctor or examined by a doctor for the certification that you lack capacity, you must say so in the document and name a person to be able to certify your lack of capacity. That person may not be your agent or alternate agent or any person ineligible to be your agent. You may attach additional pages if you need more space to complete your statement.

If you want to give your agent authority to withhold or withdraw the artificial providing of nutrition and fluids, your document must say so. Otherwise, your agent will not be able to direct that. Under no conditions will your agent be able to direct the withholding of food and drink for you to eat and drink normally.

Your agent will be obligated to follow your instructions when making decisions on your behalf. Unless you state otherwise, your agent will have the same authority to make decisions about your health care as you would have had if made consistent with state law.

It is important that you discuss this document with your physician or other health care providers before you sign it to make sure that you understand the nature and range of decisions which may be made on your behalf. If you do not have a physician, you should talk with someone else who is knowledgeable about these issues and can answer your questions. You do not need a lawyer's assistance to complete this document, but if there is anything in this document that you do not understand, you should ask a lawyer to explain it to you.

The person you appoint as agent should be someone you know and trust and must be at least 18 years old. If you appoint your health or residential care provider (e.g. your physician, or an employee of a home health agency, hospital, nursing home, or residential care home, other than a relative), that person will have to choose between acting as your agent or as your health or residential care provider; the law does not permit a person to do both at the same time.

You should inform the person you appoint that you want him or her to be your health care agent. You should discuss this document with your agent and your physician and give each a signed copy. You should indicate on the document itself the people and institutions who will have signed copies. Your agent will not be liable for health care decisions made in good faith on your behalf.

Even after you have signed this document, you have the right to make health care decisions for yourself as long as you are able to do so, and treatment cannot be given to you or stopped over your objection. You have the right to revoke the authority granted to your agent by informing him or her or your health care provider orally or in writing. This document may not be changed or modified. If you want to make changes in the document you must make an entirely new one.

You should consider designating an alternate agent in the event that your agent is unwilling, unable, unavailable, or ineligible to act as your agent. Any alternate agent you designate will have the same authority to make health care decisions for you.

THIS POWER OF ATTORNEY WILL NOT BE VALID UNLESS IT IS SIGNED IN THE PRESENCE OF TWO (2) OR MORE QUALIFIED WITNESSES WHO MUST BOTH BE PRESENT WHEN YOU SIGN AND ACKNOWLEDGE YOUR SIGNATURE. THE FOLLOWING PERSONS MAY NOT ACT AS WIT-NESSES:

      The person you have designated as your agent;

      Your spouse;

      Your lawful heirs or beneficiaries named in your will or a deed;

ONLY ONE OF THE TWO WITNESSES MAY BE YOUR HEALTH OR RESIDENTIAL CARE PROVIDER OR ONE OF THEIR EMPLOYEES.

I hereby appoint _____ (name), of _____ (address), as my agent to make any and all health care decisions for me, except to the extent I state otherwise in this document or as prohibited by law. This durable power of attorney for health care shall take effect in the event I become unable to make my own health care decisions.

OPTIONAL - DESIGNATION OF ALTERNATE AGENT: If I revoke my agent's authority or if my agent is not willing, able, or reasonably available to make a health care decision for me, I designate as my alternate agent

_____ (name of individual you choose as alternate agent)

_____ (address)

STATEMENT OF DESIRES, SPECIAL PROVISIONS, AND LIMITATIONS REGARDING HEALTH CARE DECISIONS.

For your convenience in expressing your wishes, some general statements concerning the withholding or removal of life-sustaining treatment are set forth below. (Life-sustaining treatment is defined as procedures without which a person would die, such as, but not limited to the following: cardiopulmonary resuscitation, mechanical respiration, kidney dialysis or the use of other external mechanical and technological devices, drugs to maintain blood pressure, blood transfusions, and antibiotics.) There is also a section which allows you to set forth specific directions for these or other matters. If you wish, you may indicate your agreement or disagreement with any of the following statements and give your agent power to act in those specific circumstances.

(Initial your choices):

[   ] If I become permanently incompetent to make health care decisions, and if I am also suffering from a terminal illness, I authorize my agent to direct that life-sustaining treatment be discontinued.

[   ] Whether terminally ill or not, if I become permanently unconscious, I authorize my agent to direct that life-sustaining treatment be discontinued.

[   ] I realize that situations could arise in which the only way to allow me to die would be to discontinue artificial feeding (artificial nutrition and hydration).

In carrying out any instruction I have given under this section, I authorize that **(initial your choice)**: **(If you fail to complete this section, your agent will not have the power to direct the withdrawal of artificial nutrition and hydration)**:

[   ] Artificial nutrition and hydration should NOT be started or, if started, be discontinued.

[   ] Artificial nutrition and hydration SHOULD be provided and not be removed.

Here you may include any specific desires or limitations you deem appropriate, such as when or what life-sustaining treatment you would want used or withheld, or instructions about refusing any specific types of treatment that are inconsistent with your religious beliefs or unacceptable to you for any other reason. You may leave this question blank if you desire **(attach additional pages as necessary)**:

I hereby acknowledge that I have read and understand the disclosure statement contained in this document. The original of this document will be kept at the following address:

_____ and the following persons or institutions will have signed copies: _____ .

Designation of Primary Physician

I designate the following physician as my primary physician: _____ (name)
_____ (address)
_____ (phone).

OPTIONAL- DESIGNATION OF ALTERNATE PRIMARY PHYSICIAN: If the physician I have designated above is not willing, able, or reasonably available to act as my primary physician, I designate the following physician as my primary physician:
_____ (name)
_____ (address)
_____ (phone).

Organ Donation

In the event of my death, I have placed my initials next to the following part(s) of my body that I wish donated for the purposes **that I have initialed below:**

[   ] any organs or parts **OR**
[   ] eyes   [   ] bone and connective tissue   [   ] skin
[   ] heart   [   ] kidney(s)   [   ] liver
[   ] lung(s)   [   ] pancreas   [   ] other _____
for the purposes of:
[   ] any purpose authorized by law **OR**
[   ] transplantation   [   ] research   [   ] therapy
[   ] medical education   [   ] other limitations _____

Signature

I sign this Advance Health Care Directive, consisting of the following sections, **which I have initialed below and have elected to adopt:**

[   ] Living Will Declaration
[   ] Selection of Health Care Agent (Durable Power of Attorney for Health Care)
[   ] Designation of Primary Physician
[   ] Organ Donation

BY SIGNING HERE I INDICATE THAT I UNDERSTAND THE PURPOSE AND EFFECT OF THIS DOCUMENT.

Signature _____   Date _____

City, County, and State of Residence _____

Notary Acknowledgment

State of _____

County of _____

On _____ , _____ came before me personally and, under oath, stated that he or she is the person described in the above document and he or she signed the above document in my presence. I declare under penalty of perjury that the person whose name is subscribed to this instrument appears to be of sound mind and under no duress, fraud, or undue influence.

_____
Notary Public
My commission expires _____

Witness Acknowledgment

The declarant is personally known to me and I believe him or her to be of sound mind and under no duress, fraud, or undue influence. I did not sign the declarant's signature above for or at the direction of the declarant and I am not appointed as the health care agent or attorney-in-fact herein. I am at least eighteen (18) years of age and I am not related to the declarant by blood, adoption, or marriage, entitled to any portion of the estate of the declarant according to the laws of intestate succession or under any will of declarant or codicil thereto, or directly financially responsible for declarant's medical care. **The first witness is not a health care provider of the declarant or an employee of the health facility in which the declarant is a patient.**

Witness Signature _____ Date _____

Printed Name of Witness _____

Second Witness Signature _____ Date _____

Printed Name of Second Witness _____

Acceptance of Health Care Agent and Attorney-in-Fact for Health Care

I accept my appointment as Health Care Agent and Attorney-in-Fact for Health Care:

Signature _____ Date _____

I accept my appointment as Alternate Health Care Agent and Attorney-in-Fact for Health Care:

Signature _____ Date _____

New Jersey Advance Health Care Directive

On this date of _____ , I, _____ , do hereby sign, execute, and adopt the following as my Advance Health Care Directive. I direct any and all persons or entities involved with my health care in any manner that these decisions are my wishes and were adopted without duress or force and of my own free will.

I have placed my initials next to the sections of this Directive that I have adopted:

[   ] Living Will
[   ] Appointment of Health Care Representative
[   ] Designation of Primary Physician
[   ] Organ Donation

Living Will

If I am incapable of making an informed decision regarding my health care, I direct my loved ones and health care providers to follow my instructions as set forth below:

If I am diagnosed as having an incurable and irreversible illness, disease, or condition and if my attending physician and at least one (1) additional physician who has personally examined me determine that my condition is terminal **(initial all those that apply)**:

[   ] I direct that life-sustaining treatment which would serve only to artificially prolong my dying be withheld or ended. I also direct that I be given all medically-appropriate treatment and care necessary to make me comfortable and to relieve pain.

[   ] I direct that life-sustaining treatment be continued, if medically appropriate.

If there should come a time when I become permanently unconscious, and it is determined by my attending physician and at least one (1) additional physician with appropriate expertise who has personally examined me, that I have totally and irreversibly lost consciousness and my ability to interact with other people and my surroundings **(initial all those that apply)**:

[   ] I direct that life-sustaining treatment be withheld or discontinued. I understand that I will not experience pain or discomfort in this condition, and I direct that I be given all medically-appropriate treatment and care necessary to provide for my personal hygiene and dignity.

[   ] I direct that life-sustaining treatment be continued, if medically appropriate.

If there comes a time when I am diagnosed as having an incurable and irreversible illness, disease, or condition which may not be terminal, but causes me to experience severe and worsening physical or mental deterioration, and I will never regain the ability to make decisions and express my wishes **(initial all those that apply)**:

[   ] I direct that life-sustaining measures be withheld or discontinued and that I be given all medically-appropriate care necessary to make me comfortable and to relieve pain.

[   ] I direct that life-sustaining treatment be continued, if medically appropriate.

If I am receiving life-sustaining treatment that is experimental and not a proven therapy, or is likely to be ineffective or futile in prolonging life (initial all those that apply):

[   ] I direct that such life-sustaining treatment be withheld or withdrawn. I also direct that I be given all medically-appropriate care necessary to make me comfortable and to relieve pain.

[   ] I direct that life-sustaining treatment be continued, if medically appropriate.

If I am in the condition(s) described above, I feel especially strongly about the following forms of treatment (initial all those that apply):

[   ] I do NOT want cardiopulmonary resuscitation (CPR).

[   ] I do NOT want mechanical respiration.

[   ] I do NOT want tube feeding.

[   ] I do NOT want antibiotics.

[   ] I DO want maximum pain relief, even if it may hasten my death.

PREGNANCY: If I am pregnant at the time that I am diagnosed as having any of the conditions described above, I direct that my health care provider comply with following instructions (optional):

The State of New Jersey has determined that an individual may be declared legally dead when there has been an irreversible cessation of all functions of the entire brain, including the brain stem (also known as whole-brain death). However, individuals who do not accept this definition of brain death because of their personal religious beliefs may request that it not be applied in determining their death. Initial the following statement only if it applies to you:

[   ] To declare my death on the basis of the whole-brain death standard would violate my personal religious beliefs. I therefore wish my death to be declared only when my heartbeat and breathing have irreversibly stopped.

FURTHER INSTRUCTIONS: By writing this advance directive, I inform those who may become responsible for my health care of my wishes and intend to ease the burdens of decision-making which this responsibility may impose. I have discussed the terms of this designation with my health care representative and my representative has willingly agreed to accept the responsibility for acting on my behalf in accordance with this directive and my wishes. I understand the purpose and effect of this document and sign it knowingly, voluntarily, and after careful deliberation.

Appointment of Health Care Representative

I hereby appoint _____ (name), of
_____ (address), to be my health care representative to make any and all health care decisions for me, including decisions to accept or to refuse any treatment, service, or procedure used to diagnose or treat my physical or mental condition, and decisions to provide, withhold, or withdraw life-sustaining treatment. I direct

my health care representative to make decisions on my behalf in accordance with my wishes as stated in this document, or as otherwise known to him or her. In the event my wishes are not clear, or if a situation arises that I did not anticipate, my health care representative is authorized to make decisions in my best interests. I direct that my health care representative comply with the following instructions and/or limitations (optional):

I direct that my health care representative comply with the following instructions in the event that I am pregnant when this Directive becomes effective (optional):

OPTIONAL - DESIGNATION OF ALTERNATE REPRESENTATIVE: If I revoke my representative's authority or if my representative is not willing, able, or reasonably available to make a health care decision for me, I designate as my alternate representative
_____ (name of individual you choose as alternate representative)
_____ (address)

By writing this advance directive, I inform those who may become responsible for my health care of my wishes and intend to ease the burdens of decision-making which this responsibility may impose. I have discussed the terms of this designation with my health care representative and my representative has willingly agreed to accept the responsibility for acting on my behalf in accordance with this directive and my wishes. I understand the purpose and effect of this document and sign it knowingly, voluntarily, and after careful deliberation.

Designation of Primary Physician

I designate the following physician as my primary physician: _____ (name)
_____ (address)
_____(phone).

OPTIONAL- DESIGNATION OF ALTERNATE PRIMARY PHYSICIAN: If the physician I have designated above is not willing, able, or reasonably available to act as my primary physician, I designate the following physician as my primary physician:
_____ (name)
_____ (address)
_____(phone).

Organ Donation

In the event of my death, I have placed my initials next to the following part(s) of my body that I wish donated for the purposes **that I have initialed below:**

[   ] any organs or parts **OR**

[   ] eyes   [   ] bone and connective tissue   [   ] skin

[   ] heart   [   ] kidney(s)   [   ] liver

[   ] lung(s)   [   ] pancreas   [   ] other _____

for the purposes of:

[   ] any purpose authorized by law **OR**

[   ] transplantation   [   ] research   [   ] therapy

[   ] medical education   [   ] other limitations _____

Signature

I sign this Advance Health Care Directive, consisting of the following sections, **which I have initialed below and have elected to adopt:**

[   ] Living Will

[   ] Appointment of Health Care Representative

[   ] Designation of Primary Physician

[   ] Organ Donation

BY SIGNING HERE I INDICATE THAT I UNDERSTAND THE PURPOSE AND EFFECT OF THIS DOCUMENT.

Signature _____ Date _____

City, County, and State of Residence _____

Notary Acknowledgment

State of _____
County of _____

On _____ , _____ came before me personally and, under oath, stated that he or she is the person described in the above document and he or she signed the above document in my presence. I declare under penalty of perjury that the person whose name is subscribed to this instrument appears to be of sound mind and under no duress, fraud, or undue influence.

_____
Notary Public
My commission expires _____

Witness Acknowledgment

The declarant is personally known to me and I believe him or her to be of sound mind and under no duress, fraud, or undue influence. I did not sign the declarant's signature above for or at the direction of the declarant and I am not appointed as the health care representative or attorney-in-fact herein. I am at least eighteen (18) years of age and I am not related to the declarant by blood, adoption, or marriage, entitled to any portion of the estate of the declarant according to the laws of intestate succession or under any will of declarant or codicil thereto, or directly financially responsible for declarant's medical care. I am not a health care provider of the declarant or an employee of the health facility in which the declarant is a patient.

Witness Signature _____ Date _____

Printed Name of Witness _____

Witness Signature _____ Date _____

Printed Name of Witness _____

Acceptance of Health Care Representative

I accept my appointment as Health Care Representative:

Signature _____ Date _____

I accept my appointment as Alternate Health Care Representative:

Signature _____ Date _____

New Mexico Advance Health Care Directive

On this date of _____ , I, _____ , do hereby sign, execute, and adopt the following as my Advance Health Care Directive. I direct any and all persons or entities involved with my health care in any manner that these decisions are my wishes and were adopted without duress or force and of my own free will.

I have placed my initials next to the sections of this Directive that I have adopted:

[   ] Living Will
[   ] Selection of Health Care Agent (Power of Attorney for Health Care)
[   ] Designation of Primary Physician
[   ] Organ Donation

EXPLANATION: You have the right to give instructions about your own health care. You also have the right to name someone else to make health-care decisions for you. This form lets you do either or both of these things. It also lets you express your wishes regarding the designation of your primary physician. THIS FORM IS OPTIONAL. Each paragraph and word of this form is also optional. If you use this form, you may cross out, complete or modify all or any part of it. You are free to use a different form. If you use this form, be sure to sign it and date it.

PART 1 of this form lets you give specific instructions about any aspect of your health care. Choices are provided for you to express your wishes regarding life-sustaining treatment, including the provision of artificial nutrition and hydration, as well as the provision of pain relief. In addition, you may express your wishes regarding whether you want to make an anatomical gift of some or all of your organs and tissue. Space is also provided for you to add to the choices you have made or for you to write out any additional wishes.

PART 2 of this form is a power of attorney for health care. PART 2 lets you name another individual as agent to make health-care decisions for you if you become incapable of making your own decisions or if you want someone else to make those decisions for you now even though you are still capable. You may also name an alternate agent to act for you if your first choice is not willing, able or reasonably available to make decisions for you. Unless related to you, your agent may not be an owner, operator or employee of a health-care institution at which you are receiving care. Unless the form you sign limits the authority of your agent, your agent may make all health-care decisions for you. This form has a place for you to limit the authority of your agent. You need not limit the authority of your agent if you wish to rely on your agent for all health-care decisions that may have to be made. If you choose not to limit the authority of your agent, your agent will have the right to: (a) consent or refuse consent to any care, treatment, service or procedure to maintain, diagnose or otherwise affect a physical or mental condition; (b) select or discharge health-care providers and institutions; (c) approve or disapprove diagnostic tests, surgical procedures, programs of medication and orders not to resuscitate; and (d) direct the provision, withholding or withdrawal of artificial nutrition and hydration and all other forms of health care.

PART 3 of this form lets you designate a physician to have primary responsibility for your health care.

Part 4 of this form lets you make choices regarding the donation of your organs after your death.

After completing this form, sign and date the form at the end. It is recommended but not required that you request two other individuals to sign as witnesses. Give a copy of the signed and completed form to your physician, to any other health-care providers you may have, to any health-care institution at which you are receiving care and to any health-care agents you have named. You should talk to the person you have named as agent to make sure that he or she understands your wishes and is willing to take the responsibility. You have the right to revoke this advance health-care directive or replace this form at any time.

Part 1: Living Will

If you are satisfied to allow your health care agent to determine what is best for you in making end-of-life decisions, you need not fill out this part of the form. If you do fill out this part of the form, you may cross out any wording you do not want.

END OF LIFE DECISIONS: If I am unable to make or communicate decisions regarding my health care, and if:

(1) I have an incurable or irreversible condition that will result in my death within a relatively short time, **OR**

(2) I become unconscious and, to a reasonable degree of medical certainty, I will not regain consciousness, **OR**

(3) the likely risks and burdens of treatment would outweigh the expected benefits,

THEN I direct that my health care providers and others involved in my care provide, withhold, or withdraw treatment in accordance with **the choice I have initialed below in one of the following three (3) boxes that:**

[   ] **I Choose NOT To Prolong Life**. I do not want my life to be prolonged.

[   ] **I CHOOSE To Prolong Life**. I want my life to be prolonged as long as possible within the limits of generally-accepted health care standards.

[   ] **I CHOOSE To Let My Health Care Agent Decide**. My agent under my power of attorney for health care that I designate in this document may make life-sustaining treatment decisions for me.

If I have chosen above NOT to prolong life, I also specify by marking my initials below that:

[   ] I do NOT want artificial nutrition, **OR**

[   ] I DO want artificial nutrition.

[   ] I do NOT want artificial hydration unless required for my comfort, **OR**

[   ] I DO want artificial hydration.

RELIEF FROM PAIN: Regardless of the choices I have made in this form and except as I state in the following space, I direct that the best medical care possible to keep me clean, comfortable, and free of pain or discomfort be provided at all times so that my dignity is maintained, even if this care hastens my death. **(State any additional directions if desired)**.

A copy of this form has the same effect as the original. I understand that I may revoke this Advance Health Care Directive at any time, and that if I revoke it, I should promptly notify my supervising health care provider and any health care institution where I am receiving care and any others to whom I have given copies of this power of attorney. I understand that I may revoke the designation of an agent either by a signed writing or by personally informing the supervising health care provider.

Part 2: Selection of Health Care Agent
(Power of Attorney for Health Care)

I designate the following individual as my agent to make health care decisions for me:

_____ (name), of
_____ (address).

OPTIONAL - DESIGNATION OF ALTERNATE AGENT: If I revoke my agent's authority or if my agent is not willing, able, or reasonably available to make a health care decision for me, I designate as my first alternate agent

_____ (name of individual you choose as first alternate agent)
_____ (address)

AGENT'S AUTHORITY: My agent is authorized to obtain and review medical records, reports, and information about me and to make all health care decisions for me, including decisions to provide, withhold, or withdraw artificial nutrition, hydration, and all other forms of health care to keep me alive, except as I state here **(State any limitations or exceptions. Add additional sheets if needed)**:

WHEN AGENT'S AUTHORITY BECOMES EFFECTIVE: My agent's authority becomes effective when my primary physician and one other qualified health care professional determine that I am unable to make my own health care decisions.
If I initial this box [   ], my agent's authority to make health care decisions for me takes effect immediately.

AGENT'S OBLIGATIONS: My agent shall make health care decisions for me in accordance with this power of attorney for health care, any instructions I give in this Advance Health Care Directive, and my other wishes to the extent known to my agent. To the extent my wishes are unknown, my agent shall make health care decisions for me in accordance with what my agent determines to be in my best interest. In determining my best interest, my agent shall consider my personal values to the extent known to my agent.

NOMINATION OF GUARDIAN: If a guardian of my person needs to be appointed for me by a court, I nominate the agent designated in this form.

Part 3: Designation of Primary Physician

I designate the following physician as my primary physician: _____ (name)
_____ (address)
_____ (phone).

OPTIONAL- DESIGNATION OF ALTERNATE PRIMARY PHYSICIAN: If the physician I have designated above is not willing, able, or reasonably available to act as my primary physician, I designate the following physician as my primary physician:
_____ (name)
_____ (address)
_____ (phone).

Part 4: Organ Donation

In the event of my death, I have placed my initials next to the following part(s) of my body that I wish donated for the purposes **that I have initialed below:**

[　　] any organs or parts **OR**
[　　] eyes　　　　[　　] bone and connective tissue　　　[　　] skin
[　　] heart　　　[　　] kidney(s)　　　　　　　　　　　[　　] liver
[　　] lung(s)　　[　　] pancreas　　　　　　　　　　　[　　] other _____

for the purposes of:
[　　] any purpose authorized by law **OR**
[　　] transplantation　　　[　　] research　　　　[　　] therapy
[　　] medical education　　[　　] other limitations _____

Signature

I sign this Advance Health Care Directive, consisting of the following sections, **which I have initialed below and have elected to adopt:**

[　　] Living Will
[　　] Selection of Health Care Agent (Power of Attorney for Health Care)
[　　] Designation of Primary Physician
[　　] Organ Donation

BY SIGNING HERE I INDICATE THAT I UNDERSTAND THE PURPOSE AND EFFECT OF THIS DOCUMENT.

Signature _____　Date _____

City, County, and State of Residence _____

Notary Acknowledgment

State of _____

County of _____

On _____ , _____ came before me personally and, under oath, stated that he or she is the person described in the above document and he or she signed the above document in my presence. I declare under penalty of perjury that the person whose name is subscribed to this instrument appears to be of sound mind and under no duress, fraud, or undue influence.

_____
Notary Public
My commission expires _____

Witness Acknowledgment

The declarant is personally known to me and I believe him or her to be of sound mind and under no duress, fraud, or undue influence. I did not sign the declarant's signature above for or at the direction of the declarant and I am not appointed as the health care agent or attorney-in-fact herein. I am at least eighteen (18) years of age and I am not related to the declarant by blood, adoption, or marriage, entitled to any portion of the estate of the declarant according to the laws of intestate succession or under any will of declarant or codicil thereto, or directly financially responsible for declarant's medical care. I am not a health care provider of the declarant or an employee of the health facility in which the declarant is a patient.

Witness Signature _____ Date _____

Printed Name of Witness _____

Second Witness Signature _____ Date _____

Printed Name of Second Witness _____

Acceptance of Health Care Agent and Attorney-in-Fact for Health Care

I accept my appointment as Health Care Agent and Attorney-in-Fact for Health Care:

Signature _____ Date _____

I accept my appointment as Alternate Health Care Agent and Attorney-in-Fact for Health Care:

Signature _____ Date _____

New York Advance Health Care Directive

On this date of _____ , I, _____ , do hereby sign, execute, and adopt the following as my Advance Health Care Directive. I direct any and all persons or entities involved with my health care in any manner that these decisions are my wishes and were adopted without duress or force and of my own free will.

I have placed my initials next to the sections of this Directive that I have adopted:

[   ] Living Will (Order Not to Resucitate)
[   ] Selection of Health Care Agent (Health Care Proxy)
[   ] Designation of Primary Physician
[   ] Organ Donation

Living Will (Order Not to Resucitate)

I, being of sound mind, make this statement as a directive to be followed if I become permanently unable to participate in decisions regarding my medical care. These instructions reflect my firm and settled commitment to decline medical treatment under the circumstances indicated below. I direct my attending physician to withhold or withdraw treatment that merely prolongs my dying, if I should be in an incurable or irreversible mental or physical condition with no reasonable expectation of recovery, including but not limited to:

> (1) a terminal condition,
> (2) a permanently-unconscious condition, **OR**
> (3) a minimally-conscious condition in which I am permanently unable to make decisions or express my wishes.

I direct that my treatment be limited to measures to keep me comfortable and to relieve pain, including any pain that might occur by withholding or withdrawing treatment. While I understand that I am not legally required to be specific about future treatments if I am in the condition(s) described above, I feel especially strongly about the following forms of treatment **(initial those that you choose)**:

[   ] I do NOT want cardiac resuscitation.
[   ] I do NOT want mechanical respiration.
[   ] I do NOT want artificial nutrition and hydration.
[   ] I do NOT want antibiotics.
[   ] However, I DO want maximum pain relief, even if it may hasten my death.

Other directions **(Add instructions and additional pages as needed)**:

These directions express my legal right to refuse treatment, under the law of New York. I intend my instructions to be carried out, unless I have rescinded them in a new writing or by clearly indicating that I have changed my mind.

Selection of Health Care Agent (Health Care Proxy)

I, hereby appoint _____ (name),
of _____ (address),
as my health care agent to make any and all health care decisions for me, except to the extent I state otherwise. This health care proxy shall take effect in the event I become unable to make my own health care decisions.

OPTIONAL - DESIGNATION OF ALTERNATE AGENT: If I revoke my agent's authority or if my agent is not willing, able, or reasonably available to make a health care decision for me, I designate as my alternate agent

_____ (name of individual you choose as alternate agent)
_____ (address)

(NOTE: Although not necessary, and neither encouraged nor discouraged, you may wish to state instructions or wishes, and limit your agent's authority. Unless your agent knows your wishes about artificial nutrition and hydration, he or she will not have the authority to decide about artificial nutrition and hydration. If you choose to state instructions, wishes, or limits, please do so below. Attach additional pages if needed):

I direct my agent to make health care decisions in accordance with my wishes and instructions as stated above or as otherwise known to him or her. I also direct my agent to abide by any limitations on his or her authority as stated above or as otherwise known to him or her. I understand that, unless I revoke it, this proxy will remain in effect indefinitely. **Please initial the box and complete the following only if you DO NOT want your health care proxy to remain in effect indefinitely**:

[   ] This Proxy shall expire on _____

Designation of Primary Physician

I designate the following physician as my primary physician: _____ (name)
_____ (address)
_____ (phone).

OPTIONAL- DESIGNATION OF ALTERNATE PRIMARY PHYSICIAN: If the physician I have designated above is not willing, able, or reasonably available to act as my primary physician, I designate the following physician as my primary physician:

_____ (name)
_____ (address)
_____ (phone).

Organ Donation

In the event of my death, I have placed my initials next to the following part(s) of my body that I wish donated for the purposes **that I have initialed below:**

[   ] any organs or parts **OR**

[   ] eyes   [   ] bone and connective tissue   [   ] skin

[   ] heart   [   ] kidney(s)   [   ] liver

[   ] lung(s)   [   ] pancreas   [   ] other _____

for the purposes of:

[   ] any purpose authorized by law **OR**

[   ] transplantation   [   ] research   [   ] therapy

[   ] medical education   [   ] other limitations _____

Signature

I sign this Advance Health Care Directive, consisting of the following sections, **which I have initialed below and have elected to adopt:**

[   ] Living Will (Order Not to Resucitate)

[   ] Selection of Health Care Agent (Health Care Proxy)

[   ] Designation of Primary Physician

[   ] Organ Donation

BY SIGNING HERE I INDICATE THAT I UNDERSTAND THE PURPOSE AND EFFECT OF THIS DOCUMENT.

Signature _____ Date _____

City, County, and State of Residence _____

Notary Acknowledgment

State of _____

County of _____

On _____ , _____ came before me personally and, under oath, stated that he or she is the person described in the above document and he or she signed the above document in my presence. I declare under penalty of perjury that the person whose name is subscribed to this instrument appears to be of sound mind and under no duress, fraud, or undue influence.

_____

Notary Public

My commission expires _____

Witness Acknowledgment

The declarant is personally known to me and I believe him or her to be of sound mind and under no duress, fraud, or undue influence. I did not sign the declarant's signature above for or at the direction of the declarant and I am not appointed as the health care agent or attorney-in-fact herein. I am at least eighteen (18) years of age and I am not related to the declarant by blood, adoption, or marriage, entitled to any portion of the estate of the declarant according to the laws of intestate succession or under any will of declarant or codicil thereto, or directly financially responsible for declarant's medical care. I am not a health care provider of the declarant or an employee of the health facility in which the declarant is a patient.

Witness Signature _____ Date _____

Printed Name of Witness _____

Second Witness Signature _____ Date _____

Printed Name of Second Witness _____

Acceptance of Health Care Agent (Health Care Proxy)

I accept my appointment as Health Care Agent and Health Care Proxy:

Signature _____ Date _____

I accept my appointment as Alternate Health Care Agent and Health Care Proxy

Signature _____ Date _____

North Carolina Advance Health Care Directive

On this date of _____ , I, _____ , do hereby sign, execute, and adopt the following as my Advance Health Care Directive. I direct any and all persons or entities involved with my health care in any manner that these decisions are my wishes and were adopted without duress or force and of my own free will.

I have placed my initials next to the sections of this Directive that I have adopted:

[   ] Living Will (Declaration of Desire for a Natural Death)
[   ] Selection of Health Care Agent (Health Care Power of Attorney)
[   ] Designation of Primary Physician
[   ] Organ Donation

Living Will (Declaration of Desire for a Natural Death)

I, being of sound mind, desire that, as specified below, my life not be prolonged by extraordinary means or by artificial nutrition or hydration if my condition is determined to be terminal and incurable or if I am diagnosed as being in a persistent vegetative state. I am aware and understand that this writing authorizes a physician to withhold or discontinue extraordinary means or artificial nutrition or hydration, in accordance with my specifications set forth below (**initial any of the following, as desired**):

[   ] If my condition is determined to be terminal and incurable, I authorize the following:
  [   ] My physician may withhold or discontinue extraordinary means only.
  [   ] In addition to withholding or discontinuing extraordinary means if such means are necessary, my physician may withhold or discontinue either artificial nutrition or hydration, or both.

[   ] If my physician determines that I am in a persistent vegetative state, I authorize the following:
  [   ] My physician may withhold or discontinue extraordinary means only.
  [   ] In addition to withholding or discontinuing extraordinary means if such means are necessary, my physician may withhold or discontinue either artificial nutrition or hydration, or both.

Selection of Health Care Agent
(Health Care Power of Attorney)

NOTICE: This document gives the person you designate as your health care agent broad powers to make health care decisions, including mental health treatment decisions for you. Except to the extent that you express specific limitations or restrictions on the authority of your health care agent, this power includes the power to consent to your doctor not giving treatment or stopping treatment necessary to keep you alive, admit you to a facility, and administer certain treatments and medications. This power exists only as to those health care decisions for which you are unable to give informed consent. This form does not impose a duty on your health care agent to exercise granted powers, but when a power is exercised, your health care agent will have to use due care to act in your best interests and in accordance with this document. For mental health treatment decisions, your health care agent will act according to how the health agent believes you would act if you were making the decision. This health care power of attorney may be revoked by you at any time in any manner by which you are able to communicate your intent to revoke to your health care agent and your attending physician. Because the powers granted by this document are broad and sweeping, you should discuss your wishes concerning life-sustaining procedures, mental health treatment, and other health care decisions with your health care agent. Use of this form in the creation of a health care power of attorney is lawful and is authorized pursuant to North Carolina law. However, use of this form is an optional and non-exclusive method for creating a health care power of attorney and North Carolina law does not bar the use of any other or different form of power of attorney for health care that meets the statutory requirements.

DESIGNATION OF AGENT: I, being of sound mind, hereby appoint:

_____ (name),

of _____ (address),

as my health care attorney-in-fact (herein referred to as my "health care agent") to act for me and in my name (in any way I could act in person) to make health care decisions for me as authorized in this document.

OPTIONAL - DESIGNATION OF ALTERNATE HEALTH CARE AGENT: If I revoke my health care agent's authority or if my health care agent is not willing, able, or reasonably available to make a health care decision for me, I designate as my alternate health care agent

_____ (name of individual you choose as alternate health care agent)

_____ (address)

EFFECTIVENESS OF APPOINTMENT: Unless revoked, the authority granted in this document shall become effective when and if the physician or physicians designated as my primary physicians in this document determine that I lack sufficient understanding or capacity to make or communicate decisions relating to my health care and will continue in effect during my incapacity, until my death.

For decisions related to mental health treatment, this determination shall be made by the following physician or eligible psychologist (include here a designation of your choice):

_____ (name),

of _____(address)

GENERAL STATEMENT OF AUTHORITY GRANTED: Except as indicated below, I hereby grant to my health care agent named above full power and authority to make health care decisions, including mental health treatment decisions, on my behalf, including, but not limited to, the following :

(1) To request, review, and receive any information, verbal or written, regarding my physical or mental health, including, but not limited to medical and hospital records, and to consent to the disclosure of this information,

(2) To employ or discharge my health care providers,

(3) To consent to and authorize my admission to and discharge from a hospital, nursing or convalescent home, or other institution,

(4) To consent to and authorize my admission to and retention in a facility for the care or treatment of mental illness,

(5) To consent to and authorize the administration of medications for mental health treatment and electroconvulsive treatment (ECT), commonly referred to as "shock treatment,"

(6) To give consent for, withdraw consent for, or withhold consent for x-ray, anesthesia, medication, surgery, and all other diagnostic and treatment procedures ordered by or under the authorization of a licensed physician, dentist, or podiatrist. This authorization specifically includes the power to consent to measures for relief of pain,

(7) To authorize the withholding or withdrawal of life-sustaining procedures when and if my physician determines that I am terminally ill, am permanently in a coma, suffer severe dementia, or am in a persistent vegetative state. **Life-sustaining procedures are those forms of medical care that only serve to artificially prolong the dying process and may include mechanical ventilation, dialysis, antibiotics, artificial nutrition and hydration, and other forms of medical treatment which sustain, restore, or supplant vital bodily functions. Life-sustaining procedures do not include care necessary to provide comfort or alleviate pain.**

I DESIRE THAT MY LIFE NOT BE PROLONGED BY LIFE-SUSTAINING PROCEDURES IF I AM TERMINALLY ILL, AM PERMANENTLY IN A COMA, SUFFER SEVERE DEMENTIA, OR AM IN A PERSISTENT VEGETATIVE STATE.

(8) To exercise any right I may have to make a disposition of any part or all of my body for medical purposes, donate my organs, authorize an autopsy, and direct the disposition of my remains,

(9) To take any lawful actions that may be necessary to carry out these decisions, including the granting of releases of liability to medical providers.

NOTICE: The above grant of power is intended to be as broad as possible so that your health care agent will have authority to make any decisions you could make to obtain or terminate any type of health care. If you wish to limit the scope of your health care agent's powers, you may do so in this section.

SPECIAL PROVISIONS AND LIMITATIONS: In exercising the authority to make health care decisions on my behalf, the authority of my health care agent is subject to the following special provisions and limitations **(here you may include any specific limitations you deem appropriate such as: your own definition of when life-sustaining treatment should be withheld or discontinued, or instructions to refuse any specific types of treatment that are inconsistent with your religious beliefs or unacceptable to you for any other reason. Attach additional pages if needed):**

In exercising the authority to make mental health decisions on my behalf, the authority of my health care agent is subject to the following special provisions and limitations **(here you may include any specific limitations you deem appropriate such as: limiting the grant of authority to make only mental health treatment decisions, your own instructions regarding the administration or withholding of psychotropic medications and electroconvulsive treatment (ECT), instructions regarding your admission to and retention in a health care facility for mental health treatment, or instructions to refuse any specific types of treatment that are unacceptable to you. Attach additional pages as needed):**

NOTICE: This health care power of attorney may incorporate or be combined with an advance instruction for mental health treatment, executed in accordance with Part 2 of Article 3 of Chapter 122C of the North Carolina General Statutes, which you may use to state your instructions regarding mental health treatment in the event you lack sufficient understanding or capacity to make or communicate mental health treatment decisions. Because your health care agent's decisions must be consistent with any statements you have expressed in an advance instruction, you should indicate here whether you have executed an advance instruction for mental health treatment (indicate your actions and attach additional pages if needed):

In exercising the authority to make decisions regarding autopsy, anatomical gifts and disposition of remains on my behalf, the authority of my health care agent is subject to the following special provisions and limitations. **(Here you may include any specific limitations you deem appropriate such as: limiting the grant of authority and the scope of authority, instructions regarding gifts of the body or body part, or instructions regarding burial or cremation):**

GUARDIANSHIP PROVISION: If it becomes necessary for a court to appoint a guardian of my person, I nominate my health care agent acting under this document to be the guardian of my person and to serve without bond or security. The guardian shall act consistently with N.C.G.S. 35A-1201(a)(5).

RELIANCE OF THIRD PARTIES ON HEALTH CARE AGENT: No person who relies in good faith upon the authority of or any representations by my health care agent shall be liable to me or my estate, heirs, successors, assigns, or personal representatives, for actions or omissions by my health care agent. The powers conferred on my health care agent by this document may be exercised by my health care agent alone, and my health care agent's signature or act under the authority granted in this document may be accepted by persons as fully authorized by me and with the same force and effect as if I were personally present, competent, and acting on my own behalf. All acts performed in good faith by my health care agent pursuant to this power of attorney are done with my consent and shall have the same validity and effect as if I were present and exercised the powers myself, and shall inure to the benefit of and bind me or my estate, heirs, successors, assigns, and personal representatives. The authority of my health care agent pursuant to this power of attorney shall be superior to and binding upon my family, relatives, friends, and others.

MISCELLANEOUS PROVISIONS: I revoke any prior health care power of attorney. My health care agent shall be entitled to sign, execute, deliver, and acknowledge any contract or other document that may be necessary, desirable, convenient, or proper in order to exercise and carry out any of the powers described in this document and incur reasonable costs on my behalf, incident to the exercise of these powers; provided, however, that except as shall be necessary in order to exercise the powers described in this document relating to my health care, my health care agent shall not have any authority over my property or financial affairs. My health care agent and his or her estate, heirs, successors, and assigns are hereby released and forever discharged by me or my estate, heirs, successors, assigns, and personal representatives from all liability and claims or demands of all kinds arising out of the acts or omissions of my health care agent pursuant to this document, except for willful misconduct or gross negligence. No act or omission of my health care agent, any other person, institution, or facility acting in good faith in reliance on the authority of my health care agent pursuant to this health care power of attorney shall be considered suicide, nor the cause of my death for any civil or criminal purposes, nor shall it be considered unprofessional conduct or as lack of professional competence. Any person, institution, or facility against whom criminal or civil liability is asserted because of conduct authorized by this health care power of attorney may interpose this document as a defense.

Designation of Primary Physician

I designate the following physician as my primary physician: _____ (name)
_____ (address)
_____ (phone).

OPTIONAL- DESIGNATION OF ALTERNATE PRIMARY PHYSICIAN: If the physician I have designated above is not willing, able, or reasonably available to act as my primary physician, I designate the following physician as my primary physician:
_____ (name)
_____ (address)
_____ (phone).

Organ Donation

In the event of my death, I have placed my initials next to the following part(s) of my body that I wish donated for the purposes **that I have initialed below:**

[   ] any organs or parts **OR**
[   ] eyes   [   ] bone and connective tissue   [   ] skin
[   ] heart   [   ] kidney(s)   [   ] liver
[   ] lung(s)   [   ] pancreas   [   ] other _____

for the purposes of:

[   ] any purpose authorized by law **OR**
[   ] transplantation   [   ] research   [   ] therapy
[   ] medical education   [   ] other limitations _____

Signature of Declarant/Principal

I sign this Advance Health Care Directive, consisting of the following sections, **which I have initialed below and have elected to adopt:**

[   ] Living Will (Declaration of Desire for a Natural Death)
[   ] Selection of Health Care Agent (Health Care Power of Attorney)
[   ] Designation of Primary Physician
[   ] Organ Donation

BY SIGNING HERE I INDICATE THAT I AM MENTALLY ALERT AND COMPETENT, FULLY INFORMED AS TO THE CONTENTS OF THIS DOCUMENT, AND UNDERSTAND THE FULL IMPORT AND THE PURPOSE AND EFFECT OF THIS DOCUMENT.

Signature _____   Date _____

City, County, and State of Residence _____

Notary or Superior Court Clerk Certification

State of _____

County of _____

I, _____, Clerk (Assistant Clerk) of Superior Court or Notary Public (circle one as appropriate) for _____ County hereby certify that _____, the declarant/principal, appeared before me and swore to me and to the witnesses in my presence that this instrument is his Advance Health Care Directive, consisting of a Declaration Of A Desire For A Natural Death, a Health Care Power of Attorney, a Designation of Primary Physician, and an Organ Donation, and that he had willingly and voluntarily made and executed it as his free act and deed for the purposes expressed in it.

I further certify that _____ and _____, witnesses, appeared before me and swore that they witnessed _____, the declarant/principal, sign the attached Advance Health Care Directive, consisting of a Declaration of a Desire for a Natural Death, a Health Care Power of Attorney, a Designation of Primary Physician, and an Organ Donation, believing him to be of sound mind; and also swore that at the time they witnessed the Advance Health Care Directive, consisting of a Declaration of a Desire for a Natural Death, a Health Care Power of Attorney, a Designation of Primary Physician, and an Organ Donation, (i) they were not related within the third degree to the declarant/principal or to the declarant/principal's spouse, and (ii) they did not know or have a reasonable expectation that they would be entitled to any portion of the estate of the declarant/principal upon the declarant/principal's death under any will of the declarant/principal or codicil thereto then existing or under the Intestate Succession Act as it provides at that time, and (iii) they were not a physician attending the declarant/principal or an employee of an attending physician or an employee of a health facility in which the declarant/principal was a patient or an employee of a nursing home or any group-care home in which the declarant/principal resided, and (iv) they did not have a claim against the declarant/principal. I further certify that I am satisfied as to the genuineness and due execution of the Advance Health Care Directive, consisting of a Declaration of a Desire for a Natural Death, a Health Care Power of Attorney, a Designation of Primary Physician, and an Organ Donation.

This the _____ day of _____, _____.

Clerk (Assistant Clerk) of Superior Court or Notary Public (circle one as appropriate) for the County of _____ "

_____
Official Signature
My commission expires _____

Witness Acknowledgment

I hereby state that the declarant/principal, being of sound mind signed the above Advance Health Care Directive, consisting of a Declaration of a Desire for a Natural Death, a Health Care Power of Attorney, a Designation of Primary Physician, and an Organ Donation, in my presence and that I am not related to the declarant/principal by blood or marriage and that I do not know or have a reasonable expectation that I would be entitled to any portion of the estate of the declarant/principal under any existing will or codicil of the declarant/principal or as an heir under the Intestate Succession Act if the declarant/principal died on this date without a will. I also state that I am not the declarant/principal's attending physician or an employee of the declarant/principal's attending physician, or an employee of a health facility in which the declarant/principal is a patient or an employee of a nursing home or any group-care home where the declarant/principal resides. I further state that I do not now have any claim against the declarant/principal.

Witness Signature _____ Date _____

Printed Name of Witness _____

Second Witness Signature _____ Date _____

Printed Name of Second Witness _____

Acceptance of Health Care Agent and Attorney-in-Fact for Health Care

I accept my appointment as Health Care Agent and Attorney-in-Fact for Health Care:

Signature _____ Date _____

I accept my appointment as Alternate Health Care Agent and Attorney-in-Fact for Health Care:

Signature _____ Date _____

NOTE: A copy of this document should be given to your health care agent and alternate health care agent (if an alternate has been designated), and to your primary physician (and to your alternate primary physician if one has been designated), and to family members.

North Dakota Advance Health Care Directive

On this date of _____ , I, _____ , do hereby sign, execute, and adopt the following as my Advance Health Care Directive. I direct any and all persons or entities involved with my health care in any manner that these decisions are my wishes and were adopted without duress or force and of my own free will.

I have placed my initials next to the sections of this Directive that I have adopted:

[   ] Living Will (Health Care Instructions)
[   ] Appointment of Health Care Agent
[   ] Designation of Primary Physician
[   ] Organ Donation

I understand this document allows me to do ONE OR ALL of the following:

PART I: Give health care instructions to guide others making health care decisions for me. If I have named a health care agent, these instructions are to be used by the agent. These instructions may also be used by my health care providers, others assisting with my health care and my family, in the event I cannot make and communicate decisions for myself. AND/OR

PART II: Name another person (called the health care agent) to make health care decisions for me if I am unable to make and communicate health care decisions for myself. My health care agent must make health care decisions for me based on the instructions I provide in this document (Part I), if any, the wishes I have made known to him or her, or my agent must act in my best interest if I have not made my health care wishes known. AND/OR

PART III: Designate the doctor that I wish to be considered my primary physician (and, if desired an alternate choice if my primary doctor is unavailable). AND/OR

PART IV: Allows me to make an organ and tissue donation upon my death by signing a document of anatomical gift.

Part I: Living Will (Health Care Instructions)

NOTE: Complete this Part I if you wish to give health care instructions. If you appointed an agent in Part II, completing this Part I is optional but would be very helpful to your agent. However, if you chose not to appoint an agent in Part II, you MUST complete, at a minimum, Part I (B) if you wish to make a valid health care directive.

These are instructions for my health care when I am unable to make and communicate health care decisions for myself. These instructions must be followed (so long as they address my needs).

(A) THESE ARE MY BELIEFS AND VALUES ABOUT MY HEALTH CARE
(I know I can change these choices or leave any of them blank)
I want you to know these things about me to help you make decisions about my health care:

My goals for my health care:

My fears about my health care:

My spiritual or religious beliefs and traditions:

My beliefs about when life would be no longer worth living:

My thoughts about how my medical condition might affect my family:

(B) THIS IS WHAT I WANT AND DO NOT WANT FOR MY HEALTH CARE

(I know I can change these choices or leave any of them blank) Many medical treatments may be used to try to improve my medical condition or to prolong my life. Examples include artificial breathing by a machine connected to a tube in the lungs, artificial feeding or fluids through tubes, attempts to start a stopped heart, surgeries, dialysis, antibiotics, and blood transfusions. Most medical treatments can be tried for a while and then stopped if they do not help. I have these views about my health care in these situations:
(Note: You can discuss general feelings, specific treatments, or leave any of them blank).

If I had a reasonable chance of recovery and were temporarily unable to make and communicate health care decisions for myself, I would want:

If I were dying and unable to make and communicate health care decisions for myself, I would want:

If I were permanently unconscious and unable to make and communicate health care decisions for myself, I would want:

If I were completely dependent on others for my care and unable to make and communicate health care decisions for myself, I would want:

In all circumstances, my doctors will try to keep me comfortable and reduce my pain.

This is how I feel about pain relief if it would affect my alertness or if it could shorten my life:

There are other things that I want or do not want for my health care, if possible:

Where I would like to live to receive health care:

Where I would like to die and other wishes I have about dying:

My wishes about what happens to my body when I die (cremation, burial):

Any other things:

(THIS HEALTH CARE DIRECTIVE WILL NOT BE VALID UNLESS IT IS NOTARIZED OR SIGNED BY TWO QUALIFIED WITNESSES WHO ARE PRESENT WHEN YOU SIGN OR ACKNOWLEDGE YOUR SIGNATURE. IF YOU HAVE ATTACHED ANY ADDITIONAL PAGES TO THIS FORM, YOU MUST DATE AND SIGN EACH OF THE ADDITIONAL PAGES AT THE SAME TIME YOU DATE AND SIGN THIS HEALTH CARE DIRECTIVE.)

Part II: Appointment of Health Care Agent

THIS IS WHO I WANT TO MAKE HEALTH CARE DECISIONS FOR ME IF I AM UNABLE TO MAKE AND COMMUNICATE HEALTH CARE DECISIONS FOR MYSELF
(I know I can change my agent or alternate agent at any time and I know I do not have to appoint an agent or an alternate agent)
NOTE: If you appoint an agent, you should discuss this health care directive with your agent and give your agent a copy. If you do not wish to appoint an agent, you

may leave Part II blank and go to Part III and/or Part IV. None of the following may be designated as your agent: your treating health care provider, a nonr-relative employee of your treating health care provider, an operator of a long-term care facility, or a non-relative employee of a long-term care facility.

When I am unable to make and communicate health care decisions for myself, I trust and appoint
_____ (name)
to make health care decisions for me. This person is called my health care agent.
Relationship of my health care agent to me: _____
Telephone number of my health care agent: _____
Address of my health care agent: _____

(OPTIONAL) APPOINTMENT OF ALTERNATE HEALTH CARE AGENT: If my health care agent is not reasonably available, I trust and appoint:
_____ (name)
to be my health care agent instead.
Relationship of my alternate health care agent to me: _____
Telephone number of my alternate health care agent: _____
Address of my alternate health care agent: _____

THIS IS WHAT I WANT MY HEALTH CARE AGENT TO BE ABLE TO DO IF I AM UNABLE TO MAKE AND COMMUNICATE HEALTH CARE DECISIONS FOR MYSELF
(I know I can change these choices)
My health care agent is automatically given the powers listed below in (A) through (D). My health care agent must follow my health care instructions in this document or any other instructions I have given to my agent. If I have not given health care instructions, then my agent must act in my best interest.

Whenever I am unable to make and communicate health care decisions for myself, my health care agent has the power to:
  (A) Make any health care decision for me. This includes the power to give, refuse, or withdraw consent to any care, treatment, service, or procedures. This includes deciding whether to stop or not start health care that is keeping me or might keep me alive and deciding about mental health treatment.
  (B) Choose my health care providers.
  (C) Choose where I live and receive care and support when those choices relate to my health care needs.
  (D) Review my medical records and have the same rights that I would have to give my medical records to other people.

If I DO NOT want my health care agent to have a power listed above in (A) through (D) OR if I want to LIMIT any power in (A) through (D), I MUST say that here:

My health care agent is NOT automatically given the powers listed below in (1) and (2). If I WANT my agent to have any of the powers in (1) and (2), I must INITIAL the line in front of the power; then my agent WILL HAVE that power.

[   ] (1) To decide whether to donate any parts of my body, including organs, tissues, and eyes, when I die.

[   ] (2) To decide what will happen with my body when I die (burial, cremation).

If I want to say anything more about my health care agent's powers or limits on the powers, I can say it here:

Part III: Designation of Primary Physician

I designate the following physician as my primary physician: _____ (name)
_____ (address)
_____ (phone).

OPTIONAL- DESIGNATION OF ALTERNATE PRIMARY PHYSICIAN: If the physician I have designated above is not willing, able, or reasonably available to act as my primary physician, I designate the following physician as my primary physician:
_____ (name)
_____ (address)
_____ (phone).

Part IV: Organ Donation

In the event of my death, I have placed my initials next to the following part(s) of my body that I wish donated for the purposes **that I have initialed below:**

[   ] any organs or parts **OR**
[   ] eyes   [   ] bone and connective tissue   [   ] skin
[   ] heart   [   ] kidney(s)   [   ] liver
[   ] lung(s)   [   ] pancreas   [   ] other _____

for the purposes of:

[   ] any purpose authorized by law **OR**
[   ] transplantation   [   ] research   [   ] therapy
[   ] medical education   [   ] other limitations _____

Signature

I sign this Advance Health Care Directive, consisting of the following sections, **which I have initialed below and have elected to adopt:**

[   ] Living Will (Health Care Instructions)
[   ] Appointment of Health Care Agent
[   ] Designation of Primary Physician
[   ] Organ Donation

BY SIGNING HERE I INDICATE THAT I UNDERSTAND THE PURPOSE AND EFFECT OF THIS DOCUMENT. I HAVE READ A WRITTEN EXPLANATION OF THE NATURE AND EFFECT OF AN APPOINTMENT OF A HEALTH CARE AGENT THAT IS PART OF MY HEALTH CARE DIRECTIVE.

Signature _____ Date _____

City, County, and State of Residence _____

Notary Acknowledgment

State of _____
County of _____

On _____ , _____ came before me personally and, under oath, stated that he or she is the person described in the above document and he or she signed the above document in my presence. I declare under penalty of perjury that the person whose name is subscribed to this instrument appears to be of sound mind and under no duress, fraud, or undue influence.

_____
Notary Public
My commission expires _____

Witness Acknowledgment

The declarant is personally known to me and I believe him or her to be of sound mind and under no duress, fraud, or undue influence. I did not sign the declarant's signature above for or at the direction of the declarant and I am not appointed as the health care agent herein. I am at least eighteen (18) years of age and I am not related to the declarant by blood, adoption, or marriage, entitled to any portion of the estate of the declarant according to the laws of intestate succession or under any will of declarant or codicil thereto, or directly financially responsible for declarant's medical care, or have any claim against the declarant. The first witness is not a health care provider or long-term provider of the declarant or an employee of the health facility in which the declarant is a patient.

Witness Signature _____ Date _____

Printed Name of Witness _____

Second Witness Signature _____ Date _____

Printed Name of Second Witness _____

Acceptance of Appointment of Health Care Agent

I accept this appointment and agree to serve as agent for health care decisions. I understand I have a duty to act consistently with the desires of the principal as expressed in this appointment. I understand that this document gives me authority over health care decisions for the principal only if the principal becomes incapacitated. I understand that I must act in good faith in exercising my authority under this power of attorney. I understand that the principal may revoke this power of attorney at any time in any manner. If I choose to withdraw during the time the principal is competent, I must notify the principal of my decision. If I choose to withdraw when the principal is not able to make health care decisions, I must notify the principal's physician.

Signature of Health Care Agent _____ Date _____

I accept my appointment :

Signature of Alternate Health Care Agent_____ Date _____

Ohio Advance Health Care Directive

On this date of _____ , I, _____ , do hereby sign, execute, and adopt the following as my Advance Health Care Directive. I direct any and all persons or entities involved with my health care in any manner that these decisions are my wishes and were adopted without duress or force and of my own free will.

I have placed my initials next to the sections of this Directive that I have adopted:

[   ] Living Will Declaration
[   ] Selection of Health Care Agent (Durable Power of Attorney for Health Care)
[   ] Designation of Primary Physician
[   ] Organ Donation

Living Will Declaration

NOTICE: This form of a Living Will Declaration is designed to serve as evidence of an individual's desire that life-sustaining medical treatment, including artificially- or technologically-supplied nutrition and hydration, be withheld or withdrawn if the individual is unable to communicate and is in a terminal condition or a permanently-unconscious state. If you would choose not to withhold or withdraw any or all forms of life-sustaining treatment, you have the legal right to so choose and you might want to state your medical treatment preferences in writing in another form of Declaration. Under Ohio law, a Living Will Declaration may be relied on only for individuals in a terminal condition or a permanently-unconscious state. If you wish to direct your medical treatment in other circumstances, you should consider preparing a Durable Power of Attorney for Health Care.

I, being of sound mind and not subject to duress, fraud, or undue influence, intending to create a Living Will Declaration under Chapter 2133 of the Ohio Revised Code, do voluntarily make known my desire that my dying shall not be artificially-prolonged. If I am unable to give directions regarding the use of life-sustaining treatment when I am in a terminal condition or a permanently-unconscious state, it is my intention that this Living Will Declaration shall be honored by my family and physicians as the final expression of my legal right to refuse medical or surgical treatment. I am a competent adult who understands and accepts the consequences of such refusal and the purpose and effect of this document **(initial all the following that you choose)**:

In the event I am in a terminal condition, I declare and direct that my attending physician shall **(initial all that you choose)**:

[   ] Administer NO life-sustaining treatment, including cardiopulmonary resuscitation;

[   ] Withdraw life-sustaining treatment, including cardiopulmonary resuscitation, if such treatment has commenced, and in the case of cardiopulmonary resuscitation, issue a do-not-resuscitate order;

[   ] Permit me to die naturally and provide me with only the care necessary to make me comfortable and to relieve my pain but not to postpone my death.

In the event I am in a permanently-unconscious state, I declare and direct that my attending physician shall **(initial all that you choose):**

[   ] Administer NO life-sustaining treatment, including cardiopulmonary resuscitation, except for the provision of artificially- or technologically-supplied nutrition or hydration unless, in the following paragraph, I have authorized its withholding or withdrawal;

[   ] Withdraw such treatment, including cardiopulmonary resuscitation, if such treatment has commenced, and, in the case of cardiopulmonary resuscitation, issue a do-not-resuscitate order;

[   ] Permit me to die naturally and provide me with only that care necessary to make me comfortable and to relieve my pain but not to postpone my death.

[   ] In addition, **if I have initialed the foregoing box,** I authorize my attending physician to withhold, or in the event that treatment has already commenced, to withdraw the provision of artificially- or technologically-supplied nutrition and hydration, if I am in a permanently-unconscious state and if my attending physician and at least one other physician who has examined me determine, to a reasonable degree of medical certainty and in accordance with reasonable medical standards, that such nutrition or hydration will not or will no longer serve to provide comfort to me or alleviate my pain.

OTHER DIRECTIONS: In the event my attending physician determines that life-sustaining treatment should be withheld or withdrawn, he or she shall make a good faith effort and use reasonable diligence to notify one (1) of the persons named below in the following order of priority:

(1) _____ (name), _____ (relationship), of _____ (address).

(2) _____ (name), _____ (relationship), of _____ (address).

[   ] I have a durable power of attorney for health care. **(Initial if true).**

For purposes of this Living Will Declaration:
(1) "Life-Sustaining Treatment" means any medical procedure, treatment, intervention, or other measure including artificially- or technologically-supplied nutrition and hydration that, when administered, will serve principally to prolong the process of dying.
(2) "Terminal Condition" means an irreversible, incurable, and untreatable condition caused by disease, illness, or injury from which, to a reasonable degree of medical certainty as determined in accordance with reasonable medical standards by my attending physician and one (1) other physician who has examined me, both of the following apply: (a) There can be no recovery; and (b) Death is likely to occur within a relatively short time if life-sustaining treatment is not administered.
(3) "Permanently-Unconscious State" means a state of permanent unconsciousness that, to a reasonable degree of medical certainty as determined in accordance with reasonable medical standards by my attending physician and one (1) other physician who has examined me, is characterized by both of the following: (a) I am irreversibly unaware of myself and my environment, and (b) There is a total loss of cerebral cortical functioning, resulting in my having no capacity to experience pain or suffering.

Selection of Health Care Agent
(Durable Power of Attorney for Health Care)

NOTICE: This is an important legal document. Before executing this document, you should know these facts: This document gives the person you designate (the attorney-in-fact) the power to make MOST health care decisions for you if you lose the capacity to make informed health care decisions for yourself. This power is effective only when your attending physician determines that you have lost the capacity to make informed health care decisions for yourself and, notwithstanding this document, as long as you have the capacity to make informed health care decisions for yourself, you retain the right to make all medical and other health care decisions for yourself. You may include specific limitations in this document on the authority of the attorney-in-fact to make health care decisions for you. Subject to any specific limitations you include in this document, if your attending physician determines that you have lost the capacity to make an informed decision on a health care matter, the attorney-in-fact GENERALLY will be authorized by this document to make health care decisions for you to the same extent as you could make those decisions yourself, if you had the capacity to do so. The authority of the attorney-in-fact to make health care decisions for you GENERALLY will include the authority to give informed consent, refuse to give informed consent, or withdraw informed consent to any care, treatment, service, or procedure to maintain, diagnose, or treat a physical or mental condition. HOWEVER, even if the attorney-in-fact has general authority to make health care decisions for you under this document, the attorney-in-fact NEVER will be authorized to do any of the following:

(1) Refuse or withdraw informed consent to life-sustaining treatment (unless your attending physician and one (1) other physician who examines you determine, to a reasonable degree of medical certainty and in accordance with reasonable medical standards, that either of the following applies:

(a) You are suffering from an irreversible, incurable, and untreatable condition caused by disease, illness, or injury from which: (i) there can be no recovery, and (ii) your death is likely to occur within a relatively short time if life-sustaining treatment is not administered, and your attending physician additionally determines, to a reasonable degree of medical certainty and in accordance with reasonable medical standards, that there is no reasonable possibility that you will regain the capacity to make informed health care decisions for yourself, OR

(b) You are in a state of permanent unconsciousness that is characterized by you being irreversibly unaware of yourself and your environment and by a total loss of cerebral cortical functioning, resulting in you having no capacity to experience pain or suffering, and your attending physician additionally determines, to a reasonable degree of medical certainty and in accordance with reasonable medical standards, that there is no reasonable possibility that you will regain the capacity to make informed health care decisions for yourself);

(2) Refuse or withdraw informed consent to health care necessary to provide you with comfort care (except that, if the attorney-in-fact is not prohibited from doing so under paragraph [4] below, the attorney-in-fact could refuse or withdraw informed consent to the provision of nutrition or hydration to you as described under paragraph [4] below). (You should understand that "comfort care" is defined in Ohio law to mean artificially- or technologically-administered sustenance [nutrition] or fluids [hydration] when administered to diminish your pain or discomfort, not to postpone your death, and any other medical or

nursing procedure, treatment, intervention, or other measure that would be taken to diminish your pain or discomfort, not to postpone your death. Consequently, if your attending physician were to determine that a previously-described medical or nursing procedure, treatment, intervention, or other measure will not or will no longer serve to provide comfort to you or alleviate your pain, then, subject to paragraph [4] below, your attorney-in-fact would be authorized to refuse or withdraw informed consent to the procedure, treatment, intervention, or other measure.);

(3) Refuse or withdraw informed consent to health care for you if you are pregnant and if the refusal or withdrawal would terminate the pregnancy (unless the pregnancy or health care would pose a substantial risk to your life, or unless your attending physician and at least one (1) other physician who examines you determine, to a reasonable degree of medical certainty and in accordance with reasonable medical standards, that the fetus would not be born alive);

(4) Refuse or withdraw informed consent to the provision of artificially- or technologically-administered sustenance (nutrition) or fluids (hydration) to you, unless: (a) You are in a terminal condition or in a permanently-unconscious state, (b) Your attending physician and at least one (1) other physician who has examined you determine, to a reasonable degree of medical certainty and in accordance with reasonable medical standards, that nutrition or hydration will not or will no longer serve to provide comfort to you or alleviate your pain, (c) If, but only if, you are in a permanently-unconscious state, you authorize the attorney-in-fact to refuse or withdraw informed consent to the provision of nutrition or hydration to you by doing both of the following in this document: (i) including a statement in capital letters or other conspicuous type, including, but not limited to, a different font, bigger type, or boldface type that the attorney-in-fact may refuse or withdraw informed consent to the provision of nutrition or hydration to you if you are in a permanently-unconscious state and if the determination that nutrition or hydration will not or will no longer serve to provide comfort to you or alleviate your pain is made, or checking or otherwise marking a box or line (if any) that is adjacent to a similar statement on this document; (ii) placing your initials or signature underneath or adjacent to the statement, check, or other mark previously described. (d) Your attending physician determines, in good faith, that you authorized the attorney-in-fact to refuse or withdraw informed consent to the provision of nutrition or hydration to you if you are in a permanently-unconscious state by complying with the requirements of paragraphs (4)(c)(i) and (4)(c)(ii) above.

(5) Withdraw informed consent to any health care to which you previously consented, unless a change in your physical condition has significantly decreased the benefit of that health care to you, or unless the health care is not, or is no longer significantly effective in achieving the purposes for which you consented to its use.

Additionally, when exercising authority to make health care decisions for you, the attorney-in-fact will have to act consistently with your desires or, if your desires are unknown, to act in your best interest. You may express your desires to the attorney-in-fact by including them in this document or by making them known to the attorney-in-fact in another manner. When acting pursuant to this document, the attorney-in-fact GENERALLY will have the same rights that you have to receive information about proposed health care, review health care records, and consent to the disclosure of health care records. You can limit that right in this document if you so choose. Generally, you may designate any competent adult as the attorney-in-fact under this document. However, you CANNOT designate your attending physician or the administrator of any nursing home in which you are receiving care as the attorney-in-fact under this document. Additionally, you CANNOT designate an employee or agent of your attending physician or an employee or agent of a health care facility at which you are being treated as the attorney-in-fact under this document, unless either type of employee or agent is a competent adult and related to you by blood, marriage, or adoption, or unless either type of employee or agent is a competent adult and you and the employee or agent are members of the same religious order. This document has no expiration date under Ohio law, but you may choose to specify a date upon which your Durable Power of Attorney for Health Care generally will expire. However, if you specify an expiration date and then lack the capacity to make informed health care decisions for yourself on that date, the document and the power it grants to your attorney-in-fact will continue in effect until you regain the capacity to make informed health care decisions for yourself. You have the right to revoke the designation of the attorney-in-fact and the right to revoke this entire document at any time and in any manner. Any such revocation generally will be effective when you express your intention to make the revocation. However, if you made your attending physician aware of this document, any such revocation will be effective only when you communicate it to your attending physician, or when a witness to the revocation or other health care personnel to whom the revocation is communicated by such a witness communicates it to your attending physician. If you execute this document and create a valid Durable Power of Attorney for Health Care with it, it will revoke any prior valid durable power of attorney for health care that you created, unless you indicate otherwise in this document. This document is not valid as a Durable Power of Attorney for Health Care unless it is acknowledged before a notary public or is signed by at least two (2) adult witnesses who are present when you sign or acknowledge your signature. No person who is related to you by blood, marriage, or adoption may be a witness. The attorney-in-fact, your attending physician, and the administrator of any nursing home in which you are receiving care also are ineligible to be witnesses. If there is anything in this document that you do not understand, you should ask your lawyer to explain it to you.

I, intending to create a Durable Power of Attorney for Health Care under Chapter 1337 of the Ohio Revised Code, do hereby designate and appoint:

_____ (name),
of _____ (address),
as my attorney-in-fact who shall act as my agent to make health care decisions for me as authorized in this document.

I hereby grant to my agent full power and authority to make all health care decisions for me to the same extent that I could make such decisions for myself if I had the capacity to do so, at any time during which I do not have the capacity to make or communicate informed health care decisions for myself. My agent shall have the authority to give, withdraw, or refuse to give informed consent to any medical or nursing procedure, treatment, intervention, or other measure used to maintain, diagnose, or treat my physical or mental condition. In exercising this authority, my agent shall make health care decisions that are consistent with my desires as stated in this document or otherwise made known to my agent by me or, if I have not made my desires known, that are, in the judgment of my agent, in my best interests.

Where necessary or desirable to implement the health care decisions that my agent is authorized to make pursuant to this document, my agent has the power and authority to do any and all of the following:

(1) If I am in a terminal condition, to give, withdraw, or refuse to give informed consent to life-sustaining treatment, including the provision of artificially- or technologically-supplied nutrition or hydration;

(2) If I am in a permanently-unconscious state, to give informed consent to life-sustaining treatment, withdraw, or refuse to give informed consent to life-sustaining treatment; provided, however, my agent is not authorized to refuse or direct the withdrawal of artificially- or technologically-supplied nutrition or hydration unless I have specifically authorized such refusal or withdrawal in this document;

(3) To request, review, and receive any information, verbal or written, regarding my physical or mental health, including, but not limited to, all of my medical and health care facility records;

(4) To execute on my behalf any releases or other documents that may be required in order to obtain this information;

(5) To consent to the further disclosure of this information if necessary;

(6) To select, employ, and discharge health care personnel, such as physicians, nurses, therapists, and other medical professionals, including individuals and services providing home health care, as my agent shall determine to be appropriate;

(7) To select and contract with any medical or health care facility on my behalf, including, but not limited to, hospitals, nursing homes, assisted-residence facilities, and the like; and

(8) To execute on my behalf any or all of the following: (a) documents that are written consents to medical treatment or written requests that I be transferred to another facility, (b) documents that are Do Not Resuscitate Orders, Discharge Orders, or other similar orders, and (c) any other document necessary or desirable to implement health care decisions that my agent is authorized to make pursuant to this document.

WITHDRAWAL OF NUTRITION AND HYDRATION WHEN IN A PERMANENTLY- UNCONSCIOUS STATE.

[   ] **If I have initialed the foregoing box,** my agent may refuse, or in the event treatment has already commenced, withdraw informed consent to the provision of artificially- or technologically-supplied nutrition and hydration if I am in a permanently-unconscious state and if my attending physician and at least one (1) other physician who has examined me determines, to a reasonable degree of medical certainty and in accordance with reasonable medical standards, that such nutrition or hydration will not or will no longer serve to provide comfort to me or alleviate my pain.

This Durable Power of Attorney for Health Care shall not be affected by my disability or by lapse of time. This Durable Power of Attorney for Health Care shall have no expiration date. Any invalid or unenforceable power, authority, or provision of this instrument shall not affect any other power, authority, or provision or the appointment of my agent to make health care decisions. I hereby revoke any prior Durable Powers of Attorney for Health Care executed by me under Chapter 1337 of the Ohio Revised Code.

Designation of Primary Physician

I designate the following physician as my primary physician: _____ (name)

_____ (address)

_____ (phone).

OPTIONAL- DESIGNATION OF ALTERNATE PRIMARY PHYSICIAN: If the physician I have designated above is not willing, able, or reasonably available to act as my primary physician, I designate the following physician as my primary physician:

_____ (name)

_____ (address)

_____ (phone).

Organ Donation

In the event of my death, I have placed my initials next to the following part(s) of my body that I wish donated for the purposes **that I have initialed below**:

[   ] any organs or parts **OR**

[   ] eyes   [   ] bone and connective tissue   [   ] skin

[   ] heart   [   ] kidney(s)   [   ] liver

[   ] lung(s)   [   ] pancreas   [   ] other _____

for the purposes of:

[   ] any purpose authorized by law **OR**

[   ] transplantation   [   ] research   [   ] therapy

[   ] medical education   [   ] other limitations _____

If I do not indicate a desire to donate all or part of my body by filling in the lines above, no presumption is created about my desire to make or refuse to make an anatomical gift.

Attached also please find a Donor Registry Enrollment Form. To register for the Donor Registry, please complete this form and send it to the Ohio Bureau of Motor Vehicles. This form must be signed by two witnesses. If the donor is under age eighteen, one witness must be the donor's parent or legal guardian. **The choices made on that form should be identical to the choices made in this document.**

Signature

I sign this Advance Health Care Directive, consisting of the following sections, **which I have initialed below and have elected to adopt:**

[   ] Living Will Declaration

[   ] Selection of Health Care Agent (Durable Power of Attorney for Health Care)

[   ] Designation of Primary Physician

[   ] Organ Donation

BY SIGNING HERE I INDICATE THAT I UNDERSTAND THE PURPOSE AND EFFECT OF THIS DOCUMENT.

Signature _____ Date _____

City, County, and State of Residence _____

Notary Acknowledgment

State of _____

County of _____

On _____, _____ came before me personally and, under oath, stated that he or she is the person described in the above document and he or she signed the above document in my presence. I declare under penalty of perjury that the person whose name is subscribed to this instrument appears to be of sound mind and under no duress, fraud, or undue influence.

_____

Notary Public

My commission expires _____

Witness Acknowledgment

The declarant is personally known to me and I believe him or her to be of sound mind and under no duress, fraud, or undue influence. I did not sign the declarant's signature above for or at the direction of the declarant and I am not appointed as the health care agent or attorney-in-fact herein. I am at least eighteen (18) years of age and I am not related to the declarant by blood, adoption, or marriage, entitled to any portion of the estate of the declarant according to the laws of intestate succession or under any will of declarant or codicil thereto, or directly financially responsible for declarant's medical care. I am not a health care provider of the declarant or an employee of the health facility in which the declarant is a patient.

Witness Signature _____ Date _____

Printed Name of Witness _____

Second Witness Signature _____ Date _____

Printed Name of Second Witness _____

Acceptance of Health Care Agent and Attorney-in-Fact for Health Care

I accept my appointment as Health Care Agent and Attorney-in-Fact for Health Care:

Signature _____ Date _____

Ohio Donor Registry Enrollment Form

Please initial one of the following choices:

_____Please include me in the donor registry.

_____ Please remove me from the donor registry.

Full Name (please print)_____

Mailing address_____

_____

_____

Phone _____   Date of Birth_____

Driver License or ID Card No._____

Social Security No. _____

In the event of my death, I have placed my initials next to the following part(s) of my body that I wish donated for the purposes that I have initialed below:

[   ] any organs or parts OR
[   ] eyes   [   ] bone and connective tissue   [   ] skin
[   ] heart   [   ] kidney(s)   [   ] liver
[   ] lung(s)   [   ] pancreas   [   ] other _____
for the purposes of:

[   ] any purpose authorized by law OR
[   ] transplantation   [   ] research   [   ] therapy
[   ] medical education   [   ] other limitations   _____

_____   _____
Signature of donor registrant   Date

_____
Witness signature

_____
Witness signature"

Please send this form to the Ohio Bureau of Motor Vehicles

Oklahoma Advance Health Care Directive

On this date of _____ , I, _____ , do hereby sign, execute, and adopt the following as my Advance Health Care Directive. I direct any and all persons or entities involved with my health care in any manner that these decisions are my wishes and were adopted without duress or force and of my own free will.

I have placed my initials next to the sections of this Directive that I have adopted:

[   ] Living Will
[   ] Appointment of Health Care Agent (Health Care Proxy)
[   ] Designation of Primary Physician
[   ] Organ Donation

If I am incapable of making an informed decision regarding my health care, I direct my health care providers to follow my instructions below.

Living Will

I, being of sound mind and eighteen (18) years of age or older, willfully and voluntarily make known my desire, by my instructions to others through my living will, or by my appointment of a health care proxy, or both, that my life shall not be artificially-prolonged under the circumstances set forth below. I thus do hereby declare:

If my attending physician and another physician determine that I am no longer able to make decisions regarding my medical treatment, I direct my attending physician and other health care providers, pursuant to the Oklahoma Advance Directive Act, to follow my instructions as set forth below:

If I have a terminal condition, that is, an incurable and irreversible condition that even with the administration of life-sustaining treatment will, in the opinion of the attending physician and another physician, result in death within six (6) months: **(Initial one choice only).**

[   ] I direct that my life not be extended by life-sustaining treatment, except that if I am unable to take food and water by mouth, I wish to receive artificially administered nutrition and hydration.

[   ] I direct that my life not be extended by life-sustaining treatment, including artificially administered nutrition and hydration.

[   ] I direct that I be given life-sustaining treatment and, if I am unable to take food and water by mouth, I wish to receive artificially administered nutrition and hydration.

[   ] See my more specific instructions in paragraph (4) below.

(2) If I am persistently unconscious, that is, I have an irreversible condition, as determined by the attending physician and another physician, in which thought and awareness of self and environment are absent: **(Initial one choice only)**

[   ] I direct that my life not be extended by life-sustaining treatment, except that if I am unable to take food and water by mouth, I wish to receive artificially administered nutrition and hydration.

[   ] I direct that my life not be extended by life-sustaining treatment, including artificially administered nutrition and hydration.

[   ] I direct that I be given life-sustaining treatment and, if I am unable to take food and water by mouth, I wish to receive artificially administered nutrition and hydration.

[   ] See my more specific instructions in paragraph (4) below.

(3) If I have an end-stage condition, that is, a condition caused by injury, disease, or illness, which results in severe and permanent deterioration indicated by incompetency and complete physical dependency for which treatment of the irreversible condition would be medically ineffective: **(Initial one choice only)**

[   ] I direct that my life not be extended by life-sustaining treatment, except that if I am unable to take food and water by mouth, I wish to receive artificially administered nutrition and hydration.

[   ] I direct that my life not be extended by life-sustaining treatment, including artificially administered nutrition and hydration.

[   ] I direct that I be given life-sustaining treatment and, if I am unable to take food and water by mouth, I wish to receive artificially administered nutrition and hydration.

[   ] See my more specific instructions in paragraph (4) below.

(4) OTHER. Here you may: (a) describe other conditions in which you would want life-sustaining treatment or artificially administered nutrition and hydration provided, withheld, or withdrawn, (b) give more specific instructions about your wishes concerning life-sustaining treatment or artificially administered nutrition and hydration if you have a terminal condition, are persistently unconscious, or have an end-stage condition, or (c) do both of these:

Appointment of Health Care Agent
(Health Care Proxy)

If my attending physician and another physician determine that I am no longer able to make decisions regarding my medical treatment, I direct my attending physician and other health care providers pursuant to the Oklahoma Rights of the Terminally Ill or Persistently Unconscious Act to follow the instructions of _____ (name), of _____ _____ (address), whom I appoint as my health care proxy. If my health care proxy is unable or unwilling to serve, I appoint _____ (name) as my alternate health care proxy with the same authority. My health care proxy is authorized to make whatever medical treatment decisions I could make if I were able, except that decisions regarding life-sustaining treatment and artificially administered nutrition and hydration can be made by my health care proxy or alternate health care proxy only as I have indicated in the foregoing sections.

If I fail to designate a health care proxy in this section, I am deliberately declining to designate a health care proxy.

NOTE: A physician or other health care provider who is furnished the original or a photo-copy of the advance directive shall make it a part of the declarant's medical record and if unwilling to comply with the advance directive, shall promptly so advise the declarant. In the case of a qualified patient, the patient's health care proxy, in consultation with the attending physician, shall have the authority to make treatment decisions for the patient including the withholding or withdrawal of life-sustaining procedures if so indicated in the patient's advance directive. A person executing an advanced directive appointing a health care proxy who may not have an attending physician for reasons based on established religious beliefs or tenets may designate an individual other than the designated health care proxy, in lieu of an attending physician and other physician, to determine the lack of decisional capacity of the person. Such designation shall be specified and included as part of the advanced directive executed pursuant to the provisions of this section.

Designation of Primary Physician

I designate the following physician as my primary physician: _____ (name)
_____ (address)
_____ (phone).

OPTIONAL- DESIGNATION OF ALTERNATE PRIMARY PHYSICIAN: If the physician I have designated above is not willing, able, or reasonably available to act as my primary physician, I designate the following physician as my primary physician:
_____ (name)
_____ (address)
_____ (phone).

Organ Donation

In the event of my death, I have placed my initials next to the following part(s) of my body that I wish donated for the purposes **that I have initialed below**:

[   ] any organs or parts **OR**

[   ] eyes   [   ] bone and connective tissue   [   ] skin

[   ] heart   [   ] kidney(s)   [   ] liver

[   ] lung(s)   [   ] pancreas   [   ] other _____

for the purposes of:

[   ] any purpose authorized by law **OR**

[   ] transplantation   [   ] research   [   ] therapy

[   ] medical education   [   ] other limitations _____

Signature

I sign this Advance Health Care Directive, consisting of the following sections, **which I have initialed below and have elected to adopt:**

[   ] Living Will

[   ] Appointment of Health Care Agent (Health Care Proxy)

[   ] Designation of Primary Physician

[   ] Organ Donation

a. I understand that I must be eighteen (18) years of age or older to execute this form.

b. I understand that my witnesses must be eighteen (18) years of age or older and shall not be related to me and shall not inherit from me.

c. I understand that if I have been diagnosed as pregnant and that diagnosis is known to my attending physician, I will be provided with life-sustaining treatment and artificially administered hydration and nutrition unless I have, in my own words, specifically authorized that during a course of pregnancy, life-sustaining treatment and/or artificially administered hydration and/or nutrition shall be withheld or withdrawn.

d. In the absence of my ability to give directions regarding the use of life-sustaining procedures, it is my intention that this advance directive shall be honored by my family and physicians as the final expression of my legal right to choose or refuse medical or surgical treatment including, but not limited to, the administration of life-sustaining procedures, and I accept the consequences of such choice or refusal.

e. This advance directive shall be in effect until it is revoked.

f. I understand that I may revoke this advance directive at any time.

g. I understand and agree that if I have any prior directives, and if I sign this advance directive, my prior directives are revoked.

h. I understand the full importance of this advance directive and I am emotionally and mentally competent to make this advance directive.

i. I understand that my physician(s) shall make all decisions based upon his or her best judgment applying with ordinary care and diligence the knowledge and skill that is possessed and used by members of the physician's profession in good standing engaged in the same field of practice at that time, measured by national standards.

BY SIGNING HERE I INDICATE THAT I UNDERSTAND THE PURPOSE AND EFFECT OF THIS DOCUMENT.

Signature _____ Date _____

City, County, and State of Residence _____

Notary Acknowledgment

State of _____

County of _____

On _____ , _____ came before me personally and, under oath, stated that he or she is the person described in the above document and he or she signed the above document in my presence. I declare under penalty of perjury that the person whose name is subscribed to this instrument appears to be of sound mind and under no duress, fraud, or undue influence.

_____

Notary Public

My commission expires _____

Witness Acknowledgment

The declarant is personally known to me and I believe him or her to be of sound mind and under no duress, fraud, or undue influence. I did not sign the declarant's signature above for or at the direction of the declarant and I am not appointed as the health care agent or attorney-in-fact herein. I am at least eighteen (18) years of age and I am not related to the declarant by blood, adoption, or marriage, entitled to any portion of the estate of the declarant according to the laws of intestate succession or under any will of declarant or codicil thereto, or directly financially responsible for declarant's medical care. I am not a health care provider of the declarant or an employee of the health facility in which the declarant is a patient.

Witness Signature _____ Date _____

Printed Name of Witness _____

Second Witness Signature _____ Date _____

Printed Name of Second Witness _____

Acceptance of Health Care Agent (Health Care Proxy)

I accept my appointment as Health Care Agent (Health Care Proxy):

Signature _____ Date _____

Oregon Advance Health Care Directive

On this date of _____ , I, _____ , do hereby sign, execute, and adopt the following as my Advance Health Care Directive. I direct any and all persons or entities involved with my health care in any manner that these decisions are my wishes and were adopted without duress or force and of my own free will.

I have placed my initials next to the sections of this Directive that I have adopted:

[   ] Living Will (Health Care Instructions)
[   ] Selection of Health Care Agent (Appointment of Health Care Representative)
[   ] Designation of Primary Physician
[   ] Organ Donation

IMPORTANT INFORMATION ABOUT THIS ADVANCE DIRECTIVE This is an important legal document. It can control critical decisions about your health care. Before signing, consider these important facts: YOU DO NOT HAVE TO FILL OUT AND SIGN THIS FORM UNLESS YOU WANT TO. LIVING WILL (HEALTH CARE INSTRUCTIONS): You have the right to give instructions for health care providers to follow if you become unable to direct your care.

APPOINTMENT OF HEALTH CARE REPRESENTATIVE: You have the right to name a person to direct your health care when you cannot do so. This person is called your health care representative. You can write in this document any restrictions you want on how your representative will make decisions for you. Your representative must follow your desires as stated in this document or otherwise made known. If your desires are unknown, your representative must try to act in your best interest. Your representative can resign at any time.

COMPLETING THIS FORM: This form is valid only if you sign it voluntarily and when you are of sound mind. If you do not want an advance directive, you do not have to sign this form. Unless you have limited the duration of this advance directive, it will not expire. If you have set an expiration date, and you become unable to direct your health care before that date, this advance directive will not expire until you are able to make those decisions again. You may revoke this document at any time. To do so, notify your representative and your health care provider of the revocation. Despite this document, you have the right to decide your own health care as long as you are able to do so. If there is anything in this document that you do not understand, ask a lawyer to explain it to you.

Unless revoked or suspended, this advance directive will continue for **(initial one)**:

[   ] My entire life
[   ] Other period (_____ years)

Living Will (Health Care Instructions)

NOTE: In filling out these instructions, keep the following in mind: The term "as my physician recommends" means that you want your physician to try life support if your physician believes it could be helpful and then discontinue it if it is not helping your health condition or symptoms. Life support and tube feeding are defined below. If you refuse tube feeding, you should understand that malnutrition, dehydration, and death will probably result. You will get care for your comfort and cleanliness, no matter what choices you make. You may either give specific instructions by filling out paragraphs (1) to (4) below, or you may use the general instruction provided by paragraph (5).

Here are my desires about my health care if my doctor and another knowledgeable doctor confirm that I am in a medical condition described below:

(1) CLOSE TO DEATH. If I am close to death and life support would only postpone the moment of my death:

    (a) **(initial one)**:
    [   ] I DO want to receive tube feeding.
    [   ] I want tube feeding ONLY as my physician recommends.
    [   ] I do NOT want tube feeding.
    (b) **(initial one)**:
    [   ] I DO want any other life support that may apply.
    [   ] I want life support ONLY as my physician recommends.
    [   ] I want NO life support.

(2) PERMANENTLY UNCONSCIOUS. If I am unconscious and it is very unlikely that I will ever become conscious again:

    (a) **(initial one)**:
    [   ] I DO want to receive tube feeding.
    [   ] I want tube feeding ONLY as my physician recommends.
    [   ] I do NOT want tube feeding.
    (b) **(initial one)**:
    [   ] I DO want any other life support that may apply.
    [   ] I want life support ONLY as my physician recommends.
    [   ] I want NO life support.

(3) ADVANCED PROGRESSIVE ILLNESS. If I have a progressive illness that will be fatal and is in an advanced stage, and I am consistently and permanently unable to communicate by any means, swallow food and water safely, care for myself, and recognize my family and other people, and it is very unlikely that my condition will substantially improve:

    (a) **(initial one)**:
    [   ] I DO want to receive tube feeding.
    [   ] I want tube feeding ONLY as my physician recommends.
    [   ] I do NOT want tube feeding.
    (b) **(initial one)**:
    [   ] I DO want any other life support that may apply.
    [   ] I want life support ONLY as my physician recommends.
    [   ] I want NO life support.

(4) EXTRAORDINARY SUFFERING. If life support would not help my medical condition and would make me suffer permanent and severe pain:

(a) **(initial one):**
[   ] I DO want to receive tube feeding.
[   ] I want tube feeding ONLY as my physician recommends.
[   ] I do NOT want tube feeding.
(b) **(initial one):**
[   ] I DO want any other life support that may apply.
[   ] I want life support ONLY as my physician recommends.
[   ] I want NO life support.

(5) GENERAL INSTRUCTION **(initial if this applies)**:

[   ] I do NOT want my life to be prolonged by life support. I also do NOT want tube feeding as life support. I want my doctors to allow me to die naturally if my doctor and another knowledgeable doctor confirm I am in any of the medical conditions listed in paragraphs (1) to (4) above.

(6) ADDITIONAL CONDITIONS OR INSTRUCTIONS
(insert description of what you want done):

(7) OTHER DOCUMENTS. A health care power of attorney is any document you may have signed to appoint a representative to make health care decisions for you **(initial one)**:

[   ] I have not previously signed a health care power of attorney and I am appointing a health care representative in this document.

[   ] I HAVE previously signed a health care power of attorney and I want it to remain in effect and I am not appointing a different health care representative in this document.

[   ] I have previously signed a health care power of attorney, and I REVOKE it and I am appointing a health care representative in this document.

[   ] I do NOT have a health care power of attorney and I am not appointing a health care representative in this document.

Selection of Health Care Agent
(Appointment of Health Care Representative)

NOTE: You may not appoint your doctor, an employee of your doctor, or an owner, operator, or employee of your health care facility, unless that person is related to you by blood, marriage, or adoption, or that person was appointed before your admission into the health care facility.

I appoint _____ (name),
of _____ (address),
as my health care representative. I authorize my representative to direct my health care when I cannot do so.

OPTIONAL - DESIGNATION OF ALTERNATE AGENT: If I revoke my agent's authority or if my agent is not willing, able, or reasonably available to make a health care decision for me, I designate as my alternate agent

_____ (name of individual you choose as alternate agent)

_____ (address)

LIVING WILL IN EFFECT: **(Initial if this applies):**
[   ] I have executed a Living Will Health Care Instruction or Directive to Physicians. My representative is to honor it. (This includes any Living Will that is part of this document)

LIFE SUPPORT. Life support refers to any medical means for maintaining life, including procedures, devices, and medications. If you refuse life support, you will still get routine measures to keep you clean and comfortable **(Initial if this applies): (If you don't initial this space, then your representative may NOT decide about tube feeding.)**

[   ] My representative MAY decide about life support for me.

TUBE FEEDING. One sort of life support is food and water supplied artificially by medical device, known as tube feeding **(Initial if this applies): (If you don't initial this space, then your representative may NOT decide about tube feeding.)**

[   ] My representative MAY decide about tube feeding for me.

LIMITS. Special Conditions or Instructions to my Health Care Agent:
(Insert any conditions or instructions):

Designation of Primary Physician

I designate the following physician as my primary physician: _____ (name)
_____ (address)
_____ (phone).

OPTIONAL- DESIGNATION OF ALTERNATE PRIMARY PHYSICIAN: If the physician I have designated above is not willing, able, or reasonably available to act as my primary physician, I designate the following physician as my primary physician:

_____ (name)
_____ (address)
_____ (phone).

Organ Donation

In the event of my death, I have placed my initials next to the following part(s) of my body that I wish donated for the purposes **that I have initialed below:**

[   ] any organs or parts **OR**
[   ] eyes   [   ] bone and connective tissue   [   ] skin
[   ] heart   [   ] kidney(s)   [   ] liver
[   ] lung(s)   [   ] pancreas   [   ] other _____
for the purposes of:
[   ] any purpose authorized by law **OR**
[   ] transplantation   [   ] research   [   ] therapy
[   ] medical education   [   ] other limitations _____

Signature

I sign this Advance Health Care Directive, consisting of the following sections, **which I have initialed below and have elected to adopt:**

[   ] Living Will (Health Care Instructions)
[   ] Selection of Health Care Agent (Appointment of Health Care Representative)
[   ] Designation of Primary Physician
[   ] Organ Donation

BY SIGNING HERE I INDICATE THAT I UNDERSTAND THE PURPOSE AND EFFECT OF THIS DOCUMENT.

Signature _____   Date _____

City, County, and State of Residence _____

Notary Acknowledgment

State of _____

County of _____

On _____ , _____ came before me personally and, under oath, stated that he or she is the person described in the above document and he or she signed the above document in my presence. I declare under penalty of perjury that the person whose name is subscribed to this instrument appears to be of sound mind and under no duress, fraud, or undue influence.

_____

Notary Public

My commission expires _____

Witness Acknowledgment

The declarant is personally known to me and I believe him or her to be of sound mind and under no duress, fraud, or undue influence. I did not sign the declarant's signature above for or at the direction of the declarant and I am not appointed as the health care agent or attorney-in-fact herein. I am at least eighteen (18) years of age and I am not related to the declarant by blood, adoption, or marriage, entitled to any portion of the estate of the declarant according to the laws of intestate succession or under any will of declarant or codicil thereto, or directly financially responsible for declarant's medical care. I am not a health care provider of the declarant or an employee of the health facility in which the declarant is a patient.

Witness Signature _____ Date _____

Printed Name of Witness _____

Witness Signature _____ Date _____

Printed Name of Witness _____

Acceptance of Health Care Agent (Health Care Representative)

I accept my appointment as Health Care Agent (Health Care Representative):

Signature _____ Date _____

I accept my appointment as Alternate Health Care Agent (Health Care Representative):

Signature _____ Date _____

Pennsylvania Advance Health Care Directive

On this date of _____ , I, _____ , do hereby sign, execute, and adopt the following as my Advance Health Care Directive. I direct any and all persons or entities involved with my health care in any manner that these decisions are my wishes and were adopted without duress or force and of my own free will.

I have placed my initials next to the sections of this Directive that I have adopted:

[   ] Living Will (Declaration)
[   ] Selection of Health Care Agent (Health Care Surrogate)
[   ] Designation of Primary Physician
[   ] Organ Donation

Living Will (Declaration)

I, being of sound mind, willfully and voluntarily make this declaration to be followed if I become incompetent. This declaration reflects my firm and settled commitment to refuse life-sustaining treatment under the circumstances indicated below.

I direct my attending physician to withhold or withdraw life-sustaining treatment that serves only to prolong the process of my dying, if I should be in a terminal condition or in a state of permanent unconsciousness.

I direct that treatment be limited to measures to keep me comfortable and to relieve pain, including any pain that might occur by withholding or withdrawing life-sustaining treatment.

In addition, if I am in the condition described above, I feel especially strong about the following forms of treatment (**initial "I DO" or "I do NOT"**):

I [   ] DO **OR** [   ] do NOT want cardiac resuscitation.
I [   ] DO **OR** [   ] do NOT want mechanical respiration.
I [   ] DO **OR** [   ] do NOT want tube feeding or any other artificial or invasive
                                      form of nutrition (food) or hydration (water).
I [   ] DO **OR** [   ] do NOT want blood or blood products.
I [   ] DO **OR** [   ] do NOT want any form of surgery or invasive diagnostic tests.
I [   ] DO **OR** [   ] do NOT want kidney dialysis.
I [   ] DO **OR** [   ] do NOT want antibiotics.

I realize that if I do not specifically indicate my preference regarding any of the forms of treatment listed above, I may receive that form of treatment.

OTHER INSTRUCTIONS (**include any other instructions**):

Selection of Health Care Agent
(Appointment of Health Care Surrogate)

(Initial "I DO" or "I do NOT"):

I [　　] DO **OR** [　　] do NOT want to designate another person as my surrogate to make medical treatment decisions for me if I should be incompetent and in a terminal condition or in a state of permanent unconsciousness. **(List name and address of surrogate, if applicable):**

_____ (name),

of _____ (address)

OPTIONAL - DESIGNATION OF ALTERNATE AGENT: If I revoke my agent's authority or if my agent is not willing, able, or reasonably available to make a health care decision for me, I designate as my first alternate agent

_____ (name of individual you choose as first alternate agent)

_____ (address)

Designation of Primary Physician

I designate the following physician as my primary physician: _____ (name)

_____ (address)

_____ (phone).

OPTIONAL- DESIGNATION OF ALTERNATE PRIMARY PHYSICIAN: If the physician I have designated above is not willing, able, or reasonably available to act as my primary physician, I designate the following physician as my primary physician:

_____ (name)

_____ (address)

_____ (phone).

Organ Donation

In the event of my death, I have placed my initials next to the following part(s) of my body that I wish donated for the purposes **that I have initialed below:**

[　　] any organs or parts **OR**

[　　] eyes	[　　] bone and connective tissue	[　　] skin
[　　] heart	[　　] kidney(s)	[　　] liver
[　　] lung(s)	[　　] pancreas	[　　] other _____

for the purposes of:

[　　] any purpose authorized by law **OR**

[　　] transplantation	[　　] research	[　　] therapy
[　　] medical education	[　　] other limitations _____	

Signature

I sign this Advance Health Care Directive, consisting of the following sections, **which I have initialed below and have elected to adopt:**

[   ] Living Will (Declaration)
[   ] Selection of Health Care Agent (Health Care Surrogate)
[   ] Designation of Primary Physician
[   ] Organ Donation

BY SIGNING HERE I INDICATE THAT I UNDERSTAND THE PURPOSE AND EFFECT OF THIS DOCUMENT.

Signature _____ Date _____

City, County, and State of Residence _____

Notary Acknowledgment

State of _____
County of _____

On _____ , _____ came before me personally and, under oath, stated that he or she is the person described in the above document and he or she signed the above document in my presence. I declare under penalty of perjury that the person whose name is subscribed to this instrument appears to be of sound mind and under no duress, fraud, or undue influence.

_____
Notary Public
My commission expires _____

Witness Acknowledgment

The declarant is personally known to me and I believe him or her to be of sound mind and under no duress, fraud, or undue influence. I did not sign the declarant's signature above for or at the direction of the declarant and I am not appointed as the health care agent or attorney-in-fact herein. I am at least eighteen (18) years of age and I am not related to the declarant by blood, adoption, or marriage, entitled to any portion of the estate of the declarant according to the laws of intestate succession or under any will of declarant or codicil thereto, or directly financially responsible for declarant's medical care. I am not a health care provider of the declarant or an employee of the health facility in which the declarant is a patient.

Witness Signature _____ Date _____

Printed Name of Witness _____

Second Witness Signature _____ Date _____

Printed Name of Second Witness _____

Acceptance of Health Care Agent (Health Care Surrogate)

I accept my appointment as Health Care Agent (Health Care Surrogate):

Signature _____ Date _____

I accept my appointment as Alternate Health Care Agent (Health Care Surrogate)

Signature _____ Date _____

Rhode Island Advance Health Care Directive

On this date of _____ , I, _____ , do hereby sign, execute, and adopt the following as my Advance Health Care Directive. I direct any and all persons or entities involved with my health care in any manner that these decisions are my wishes and were adopted without duress or force and of my own free will.
 I have placed my initials next to the sections of this Directive that I have adopted:

[   ] Living Will (Declaration)
[   ] Selection of Health Care Agent (Durable Power of Attorney for Health Care)
[   ] Designation of Primary Physician
[   ] Organ Donation

Living Will (Declaration)

I, being of sound mind, willfully and voluntarily make known my desire that my dying shall not be artificially-prolonged under the circumstances set forth below, and do hereby declare:

If I should have an incurable or irreversible condition that will cause my death, and if I am unable to make decisions regarding my medical treatment, I direct my attending physician to withhold or withdraw procedures that merely prolong the dying process and are not necessary to my comfort, or to alleviate pain.

OTHER DIRECTIONS **(include any other directions)**:

This authorization DOES include [   ] or does NOT include [   ] the withholding or withdrawal of artificial feeding **(initial only one box above)**.

Selection of Health Care Agent
(Durable Power of Attorney for Health Care)

WARNING TO PERSON EXECUTING THIS DOCUMENT: This is an important legal document which is authorized by the general laws of this state. Before executing this document, you should know these important facts: You must be at least eighteen (18) years of age and a resident of the state of Rhode Island for this document to be legally valid and binding.

None of the following may be designated as your agent: (1) your treating health care provider, (2) a non-relative employee of your treating health care provider, (3) an operator of a community care facility, OR (4) a non-relative employee of an operator of a community care facility.

For the purposes of this document, "health care decision" means consent, refusal of consent, or withdrawal of consent to any care, treatment, service, or procedure to maintain, diagnose, or treat an individual's physical or mental condition.

This document gives the person you designate as your agent (the attorney-in-fact) the power to make health care decisions for you. Your agent must act consistently with your desires as stated in this document or otherwise made known. Except as you otherwise specify in this document, this document gives your agent the power to consent to your doctor not giving treatment or stopping treatment necessary to keep you alive. Notwithstanding this document, you have the right to make medical and other health care decisions for yourself so long as you can give informed consent with respect to the particular decision. In addition, no treatment may be given to you over your objection at the time, and health care necessary to keep you alive may not be stopped or withheld if you object at the time. This document gives your agent authority to consent, refuse to consent, or withdraw consent to any care, treatment, service, or procedure to maintain, diagnose, or treat a physical or mental condition. This power is subject to any statement of your desires and any limitation that you include in this document. You may state in this document any types of treatment that you do not desire. In addition, a court can take away the power of your agent to make health care decisions for you if your agent:

(1) authorizes anything that is illegal,

(2) acts contrary to your known desires, OR

(3) where your desires are not known, does anything that is clearly contrary to your best interests.

Unless you specify a specific period, this power will exist until you revoke it. Your agent's power and authority ceases upon your death except to inform your next of kin of your desire to be an organ and tissue donor.

You have the right to revoke the authority of your agent by notifying your agent or your treating doctor, hospital, or other health care provider orally or in writing of the revocation. Your agent has the right to examine your medical records and consent to their disclosure unless you limit this right in this document. This document revokes any prior durable power of attorney for health care. You should carefully read and follow the witnessing procedure described at the end of this form. This document will not be valid unless you comply with the witnessing procedure. If there is anything in this document that you do not understand, you should ask a lawyer to explain it to you. Your agent may need this document immediately in case of an emergency that requires a decision concerning your health care. Either keep this document where it is immediately available to your agent or give him or her an executed copy of this document. You may also want to give your doctor an executed copy of this document.

DESIGNATION OF HEALTH CARE AGENT: I do hereby designate and appoint:

_____ (name), of

_____ (address), as

my attorney-in-fact (agent) to make health care decisions for me as authorized in this document.

CREATION OF DURABLE POWER OF ATTORNEY FOR HEALTH CARE: By this document I intend to create a durable power of attorney for health care.

GENERAL STATEMENT OF AUTHORITY GRANTED: Subject to any limitations in this document, I hereby grant to my agent full power and authority to make health care decisions for me to the same extent that I could make such decisions for myself if I had the capacity to do so. In exercising this authority, my agent shall make health care decisions that are consistent with my desires as stated in this document or otherwise made known to my agent, including, but not limited to, my desires concerning obtaining, refusing, or withdrawing life-prolonging care, treatment, services, and procedures. **(If you want to limit the authority of your agent to make health care decisions for you, you can state the limitations below. You can indicate your desires by including a statement of your desires in the same paragraph.)**

STATEMENT OF DESIRES, SPECIAL PROVISIONS, AND LIMITATIONS. **(Your agent must make health care decisions that are consistent with your known desires. You can, but are not required to state your desires in the space provided below. You should consider whether you want to include a statement of your desires concerning life-prolonging care, treatment, services, and procedures. You can also include a statement of your desires concerning other matters relating to your health care. You can also make your desires known to your agent by discussing your desires with your agent or by some other means. If there are any types of treatment that you do not want to be used, you should state them in the space below. If you want to limit in any other way the authority given your agent by this document, you should state the limits in the space below. If you do not state any limits, your agent will have broad powers to make health care decisions for you, except to the extent that there are limits provided by law.)**

In exercising the authority under this durable power of attorney for health care, my agent shall act consistently with my desires as stated below and is subject to the special provisions and limitations stated below **(List desires and limits) (Attach additional pages if necessary)**:
Statement of desires concerning life-prolonging care, treatment, services, and procedures

Additional statement of desires, special provisions, and limitations regarding health care decisions:

You may attach additional pages if you need more space to complete your statement. If you attach additional pages, you must date and sign EACH of the additional pages at the same time you date and sign this document.)

INSPECTION AND DISCLOSURE OF INFORMATION RELATING TO MY PHYSICAL AND MENTAL HEALTH: Subject to any limitations in this document, my agent has the power and authority to do all of the following: (1) Request, review, and receive any information, verbal or written, regarding my physical or mental health, including, but not limited to medical and hospital records. (2) Execute on my behalf any releases or other documents that may be required in order to obtain this information. (3) Consent to the disclosure of this information.
(If you want to limit the authority of your agent to receive and disclose information relating to your health, you must state the limitations in the "Additional Statement..." space above.)

SIGNING DOCUMENTS, WAIVERS, AND RELEASES: Where necessary to implement the health care decisions that my agent is authorized by this document to make, my agent has the power and authority to execute on my behalf all of the following: (1) Documents titled or purporting to be a "Refusal to Permit Treatment" and "Leaving Hospital Against Medical Advice." (2) Any necessary waiver or release from liability required by a hospital or physician.

DURATION. **(Unless you specify a shorter period in the space below, this power of attorney will exist until it is revoked.) (Initial the box and fill in a date ONLY if you want the authority of your agent to end on a specific date.)**

[   ] This durable power of attorney for health care expires on_____

OPTIONAL - DESIGNATION OF ALTERNATE AGENT: If I revoke my agent's authority or if my agent is not willing, able, or reasonably available to make a health care decision for me, I designate as my alternate agent

_____ (name of individual you choose as alternate agent)
_____ (address)

PRIOR DESIGNATIONS REVOKED: I revoke any prior durable powers of attorney for health care.

Designation of Primary Physician

I designate the following physician as my primary physician: _____ (name)
_____ (address)
_____ (phone).

OPTIONAL- DESIGNATION OF ALTERNATE PRIMARY PHYSICIAN: If the physician I have designated above is not willing, able, or reasonably available to act as my primary physician, I designate the following physician as my primary physician:
_____ (name)
_____ (address)
_____ (phone).

Organ Donation

In the event of my death, I have placed my initials next to the following part(s) of my body that I wish donated for the purposes **that I have initialed below:**

[   ] any organs or parts **OR**

[ ] eyes	[ ] bone and connective tissue	[ ] skin
[ ] heart	[ ] kidney(s)	[ ] liver
[ ] lung(s)	[ ] pancreas	[ ] other _____

for the purposes of:

[   ] any purpose authorized by law **OR**

[ ] transplantation	[ ] research	[ ] therapy
[ ] medical education	[ ] other limitations _____	

Signature

I sign this Advance Health Care Directive, consisting of the following sections, **which I have initialed below and have elected to adopt:**

[   ] Living Will (Declaration)

[   ] Selection of Health Care Agent (Durable Power of Attorney for Health Care)

[   ] Designation of Primary Physician

[   ] Organ Donation

BY SIGNING HERE I INDICATE THAT I UNDERSTAND THE PURPOSE AND EFFECT OF THIS DOCUMENT.

Signature _____   Date _____

City, County, and State of Residence _____

Notary Acknowledgment

State of _____

County of _____

On _____ , _____ came before me personally and, under oath, stated that he or she is the person described in the above document and he or she signed the above document in my presence. I declare under penalty of perjury that the person whose name is subscribed to this instrument appears to be of sound mind and under no duress, fraud, or undue influence.

_____

Notary Public

My commission expires _____

Witness Acknowledgment

The declarant is personally known to me and I believe him or her to be of sound mind and under no duress, fraud, or undue influence. I did not sign the declarant's signature above for or at the direction of the declarant and I am not appointed as the health care agent or attorney-in-fact herein. I am at least eighteen (18) years of age and I am not related to the declarant by blood, adoption, or marriage, entitled to any portion of the estate of the declarant according to the laws of intestate succession or under any will of declarant or codicil thereto, or directly financially responsible for declarant's medical care. I am not a health care provider of the declarant or an employee of the health facility in which the declarant is a patient.

Witness Signature _____ Date _____

Printed Name of Witness _____

Second Witness Signature _____ Date _____

Printed Name of Second Witness _____

Acceptance by Health Care Agent (Attorney-in-Fact for Health Care)

I accept my appointment as Health Care Agent (Attorney-in-Fact for Health Care):

Signature _____ Date _____

I accept my appointment as Alternate Health Care Agent (Attorney-in-Fact for Health Care)

Signature _____ Date _____

South Carolina Advance Health Care Directive

On this date of _____ , I, _____ , being at least 18 years of age, and a resident of and domiciled in the State of South Carolina at the following address:

_____

do hereby sign, execute, and adopt the following as my Advance Health Care Directive. I direct any and all persons or entities involved with my health care in any manner that these decisions are my wishes and were adopted without duress or force and of my own free will.
I have placed my initials next to the sections of this Directive that I have adopted:

[   ]   Living Will (Declaration of Desire for a Natural Death)
[   ]   Selection of Health Care Agent (Health Care Power of Attorney)
[   ]   Designation of Primary Physician
[   ]   Organ Donation

Living Will (Declaration of Desire for a Natural Death)

I willfully and voluntarily make known my desire that no life-sustaining procedures be used to prolong my dying if my condition is terminal or if I am in a state of permanent unconsciousness, and I declare:

If at any time I have a condition certified to be a terminal condition by two (2) physicians who have personally examined me, one (1) of whom is my attending physician, and the physicians have determined that my death could occur within a reasonably short period of time without the use of life-sustaining procedures or if the physicians certify that I am in a state of permanent unconsciousness and where the application of life-sustaining procedures would serve only to prolong the dying process, I direct that the procedures be withheld or withdrawn, and that I be permitted to die naturally with only the administration of medication or the performance of any medical procedure necessary to provide me with comfort care.

INSTRUCTIONS CONCERNING ARTIFICIAL NUTRITION AND HYDRATION: If my condition is terminal and could result in death within a reasonably short time:
(Initial one of the following statements)
[   ] I direct that nutrition and hydration BE provided through any medically-indicated means, including medically- or surgically-implanted tubes.
[   ] I direct that nutrition and hydration NOT be provided through any medically-indicated means, including medically- or surgically-implanted tubes.

If I am in a persistent vegetative state or other condition of permanent unconsciousness :
(Initial one of the following statements)
[   ] I direct that nutrition and hydration BE provided through any medically-indicated means, including medically- or surgically-implanted tubes.
[   ] I direct that nutrition and hydration NOT be provided through any medically-indicated means, including medically- or surgically-implanted tubes.

In the absence of my ability to give directions regarding the use of life-sustaining procedures, it is my intention that this Declaration be honored by my family and physicians and any health facility in which I may be a patient as the final expression of my legal right to refuse medical or surgical treatment, and I accept the consequences from the refusal. I am aware that this Declaration authorizes a physician to withhold or withdraw life-sustaining procedures. I am emotionally and mentally competent to make this Declaration.

APPOINTMENT OF AN AGENT FOR REVOCATION: You may give another person authority to revoke this declaration on your behalf. If you wish to do so, please enter that person's name in the space below **(optional)**:

Name of Agent with Power to Revoke _____
Address _____

REVOCATION PROCEDURES: This declaration may be revoked by any one (1) of the following methods. However, a revocation is not effective until it is communicated to the attending physician:
(1) by being defaced, torn, obliterated, or otherwise destroyed, in expression of your intent to revoke, by you or by some person in your presence and by your direction. Revocation by destruction of one or more of multiple original declarations revokes all of the original declarations,
(2) by a written revocation signed and dated by you expressing your intent to revoke,
(3) by your oral expression of your intent to revoke the declaration. An oral revocation communicated to the attending physician by a person other than you is effective only if:
(a) the person was present when the oral revocation was made;
(b) the revocation was communicated to the physician within a reasonable time; OR
(c) your physical or mental condition makes it impossible for the physician to confirm through subsequent conversation with you that the revocation has occurred. To be effective as a revocation, the oral expression clearly must indicate your desire that the declaration not be given effect or that life-sustaining procedures be administered.
(4) if you, in the space above, have authorized an agent to revoke the declaration, then the agent may revoke orally or by a written, signed, and dated instrument. An agent may revoke only if you are incompetent to do so. An agent may revoke the declaration permanently or temporarily,
(5) by your executing another declaration at a later time.

Selection of Health Care Agent
(Health Care Power of Attorney)

Information about this document: This is an important legal document. Before signing this document, you should know these important facts:

1. This document gives the person you name as your agent the power to make health care decisions for you if you cannot make the decision for yourself. This power includes the power to make decisions about life-sustaining treatment. Unless you state other-

wise, your agent will have the same authority to make decisions about your health care as you would have.

2. This power is subject to any limitations or statements of your desires that you include in this document. You may state in this document any treatment you do not desire or treatment you want to be sure you receive. Your agent will be obligated to follow your instructions when making decisions on your behalf. You may attach additional pages if you need more space to complete the statement.

3. After you have signed this document, you have the right to make health care decisions for yourself if you are mentally competent to do so. After you have signed this document, no treatment may be given to you or stopped over your objection if you are mentally competent to make that decision.

4. You have the right to revoke this document, and terminate your agent's authority, by informing either your agent or your health care provider orally or in writing.

5. If there is anything in this document that you do not understand, you should ask a social worker, lawyer, or other person to explain it to you.

6. This power of attorney will not be valid unless two persons sign as witnesses. Each of these persons must either witness your signing of the power of attorney or witness your acknowledgment that the signature on the power of attorney is yours.

The following persons may not act as witnesses: A. Your spouse, your children, grandchildren, and other lineal descendants; your parents, grandparents, and other lineal ancestors; your siblings and their lineal descendants; or a spouse of any of these persons. B. A person who is directly financially responsible for your medical care.
C. A person who is named in your will, or, if you have no will, who would inherit your property by intestate succession. D. A beneficiary of a life insurance policy on your life. E. The persons named in the health care power of attorney as your agent or successor agent. F. Your physician or an employee of your physician. G. Any person who would have a claim against any portion of your estate (persons to whom you owe money). If you are a patient in a health facility, no more than one witness may be an employee of that facility.

7. Your agent must be a person who is 18 years old or older and of sound mind. It may not be your doctor or any other health care provider that is now providing you with treatment; or an employee of your doctor or provider; or a spouse of the doctor, provider, or employee; unless the person is a relative of yours.

8. You should inform the person that you want him or her to be your health care agent. You should discuss this document with your agent and your physician and give each a signed copy. If you are in a health care facility or a nursing care facility, a copy of this document should be included in your medical record.

DESIGNATION OF HEALTH CARE AGENT (South Carolina Statutory Form): I hereby appoint:

_____ (Name)

_____ (Address)

Telephone: home: _____ work: _____ mobile: _____

as my agent to make health care decisions for me as authorized in this document.

SUCCESSOR AGENT: If an agent named by me dies, becomes legally disabled, resigns, refuses to act, becomes unavailable, or if an agent who is my spouse is divorced or separated from me, I name the following as successor to my agent:

_____ (Name)

_____ (Address)

Telephone: home: _____ work: _____ mobile: _____

UNAVAILABILITY OF AGENT(S): If at any relevant time the agent or successor agents named here are unable or unwilling to make decisions concerning my health care, and those decisions are to be made by a guardian, by the Probate Court, or by a surrogate pursuant to the Adult Health Care Consent Act, it is my intention that the guardian, Probate Court, or surrogate make those decisions in accordance with my directions as stated in this document.

EFFECTIVE DATE AND DURABILITY: By this document I intend to create a durable power of attorney effective upon, and only during, any period of mental incompetence, except as provided in Paragraph 3 below.

HIPAA AUTHORIZATION: When considering or making health care decisions for me, all individually identifiable health information and medical records shall be released without restriction to my health care agent(s) and/or my alternate health care agent(s) named above including, but not limited to, (i) diagnostic, treatment, other health care, and related insurance and financial records and information associated with any past, present, or future physical or mental health condition including, but not limited to, diagnosis or treatment of HIV/AIDS, sexually transmitted disease(s), mental illness, and/or drug or alcohol abuse and (ii) any written opinion relating to my health that such health care agent(s) and/or alternate health care agent(s) may have requested. Without limiting the generality of the foregoing, this release authority applies to all health information and medical records governed by the Health Insurance Portability and Accountability Act of 1996 (HIPAA), 42 USC 1320d and 45 CFR 160-164; is effective whether or not I am mentally competent; has no expiration date; and shall terminate only in the event that I revoke the authority in writing and deliver it to my health care provider.

AGENT'S POWERS: I grant to my agent full authority to make decisions for me regarding my health care. In exercising this authority, my agent shall follow my desires as stated in this document or otherwise expressed by me or known to my agent. In making any decision, my agent shall attempt to discuss the proposed decision with me to determine my desires if I am able to communicate in any way. If my agent cannot determine the choice I would want made, then my agent shall make a choice for me based upon what my agent believes to be in my best interests. My agent's authority to interpret my desires is intended to be as broad as possible, except for any restrictions or limitations I may state below.

Accordingly, unless specifically limited by the provisions specified below, my agent is authorized as follows: A. To consent, refuse, or withdraw consent to any and all types of medical care, treatment, surgical procedures, diagnostic procedures, medication, and the use of mechanical or other procedures that affect any bodily function, including, but not limited to, artificial respiration, nutritional support and hydration, and cardiopulmonary resuscitation. B. To authorize, or refuse to authorize, any medication or procedure intended to relieve pain, even though such use may lead to physical damage, addiction, or hasten the moment of, but not intentionally cause, my death. C. To authorize my admission to or discharge, even against medical advice, from any hospital, nursing care facility, or similar facility or service. D. To take any other action necessary to making, documenting, and assuring implementation of decisions concerning my health care, including, but not limited to, granting any waiver or release from liability required by any hospital, physician, nursing care provider, or other health care provider; signing any documents relating to refusals of treatment or the leaving of a facility against medical advice, and pursuing any legal action in my name, and at the expense of my estate to force compliance with my wishes as determined by my agent, or to seek actual or punitive damages for the failure to comply. E. The powers granted above do not include the following powers or are subject to the following rules or limitations:

ORGAN DONATION: **(Initial one only)** My agent [   ] may OR [   ] may not consent to the donation of all or any of my tissue or organs for purposes of transplantation, consistent with my wishes as known to my agent and/or as stated in this document.

EFFECT ON DECLARATION OF A DESIRE FOR A NATURAL DEATH (LIVING WILL): I understand that if I have a valid Declaration of a Desire for a Natural Death, the instructions contained in the Declaration will be given effect in any situation to which they are applicable. My agent will have authority to make decisions concerning my health care only in situations to which the Declaration does not apply.

STATEMENT OF DESIRES CONCERNING LIFE-SUSTAINING TREATMENT: With respect to any Life-Sustaining Treatment, I direct the following: **(Initial only one of the following 3 paragraphs)**

[   ] GRANT OF DISCRETION TO AGENT. I do not want my life to be prolonged nor do I want life-sustaining treatment to be provided or continued if my agent believes the burdens of the treatment outweigh the expected benefits. I want my agent to consider the relief of suffering, my personal beliefs, the expense involved and the quality as well as the possible extension of my life in making decisions concerning life-sustaining treatment. OR

[   ] DIRECTIVE TO WITHHOLD OR WITHDRAW TREATMENT. I do not want my life to be prolonged and I do not want life-sustaining treatment: (a). If I have a condition that is incurable or irreversible and, without the administration of life-sustaining procedures, expected to result in death within a relatively short period of time; or (b). If I am in a state of permanent unconsciousness. OR

[   ] DIRECTIVE FOR MAXIMUM TREATMENT. I want my life to be prolonged to the greatest extent possible, within the standards of accepted medical practice, without regard to my condition, the chances I have for recovery, or the cost of the procedures.

STATEMENT OF DESIRES REGARDING TUBE FEEDING: With respect to Nutrition and Hydration provided by means of a nasogastric tube or tube into the stomach, intestines, or veins, I wish to make clear that in situations where life-sustaining treatment is being withheld or withdrawn pursuant to my desires stated above. **(Initial only one of the following 3 paragraphs)**

[   ] GRANT OF DISCRETION TO AGENT. I do not want my life to be prolonged by tube feeding if my agent believes the burdens of tube feeding outweigh the expected benefits. I want my agent to consider the relief of suffering, my personal beliefs, the expense involved, and the quality as well as the possible extension of my life in making this decision. OR

[   ] DIRECTIVE TO WITHHOLD OR WITHDRAW TUBE FEEDING. I do not want my life prolonged by tube feeding. OR

[   ] DIRECTIVE FOR PROVISION OF TUBE FEEDING. I want tube feeding to be provided within the standards of accepted medical practice, without regard to my condition, the chances I have for recovery, or the cost of the procedure, and without regard to whether other forms of life-sustaining treatment are being withheld or withdrawn.

IF YOU DO NOT INITIAL ANY OF THE ABOVE 3 STATEMENTS, YOUR AGENT WILL NOT HAVE AUTHORITY TO DIRECT THAT NUTRITION AND HYDRATION NECESSARY FOR COMFORT CARE OR ALLEVIATION OF PAIN BE WITHDRAWN.

STATEMENT OF ANY RESTRICTIONS OR LIMITATIONS: **(Optional. Use additional pages if necessary-However, any additional pages must be signed and dated).**

ADMINISTRATIVE PROVISIONS: I revoke any prior Health Care Power of Attorney and any provisions relating to health care of any other prior power of attorney. This power of attorney is intended to be valid in any jurisdiction in which it is presented.

Designation of Primary Physician

I designate the following physician as my primary physician: _____ (name)
_____ (address)
_____(phone).

OPTIONAL- DESIGNATION OF ALTERNATE PRIMARY PHYSICIAN: If the physician I have designated above is not willing, able, or reasonably available to act as my primary physician, I designate the following physician as my primary physician:
_____ (name)
_____ (address)
_____(phone).

Organ Donation

In the event of my death, I have placed my initials next to the following part(s) of my body that I wish donated for the purposes **that I have initialed below**:

[   ] any organs or parts **OR**

[   ] eyes   [   ] bone and connective tissue   [   ] skin

[   ] heart   [   ] kidney(s)   [   ] liver

[   ] lung(s)   [   ] pancreas   [   ] other _____

for the purposes of:

[   ] any purpose authorized by law **OR**

[   ] transplantation   [   ] research   [   ] therapy

[   ] medical education   [   ] other limitations _____

Signature

I sign this Advance Health Care Directive, consisting of the following sections, **which I have initialed below and have elected to adopt:**

[   ] Living Will (Declaration of Desire for a Natural Death)

[   ] Selection of Health Care Agent (Health Care Power of Attorney)

[   ] Designation of Primary Physician

[   ] Organ Donation

BY SIGNING HERE I INDICATE THAT I UNDERSTAND THE PURPOSE AND EFFECT OF THIS DOCUMENT.

Signature _____ Date _____

City, County, and State of Residence _____

Notary Acknowledgment

State of South Carolina

County of _____

On _____, _____ came before me personally and, under oath, subscribed to, acknowledged, and stated that he or she is the person described in the above document and he or she signed the above document in my presence. I declare under penalty of perjury that the person whose name is subscribed to this instrument appears to be of sound mind and under no duress, fraud, or undue influence.

Additionally subscribed and sworn to before me by _____
and_____, the witnesses on the same date noted above.

_____

Notary Public

My commission expires _____

Witness Acknowledgment and Affidavit

State of South Carolina Affidavit
County of _____

We, _____ and _____, the undersigned witnesses to the foregoing Advance Health Care Directive, consisting of a Declaration of a Desire for a Natural Death, an Designation of Health Care Power of Attorney, a Designation of Primary Physician, and an Organ Donation, dated the ____ day of _____, _____, at least one of us being first duly sworn, declare to the undersigned authority, on the basis of our best information and belief, that the Advance Health Care Directive was on that date signed by the declarant/principal as and for his Advance Health Care Directive, consisting of a Declaration of a Desire for a Natural Death, an Designation of Health Care Power of Attorney, a Designation of Primary Physician, and an Organ Donation, in our presence and we, at his request and in his presence, and in the presence of each other, subscribe our names as witnesses on that date. The declarant/principal is personally known to us, and we believe him to be of sound mind and under no duress, fraud, or undue influence. Each of us affirms that he is qualified as a witness to this Advance Health Care Directive under the provisions of the South Carolina Death With Dignity Act and any other relevant provision of South Carolina law, that he or she is not related to the declarant/principal by blood, marriage, or adoption, either as a spouse, lineal ancestor, descendant of the parents of the declarant/principal, or spouse of any of them; nor directly financially responsible for the declarant/principal's medical care; nor entitled to any portion of the declarant/principal's estate upon his decease, whether under any will or as an heir by intestate succession; nor the beneficiary of a life insurance policy of the declarant/principal; nor the declarant/principal's attending physician; nor an employee of the attending physician; nor a person who has a claim against the declarant/principal's decedent's estate as of this time. Neither of us has been appointed as Health Care Agent or Successor Health Care Agent by this document. No more than one of us is an employee of a health facility in which the declarant/principal is a patient. If the declarant/principal is a resident in a hospital or nursing care facility at the date of execution of this Advance Health Care Directive, at least one of us is an ombudsman designated by the State Ombudsman, Office of the Governor.

Witness Signature _____ Date _____

Printed Name and Address of Witness _____

Second Witness Signature _____ Date _____

Printed Name and Address of Second Witness _____

Acceptance of Health Care Agent and Attorney-in-Fact for Health Care

I accept my appointment as Health Care Agent and Attorney-in-Fact for Health Care:

Signature _____ Date _____

Signature of Successor_____ Date _____

South Dakota Advance Health Care Directive

On this date of _____ , I, _____ , do hereby sign, execute, and adopt the following as my Advance Health Care Directive. I direct any and all persons or entities involved with my health care in any manner that these decisions are my wishes and were adopted without duress or force and of my own free will.

I have placed my initials next to the sections of this Directive that I have adopted:

[   ] Living Will Declaration
[   ] Selection of Health Care Agent (Durable Power of Attorney for Health Care)
[   ] Designation of Primary Physician
[   ] Organ Donation

Living Will Declaration

This is an important legal document. A living will directs the medical treatment you are to receive in the event you are in a terminal condition and are unable to participate in your own medical decisions. This living will may state what kind of treatment you want or do not want to receive. Prepare this living will carefully. If you use this form, read it completely. You may want to seek professional help to make sure the form does what you intend and is completed without mistakes. This living will remains valid and in effect until and unless you revoke it. Review this living will periodically to make sure it continues to reflect your wishes. You may amend or revoke this living will at any time by notifying your physician and other health care providers. You should give copies of this living will to your family, your physician, and your health care facility. This form is entirely optional. If you choose to use this form, please note that the form provides signature lines for you, the two witnesses whom you have selected, and a notary public.

TO MY FAMILY, HEALTH CARE PROVIDER, AND ALL THOSE CONCERNED WITH MY CARE: I direct you to follow my wishes for care if I am in a terminal condition, my death is imminent, and I am unable to communicate my decisions about my medical care. With respect to any life-sustaining treatment, I direct the following: **(Initial only one of the following options. If you do not agree with either of the first two options, space is provided below, in the third option, for you to write your own instructions.)**

[   ] If my death is imminent or I am permanently unconscious, I choose not to prolong my life. If life sustaining treatment has been started, stop it, but keep me comfortable and control my pain.

[   ] Even if my death is imminent or I am permanently unconscious, I choose to prolong my life.

[   ] I choose neither of the above options, and here are my instructions should I become terminally ill and my death is imminent or I am permanently unconscious: **(Insert instructions)**

Artificial Nutrition and Hydration: food and water provided by means of a tube inserted into the stomach or intestine or needle into a vein. With respect to artificial nutrition and hydration, I Direct the following: **(Initial only one)**

[   ] If my death is imminent or I am permanently unconscious, I do not want artificial nutrition and hydration. If it has been started, stop it.

[   ] Even if my death is imminent or I am permanently unconscious, I want artificial nutrition and hydration.

Selection of Health Care Agent
(Durable Power of Attorney for Health Care)

I hereby appoint _____ (name), of _____ (address), as my attorney-in-fact to consent to, reject, or withdraw consent for medical procedures, treatment, or intervention.

OPTIONAL: If I revoke my agent's authority or if my agent is not willing, able, or reasonably available to make a health care decision for me, I designate as my alternate agent:
_____ (name of individual you choose as alternate agent)
_____ (address)
_____

I have discussed my wishes with my attorney-in-fact and my alternate attorney-in-fact, and authorize him or her to make all and any health care decisions for me, including decisions to withhold or withdraw any form of life support. I expressly authorize my agent to make decisions for me regarding the withholding or withdrawal of artificial nutrition and hydration in all medical circumstances.

This power of attorney becomes effective when I can no longer make my own medical decisions and is not affected by physical disability or mental incompetence. The determination of whether I can make my own medical decisions is to be made by my attorney-in-fact, or if he or she is unable, unwilling, or unavailable to act, by my alternate attorney-in-fact, unless the attending physician determines that I have the capacity to make my own decisions.

Designation of Primary Physician

I designate the following physician as my primary physician: _____ (name)
_____ (address)
_____ (phone).

OPTIONAL- DESIGNATION OF ALTERNATE PRIMARY PHYSICIAN: If the physician I have designated above is not willing, able, or reasonably available to act as my primary physician, I designate the following physician as my primary physician:
_____ (name)
_____ (address)
_____ (phone).

Organ Donation

In the event of my death, I have placed my initials next to the following part(s) of my body that I wish donated for the purposes **that I have initialed below:**

[   ] any organs or parts **OR**

[   ] eyes   [   ] bone and connective tissue   [   ] skin

[   ] heart   [   ] kidney(s)   [   ] liver

[   ] lung(s)   [   ] pancreas   [   ] other _____

for the purposes of:

[   ] any purpose authorized by law **OR**

[   ] transplantation   [   ] research   [   ] therapy

[   ] medical education   [   ] other limitations _____

Signature

I sign this Advance Health Care Directive, consisting of the following sections, **which I have initialed below and have elected to adopt:**

[   ] Living Will Declaration

[   ] Selection of Health Care Agent (Durable Power of Attorney for Health Care)

[   ] Designation of Primary Physician

[   ] Organ Donation

BY SIGNING HERE I INDICATE THAT I UNDERSTAND THE PURPOSE AND EFFECT OF THIS DOCUMENT.

Signature _____ Date _____

City, County, and State of Residence _____

Notary Acknowledgment

State of _____

County of _____

On _____ , _____ came before me personally and, under oath, stated that he or she is the person described in the above document and he or she signed the above document in my presence. I declare under penalty of perjury that the person whose name is subscribed to this instrument appears to be of sound mind and under no duress, fraud, or undue influence.

_____

Notary Public

My commission expires _____

Witness Acknowledgment

The declarant is personally known to me and I believe him or her to be of sound mind and under no duress, fraud, or undue influence. I did not sign the declarant's signature above for or at the direction of the declarant and I am not appointed as the health care agent or attorney-in-fact herein. I am at least eighteen (18) years of age and I am not related to the declarant by blood, adoption, or marriage, entitled to any portion of the estate of the declarant according to the laws of intestate succession or under any will of declarant or codicil thereto, or directly financially responsible for declarant's medical care. I am not a health care provider of the declarant or an employee of the health facility in which the declarant is a patient.

Witness Signature _____   Date _____

Printed Name of Witness _____

Second Witness Signature _____   Date _____

Printed Name of Second Witness _____

Acceptance of Health Care Agent and Attorney-in-Fact for Health Care

I accept my appointment as Health Care Agent and Attorney-in-Fact for Health Care:

Signature _____   Date _____

I accept my appointment as Alternate Health Care Agent and Attorney-in-Fact for Health Care:

Signature _____   Date _____

Tennessee Advance Health Care Directive

On this date of _____ , I, _____ , do hereby sign, execute, and adopt the following as my Advance Health Care Directive. I direct any and all persons or entities involved with my health care in any manner that these decisions are my wishes and were adopted without duress or force and of my own free will.

I have placed my initials next to the sections of this Directive that I have adopted:

[　　] Living Will
[　　] Selection of Health Care Agent (Durable Power of Attorney for Health Care)
[　　] Designation of Primary Physician
[　　] Organ Donation

Living Will

I, willfully and voluntarily make known my desire that my dying shall not be artificially prolonged under the circumstances set forth below, and do hereby declare:

If at any time I should have a terminal condition and my attending physician has determined there is no reasonable medical expectation of recovery and which, as a medical probability, will result in my death, regardless of the use or discontinuance of medical treatment implemented for the purpose of sustaining life or the life process, I direct that medical care be withheld or withdrawn, and that I be permitted to die naturally with only the administration of medications or the performance of any medical procedure deemed necessary to provide me with comfortable care or to alleviate pain.

ARTIFICIALLY-PROVIDED NOURISHMENT AND FLUIDS: **By initialing the appropriate box below, I specifically:**

[　　] DO authorize the withholding or withdrawal of artificially-provided food, water, or other nourishment or fluids.

[　　] do NOT authorize the withholding or withdrawal of artificially-provided food, water, or other nourishment or fluids.

In the absence of my ability to give directions regarding my medical care, it is my intention that this declaration shall be honored by my family and physician as the final expression of my legal right to refuse medical care and accept the consequences of such refusal. The definitions of terms used herein shall be as set forth in the Tennessee Right to Natural Death Act, Tennessee Code Annotated, § 32-11-103. I understand the full import of this declaration, and I am emotionally and mentally competent to make this declaration.

Selection of Health Care Agent
(Durable Power of Attorney for Health Care)

This is an important legal document. Before executing this document, you should know these important facts: This document gives the person you designate as your agent (the attorney-in-fact) the power to make health care decisions for you. Your agent must act consistently with your desires as stated in this document. Except as you otherwise specify in this document, this document gives your agent the power to consent to your doctor not giving treatment or stopping treatment necessary to keep you alive. Notwithstanding this document, you have the right to make medical and other health care decisions for yourself so long as you can give informed consent with respect to the particular decision. In addition, no treatment may be given to you over your objection and health care necessary to keep you alive may not be stopped or withheld if you object at the time. This document gives your agent authority to consent, refuse to consent, or withdraw consent to any care, treatment, service, or procedure to maintain, diagnose, or treat a physical or mental condition. This power is subject to any limitations that you include in this document. You may state in this document any types of treatment that you do not desire. In addition, a court can take away the power of your agent to make health care decisions for you if your agent: (1) authorizes anything that is illegal, OR (2) acts contrary to your desires as stated in this document. You have the right to revoke the authority of your agent by notifying your agent or your treating physician, hospital, or other health care provider orally or in writing of the revocation. Your agent has the right to examine your medical records and consent to their disclosure unless you limit this right in this document. Unless you otherwise specify in this document, this document gives your agent the power after you die to: (1) authorize an autopsy, (2) donate your body or parts thereof for transplant, therapeutic, educational, or scientific purposes, and (3) direct the disposition of your remains. If there is anything in this document that you do not understand, you should ask an attorney to explain it to you.

I state and affirm that I have read the foregoing paragraphs concerning the legal consequences of my executing this document, and I do hereby appoint:

_____ (name),

of _____(address),

as my attorney-in-fact to have the authority to express and carry out my specific and general instructions and desires with respect to medical treatment.

OPTIONAL - DESIGNATION OF ALTERNATE AGENT: If I revoke my agent's authority or if my agent is not willing, able, or reasonably available to make a health care decision for me, I designate as my first alternate agent

_____ (name of individual you choose as first alternate agent)

_____ (address)

I have discussed my wishes with my attorney-in-fact, and authorize him or her to make all and any health care decisions (as defined by Tennessee law) for me, including decisions to withhold or withdraw any form of life support. I expressly authorize my agent to make decisions for me about tube feeding and medication.

This power of attorney becomes effective when I can no longer make my own medical decisions and shall not be affected by my subsequent disability or incompetence. The determination of whether I can make my own medical decisions is to be made by my attorney-in-fact.

Designation of Primary Physician

I designate the following physician as my primary physician: _____ (name)

_____ (address)

_____ (phone).

OPTIONAL- DESIGNATION OF ALTERNATE PRIMARY PHYSICIAN: If the physician I have designated above is not willing, able, or reasonably available to act as my primary physician, I designate the following physician as my primary physician:

_____ (name)

_____ (address)

_____ (phone).

Organ Donation

In the event of my death, I have placed my initials next to the following part(s) of my body that I wish donated for the purposes **that I have initialed below:**

[   ] any organs or parts **OR**

[   ] eyes   [   ] bone and connective tissue   [   ] skin

[   ] heart   [   ] kidney(s)   [   ] liver

[   ] lung(s)   [   ] pancreas   [   ] other _____

for the purposes of:

[   ] any purpose authorized by law **OR**

[   ] transplantation   [   ] research   [   ] therapy

[   ] medical education   [   ] other limitations _____

Signature

I sign this Advance Health Care Directive, consisting of the following sections, **which I have initialed below and have elected to adopt:**

[   ] Living Will

[   ] Selection of Health Care Agent (Durable Power of Attorney for Health Care)

[   ] Designation of Primary Physician

[   ] Organ Donation

BY SIGNING HERE I INDICATE THAT I UNDERSTAND THE PURPOSE AND EFFECT OF THIS DOCUMENT.

Signature _____   Date _____

City, County, and State of Residence _____

Notary Acknowledgment

State of _____

County of _____

On _____ , _____ came before me personally and, under oath, acknowledged and stated that he or she is the person described in the above document and he or she signed the above document in my presence. I declare under penalty of perjury that the person whose name is subscribed to this instrument appears to be of sound mind and under no duress, fraud, or undue influence.

_____

Notary Public
My commission expires _____

Witness Acknowledgment

The declarant is personally known to me and I believe him or her to be of sound mind and under no duress, fraud, or undue influence. I did not sign the declarant's signature above for or at the direction of the declarant and I am not appointed as the health care agent or attorney-in-fact herein. I am at least eighteen (18) years of age and I am not related to the declarant by blood, adoption, or marriage, entitled to any portion of the estate of the declarant according to the laws of intestate succession or under any will of declarant or codicil thereto, or directly financially responsible for declarant's medical care. I am not a health care provider of the declarant or an employee of the health facility in which the declarant is a patient.

Witness Signature _____ Date _____

Printed Name of Witness _____

Second Witness Signature _____ Date _____

Printed Name of Second Witness _____

Acceptance of Health Care Agent and Attorney-in-Fact for Health Care

I accept my appointment as Health Care Agent and Attorney-in-Fact for Health Care.

Signature _____ Date _____

I accept my appointment as Alternate Health Care Agent and Attorney-in-Fact for Health Care.:

Signature _____ Date _____

Texas Advance Health Care Directive

On this date of _____ , I, _____ , do hereby sign, execute, and adopt the following as my Advance Health Care Directive. I direct any and all persons or entities involved with my health care in any manner that these decisions are my wishes and were adopted without duress or force and of my own free will.

I have placed my initials next to the sections of this Directive that I have adopted:

[   ] Living Will (Directive to Physicians and Family or Surrogates)
[   ] Selection of Health Care Agent (Medical Power of Attorney)
[   ] Designation of Primary Physician
[   ] Organ Donation

Living Will (Directive to Physicians and Family or Surrogates)

INSTRUCTIONS FOR COMPLETING THIS DOCUMENT: This is an important legal document known as an Advance Directive. It is designed to help you communicate your wishes about medical treatment at some time in the future when you are unable to make your wishes known because of illness or injury. These wishes are usually based on personal values. In particular, you may want to consider what burdens or hardships of treatment you would be willing to accept for a particular amount of benefit obtained if you were seriously ill. You are encouraged to discuss your values and wishes with your family or chosen spokesperson, as well as your physician. Your physician, other health care provider, or medical institution may provide you with various resources to assist you in completing your advance directive. Brief definitions are listed on the following pages and may aid you in your discussions and advance planning. Initial the treatment choices that best reflect your personal preferences. Provide a copy of your directive to your physician, usual hospital, and family or spokesperson. Consider a periodic review of this document. By periodic review, you can best assure that the directive reflects your preferences. In addition to this advance directive, Texas law provides for other types of directives that can be important during a serious illness. These are the Medical Power of Attorney and the Out-of-Hospital Do-Not-Resuscitate Order. You may wish to discuss these with your physician, family, hospital representative, or other advisers. You may also wish to complete a directive related to the donation of organs and tissues, which is included in this document.

I recognize that the best health care is based upon a partnership of trust and communication with my physician. My physician and I will make health care decisions together as long as I am of sound mind and able to make my wishes known. If there comes a time that I am unable to make medical decisions about myself because of illness or injury, I direct that the following treatment preferences be honored:

If, in the judgment of my physician, I am suffering with a terminal condition from which I am expected to die within six (6) months, even with available life-sustaining treatment provided in accordance with prevailing standards of medical care (**initial one**):

[   ] I request that all treatments other than those needed to keep me comfortable be discontinued or withheld and my physician allow me to die as gently as possible; **OR**

[   ] I request that I be kept alive in this terminal condition using available life-sustaining treatment. (THIS SELECTION DOES NOT APPLY TO HOSPICE CARE.)

If, in the judgment of my physician, I am suffering with an irreversible condition so that I cannot care for myself or make decisions for myself and am expected to die without life-sustaining treatment provided in accordance with prevailing standards of care **(initial one):**

[   ] I request that all treatments other than those needed to keep me comfortable be discontinued or withheld and my physician allow me to die as gently as possible; **OR**

[   ] I request that I be kept alive in this irreversible condition using available life-sustaining treatment. (THIS SELECTION DOES NOT APPLY TO HOSPICE CARE.)

ADDITIONAL REQUESTS: **(After discussion with your physician, you may wish to consider listing particular treatments in this space that you do or do not want in specific circumstances, such as artificial nutrition and fluids, intravenous antibiotics, etc. Be sure to state whether you do or do not want the particular treatment):**

OPTIONAL- If I do not have a Medical Power of Attorney, and I am unable to make my wishes known, I designate the following person to make treatment decisions with my physician compatible with my personal values:

_____ (name)
_____ (address)

If the above person is not available, or if I have not designated a spokesperson, I understand that a spokesperson will be chosen for me following standards specified in the laws of Texas. **NOTE: If a Medical Power of Attorney has been executed (including the Medical Power of Attorney that you may adopt as part of this document), then an agent already has been named and you should not list additional names in this document.**

After signing this directive, if my representative or I elect hospice care, I understand and agree that only those treatments needed to keep me comfortable would be provided and I would not be given available life-sustaining treatments.

If, in the judgment of my physician, my death is imminent within minutes to hours, even with the use of all available medical treatment provided within the prevailing standard of care, I acknowledge that all treatments may be withheld or removed except those needed to maintain my comfort.

I understand that under Texas law this directive has no effect if I have been diagnosed as pregnant.

This directive will remain in effect until I revoke it. No other person may do so.

Selection of Health Care Agent (Medical Power of Attorney)

DISCLOSURE STATEMENT: THIS IS AN IMPORTANT LEGAL DOCUMENT. BEFORE SIGNING THIS DOCUMENT, YOU SHOULD KNOW THESE IMPORTANT FACTS: Except to the extent you state otherwise, this document gives the person you name as your agent the authority to make any and all health care decisions for you in accordance with your wishes, including your religious and moral beliefs, when you are no longer capable of making them yourself. Because "health care" means any treatment, service, or procedure to maintain, diagnose, or treat your physical or mental condition, your agent has the power to make a broad range of health care decisions for you. Your agent may consent, refuse to consent, or withdraw consent to medical treatment and may make decisions about withdrawing or withholding life-sustaining treatment. Your agent may not consent to voluntary inpatient mental health services, convulsive treatment, psychosurgery, or abortion. A physician must comply with your agent's instructions or allow you to be transferred to another physician. Your agent's authority begins when your doctor certifies that you lack the competence to make health care decisions. Your agent is obligated to follow your instructions when making decisions on your behalf. Unless you state otherwise, your agent has the same authority to make decisions about your health care as you would have had. It is important that you discuss this document with your physician or other health care provider before you sign it to make sure that you understand the nature and range of decisions that may be made on your behalf. If you do not have a physician, you should talk with someone else who is knowledgeable about these issues and can answer your questions. You do not need a lawyer's assistance to complete this document, but if there is anything in this document that you do not understand, you should ask a lawyer to explain it to you. The person you appoint as agent should be someone you know and trust. The person must be eighteen (18) years of age or older or a person under eighteen (18) years of age who has had the disabilities of minority removed. If you appoint your health or residential care provider (e.g., your physician or an employee of a home health agency, hospital, nursing home, or residential care home, other than a relative), that person has to choose between acting as your agent or as your health or residential care provider; the law does not permit a person to do both at the same time. You should inform the person you appoint that you want the person to be your health care agent. You should discuss this document with your agent and your physician and give each a signed copy. You should indicate on the document itself the people and institutions who have signed copies. Your agent is not liable for health care decisions made in good faith on your behalf. Even after you have signed this document, you have the right to make health care decisions for yourself as long as you are able to do so and treatment cannot be given to you or stopped over your objection. You have the right to revoke the authority granted to your agent by informing your agent or your health or residential care provider orally or in writing, or by your execution of a subsequent medical power of attorney. Unless you state otherwise, your appointment of a spouse dissolves on divorce. This document may not be changed or modified. If you want to make changes in the document, you must make an entirely new one.

THIS POWER OF ATTORNEY IS NOT VALID UNLESS IT IS SIGNED IN THE PRESENCE OF TWO (2) COMPETENT ADULT WITNESSES. THE FOLLOWING PERSONS MAY NOT ACT AS ONE (1) OF THE WITNESSES:

(1) the person you have designated as your agent, (2) a person related to you by blood or marriage, (3) a person entitled to any part of your estate after your death under a will or codicil executed by you or by operation of law, (4) your attending physician, (5) an employee of your attending physician, (6) an employee of your health care facility in which you are a patient if the employee is providing direct patient care to you or is an officer, director, partner, or business office employee of the health care facility or of any parent organization of the health care facility, OR (7) a person who, at the time this power of attorney is executed, has a claim against any part of your estate after your death.

I appoint _____ (name),
of _____ (address),
as my agent to make any and all health care decisions for me, except to the extent I state otherwise in this document. This medical power of attorney takes effect if I become unable to make my own health care decisions and this fact is certified in writing by my physician.

OPTIONAL - DESIGNATION OF ALTERNATE AGENT: If I revoke my agent's authority or if my agent is not willing, able, or reasonably available to make a health care decision for me, I designate as my alternate agent
_____ (name of individual you choose as alternate agent)
_____ (address)

LIMITATIONS ON THE DECISION-MAKING AUTHORITY OF MY AGENT ARE AS FOLLOWS (*insert limitations*):

LOCATION OF COPIES. The original of this document is kept at:
_____ (address).
The following individuals or institutions have signed copies (*list individuals and/or institutions*):

DURATION. I understand that this power of attorney exists indefinitely from the date I execute this document unless I establish a shorter time or revoke the power of attorney. If I am unable to make health care decisions for myself when this power of attorney expires, the authority I have granted my agent continues to exist until the time I become able to make health care decisions for myself.

PRIOR DESIGNATIONS REVOKED. I revoke any prior medical power of attorney.

ACKNOWLEDGMENT OF DISCLOSURE STATEMENT. A disclosure statement explaining the effect of this document is part of this document. I have read and understood that information contained in the disclosure statement.

Designation of Primary Physician

I designate the following physician as my primary physician: _____ (name)

_____ (address)

_____ (phone).

OPTIONAL- DESIGNATION OF ALTERNATE PRIMARY PHYSICIAN: If the physician I have designated above is not willing, able, or reasonably available to act as my primary physician, I designate the following physician as my primary physician:

_____ (name)

_____ (address)

_____ (phone).

Organ Donation

In the event of my death, I have placed my initials next to the following part(s) of my body that I wish donated for the purposes **that I have initialed below:**

[   ] any organs or parts **OR**

[   ] eyes   [   ] bone and connective tissue   [   ] skin

[   ] heart   [   ] kidney(s)   [   ] liver

[   ] lung(s)   [   ] pancreas   [   ] other _____

for the purposes of:

[   ] any purpose authorized by law **OR**

[   ] transplantation   [   ] research   [   ] therapy

[   ] medical education   [   ] other limitations _____

Signature

I sign this Advance Health Care Directive, consisting of the following sections, **which I have initialed below and have elected to adopt:**

[   ] Living Will (Directive to Physicians and Family or Surrogates)

[   ] Selection of Health Care Agent (Medical Power of Attorney)

[   ] Designation of Primary Physician

[   ] Organ Donation

BY SIGNING HERE I INDICATE THAT I UNDERSTAND THE PURPOSE AND EFFECT OF THIS DOCUMENT.

Signature _____ Date _____

City, County, and State of Residence _____

Notary Acknowledgment

State of _____

County of _____

On _____ , _____ came before me personally and, under oath, stated that he or she is the person described in the above document and he or she signed the above document in my presence. I declare under penalty of perjury that the person whose name is subscribed to this instrument appears to be of sound mind and under no duress, fraud, or undue influence.

_____

Notary Public

My commission expires _____

Witness Acknowledgment

The declarant is personally known to me and I believe him or her to be of sound mind and under no duress, fraud, or undue influence. I did not sign the declarant's signature above for or at the direction of the declarant and I am not appointed as the health care agent or attorney-in-fact herein. I am at least eighteen (18) years of age and I am not related to the declarant by blood, adoption, or marriage, entitled to any portion of the estate of the declarant according to the laws of intestate succession or under any will of declarant or codicil thereto, or directly financially responsible for declarant's medical care. I do not have a claim against any part of the estate of the declarant. I am not a health care provider of the declarant or an employee of the health facility in which the declarant is a patient.

Witness Signature _____ Date _____

Printed Name of Witness _____

Second Witness Signature _____ Date _____

Printed Name of Second Witness _____

Acceptance of Health Care Agent and Attorney-in-Fact for Health Care

I accept my appointment as Health Care Agent and Attorney-in-Fact for Health Care:

Signature _____ Date _____

Signature of Alternate _____ Date _____

Utah Advance Health Care Directive

On this date of _____ , I, _____ , do hereby sign, execute, and adopt the following as my Advance Health Care Directive. I direct any and all persons or entities involved with my health care in any manner that these decisions are my wishes and were adopted without duress or force and of my own free will.

I have placed my initials next to the sections of this Directive that I have adopted:

[   ] Living Will (My Health Care Wishes
[   ] Selection of Health Care Agent (My Agent)
[   ] Designation of Primary Physician
[   ] Organ Donation

PURSUANT TO UTAH CODE SECTION 75-2A-117

Part I: Allows you to record your wishes about health care in writing.
Part II: Allows you to name another person (and an alternate, if desired) to make health care decisions for you when you cannot make decisions or speak for yourself.
Part III: Tells you how to revoke the form.
Part IV: Allows you to designate your primary (and alternate , if desired) physician
Part V: Allows you to make an organ donation
Part VI: Makes your directive legal.

My Personal Information

Name: _____

Street Address: _____

City, State, Zip: _____

Telephone: _____ Cell Phone: _____

Birth date: _____

Part I: Living Will (My Health Care Wishes)

I want my health care providers to follow the instructions I give them when I am being treated, so long as I can make health care decisions, even if the instructions appear to conflict with these or other advance directives. My health care providers should always provide comfort measures and health care to keep me as comfortable and functional as possible.

Choose one of the following by placing your initials before one of the four the statements that reflects your wishes.

[   ] I choose to let my agent decide. I have chosen my agent carefully. I have talked with my agent about my health care wishes. I trust my agent to make the health care decisions for me that I would make under the circumstances. My agent may stop care that is prolonging my life only after the conditions checked "yes" below are met.

Yes _____ No _____ I have a progressive illness that will cause death.

Yes _____ No _____ I am close to death and am unlikely to recover.

Yes _____ No _____ I cannot communicate and it is unlikely that my condition will improve.

Yes _____ No _____ I am in a persistent vegetative state.

Yes _____ No _____ I do not recognize my friends or family and it is unlikely that my condition will improve.

[   ] I want to prolong life. Regardless of my condition or prognosis, I want my health care providers to try to keep me alive as long as possible, within the limits of generally accepted health care standards.

[   ] I choose NOT to receive care for the purpose of prolonging life, including food and fluids by tube, antibiotics, CPR, or dialysis used to prolong my life. I always want comfort care and routine medical care that will keep me as comfortable and functional as possible, even if that care may prolong my life. My health care provider may stop care that is prolonging my life only after the conditions checked "yes" below are met. If I check "no" to all the conditions, my health care provider should not provide care to prolong my life.

Yes _____ No _____ I have a progressive illness that will cause death.

Yes _____ No _____ I am close to death and am unlikely to recover.

Yes _____ No _____ I cannot communicate and it is unlikely that my condition will improve.

Yes _____ No _____ I am in a persistent vegetative state.

Yes _____ No _____ I do not recognize my friends or family and it is unlikely that my condition will improve.

[   ] I choose not to provide instructions about end-of-life care in this directive.

Additional or Other Instructions Regarding Choices: **(Add additional instructions if desired)**

Part II: My Agent

NO AGENT

[   ] I do not want to choose an agent. **Initial this paragraph if you do not want to name an agent, then go to Part III.** Do not name an agent below. No individual, organization, family member, health care provider, lawyer, or insurer should force you to name an agent.

If you would like to name a Health Care Agent, you may do so below:

MY AGENT
Agent's Name:: _____
Street Address: _____
City, State, Zip: _____
Home Phone: (___) _____ Cell Phone: (___) _____ Work Phone: (___) _____

ALTERNATE AGENT
Alternate Agent's Name: _____
Street Address: _____
City, State, Zip: _____
Home Phone: (___) _____ Cell Phone: (___) _____ Work Phone: (___) _____

AGENT'S AUTHORITY: If I cannot make decisions or speak for myself, my agent can make any health care decision I could have made such as:

1. Consent to, refuse, or withdraw any health care. This may include care to prolong my life such as food and fluids by tube, use of antibiotics, CPR (cardiopulmonary resuscitation), and dialysis, and mental health care, such as convulsive therapy and psychoactive medications. This authority is subject to any limits later in Part II or in previously in Part I of this directive.

2. Hire and fire health care providers.

3. Ask questions and get answers from health care providers.

4. Consent to admission or transfer to a health care provider or health care facility, including a mental health facility, subject to any limits in paragraphs E or F of this section.

5. Get copies of my medical records.

6. Ask for consultations or second opinions.

OTHER AUTHORITY: My agent has the powers below ONLY IF I place a check next to "yes" in the statement. I authorize my agent to:

Yes _____ NO _____ Get copies of my medical records at any time, even when I can speak for myself.

Yes _____ No _____ Admit me to a licensed health care facility, such as a hospital, nursing home, assisted living, or other congregate facility for long-term placement other than convalescent or recuperative care, unless I agree to be admitted at that time.

EXPANSION OR LIMITATIONS OF AUTHORITY: I wish to limit or expand the powers of my healthcare agent as follows:

NOMINATION OF GUARDIAN: Check "yes" or "no".

Yes _____ No _____ By appointing an agent in this document, I intend to avoid guardianship. If I must have a guardian, I want my agent to be my guardian.

CONSENT TO PARTICIPATE IN MEDICAL RESEARCH: Check "yes" or "no".

Yes _____ No _____ I authorize my agent to consent to my participation in medical research or clinical trials, even if I may not benefit from the results.

CONSENT TO ORGAN DONATION: Check "yes" or "no".

Yes _____ No _____ If I have not otherwise agreed to organ donation (including in this document), then my agent may consent to the donation of my organs for the purpose of organ transplantation.

AGENT'S AUTHORITY TO OVERRIDE EXPRESSED WISHES: Check "yes" or "no".

Yes _____ No _____ My agent may make decisions about health care that are different from the instructions in Part I of this form.

Part III: Revoking My Directive

I may revoke this directive by:
1. Writing "void" across the form, or burning, tearing, or otherwise destroying or defacing the document or asking another person to do the same on my behalf;
2. Signing or directing another person to sign a written revocation on my behalf;
3. Stating that I wish to revoke the directive in the presence of a witness who meets the requirements of the witness in Part VI, below, and who will not be appointed as agent or become a default surrogate when the directive is revoked; or
4. Signing a new directive. (If you sign more than one Advance Health Care Directive, the most recent one applies.)

Part IV: Designation of Primary Physician

I designate the following physician as my primary physician: _____ (name)
_____ (address)
_____ (phone).

OPTIONAL- DESIGNATION OF ALTERNATE PRIMARY PHYSICIAN: If the physician I have designated above is not willing, able, or reasonably available to act as my primary physician, I designate the following physician as my primary physician:
_____ (name)
_____ (address)
_____ (phone).

Part V: Organ Donation

In the event of my death, I have placed my initials next to the following part(s) of my body that I wish donated for the purposes **that I have initialed below:**

[   ] any organs or parts **OR**

[   ] eyes   [   ] bone and connective tissue   [   ] skin

[   ] heart   [   ] kidney(s)   [   ] liver

[   ] lung(s)   [   ] pancreas   [   ] other _____

for the purposes of:

[   ] any purpose authorized by law **OR**

[   ] transplantation   [   ] research   [   ] therapy

[   ] medical education   [   ] other limitations _____

Part VI: Making My Directive Legal

I sign this Advance Health Care Directive voluntarily, consisting of the following sections, **which I have initialed below and have elected to adopt:**

[   ] Living Will (My Health Care Wishes)

[   ] Selection of Health Care Agent (My Agent)

[   ] Designation of Primary Physician

[   ] Organ Donation

I UNDERSTAND THE CHOICES I HAVE MADE. I DECLARE THAT I AM EMOTIONALLY AND MENTALLY ABLE TO MAKE THIS DIRECTIVE. BY SIGNING HERE I INDICATE THAT I UNDERSTAND THE PURPOSE AND EFFECT OF THIS DOCUMENT.

Signature _____   Date _____

City, County, and State of Residence _____

Notary Acknowledgment

State of _____

County of _____

On _____ , _____ came before me personally and, under oath, stated that he or she is the person described in the above document and he or she signed the above document in my presence. I declare under penalty of perjury that the person whose name is subscribed to this instrument appears to be of sound mind and under no duress, fraud, or undue influence.

_____

Notary Public

My commission expires _____

Witness Acknowledgment

The declarant is personally known to me and I believe him or her to be of sound mind and under no duress, fraud, or undue influence. I did not sign the declarant's signature above for or at the direction of the declarant and I am not appointed as the health care agent or attorney-in-fact herein. I am at least eighteen (18) years of age and I am not related to the declarant by blood, adoption, or marriage, entitled to any portion of the estate of the declarant according to the laws of intestate succession or under any will of declarant or codicil thereto, or directly financially responsible for declarant's medical care. I am not a health care provider of the declarant or an employee of the health facility in which the declarant is a patient.

Witness Signature _____ Date _____

Printed Name of Witness _____

Second Witness Signature _____ Date _____

Printed Name of Second Witness _____

Acceptance of Health Care Agent

I accept my appointment as Health Care Agent:

Signature _____ Date _____

I accept my appointment as Alternate Health Care Agent:

Signature _____ Date _____

Vermont Advance Health Care Directive

On this date of _____ , I, _____ , do hereby sign, execute, and adopt the following as my Advance Health Care Directive. I direct any and all persons or entities involved with my health care in any manner that these decisions are my wishes and were adopted without duress or force and of my own free will.

I have placed my initials next to the sections of this Directive that I have adopted:

[   ] Living Will (Terminal Care Document)
[   ] Selection of Health Care Agent (Durable Power of Attorney for Health Care)
[   ] Designation of Primary Physician
[   ] Organ Donation

Living Will (Terminal Care Document)

To my family, my physician, my lawyer, my clergyman. To any medical facility in whose care I happen to be. To any individual who may become responsible for my health, welfare, or affairs.

Death is as much a reality as birth, growth, maturity, and old age. It is the one certainty of life. If the time comes when I can no longer take part in decisions of my own future, let this statement stand as an expression of my wishes, while I am still of sound mind.

If the situation should arise in which I am in a terminal state and there is no reasonable expectation of my recovery, I direct that I be allowed to die a natural death and that my life not be prolonged by extraordinary measures. I do, however, ask that medication be mercifully administered to me to alleviate suffering even though this may shorten my remaining life.

This statement is made after careful consideration and is in accordance with my strong convictions and beliefs. I want the wishes and directions here expressed carried out to the extent permitted by law. Insofar as they are not legally enforceable, I hope that those to whom this will is addressed will regard themselves as morally bound by these provisions.

Copies of this request have been given to (list name[s] and address[es] of person[s] and attach additional sheets if needed):

_____ (name),
of _____ (address)

_____ (name),
of _____ (address)

_____ (name),
of _____ (address)

Selection of Health Care Agent
(Durable Power of Attorney for Health Care)

DISCLOSURE STATEMENT: THIS IS AN IMPORTANT LEGAL DOCUMENT. BEFORE SIGNING THIS DOCUMENT, YOU SHOULD KNOW THESE IMPORTANT FACTS: Except to the extent you state otherwise, this document gives the person you name as your agent the authority to make any and all health care decisions for you when you are no longer capable of making them yourself. "Health care" means any treatment, service, or procedure to maintain, diagnose, or treat your physical or mental condition. Your agent therefore can have the power to make a broad range of health care decisions for you. Your agent may consent, refuse to consent, or withdraw consent to medical treatment and may make decisions about withdrawing or withholding life-sustaining treatment. You may state in this document any treatment you do not desire or treatment you want to be sure you receive. Your agent's authority will begin when your doctor certifies that you lack the capacity to make health care decisions. You may attach additional pages if you need more space to complete your statement. Your agent will be obligated to follow your instructions when making decisions on your behalf. Unless you state otherwise, your agent will have the same authority to make decisions about your health care as you would have had. It is important that you discuss this document with your physician or other health care providers before you sign it to make sure that you understand the nature and range of decisions which may be made on your behalf. If you do not have a physician, you should talk with someone else who is knowledgeable about these issues and can answer your questions. You do not need a lawyer's assistance to complete this document, but if there is anything in this document that you do not understand, you should ask a lawyer to explain it to you. The person you appoint as agent should be someone you know and trust and must be at least eighteen (18) years old. If you appoint your health or residential care provider (e.g., your physician, or an employee of a home health agency, hospital, nursing home, or residential care home, other than a relative), that person will have to choose between acting as your agent or as your health or residential care provider; the law does not permit a person to do both at the same time. You should inform the person you appoint that you want him or her to be your health care agent. You should discuss this document with your agent and your physician and give each a signed copy. You should indicate on the document itself the people and institutions who will have signed copies. Your agent will not be liable for health care decisions made in good faith on your behalf. Even after you have signed this document, you have the right to make health care decisions for yourself as long as you are able to do so, and treatment cannot be given to you or stopped over your objection. You have the right to revoke the authority granted to your agent by informing him or her or your health care provider orally or in writing. This document may not be changed or modified. If you want to make changes in the document you must make an entirely new one.

THIS POWER OF ATTORNEY WILL NOT BE VALID UNLESS IT IS SIGNED IN THE PRESENCE OF TWO (2) OR MORE QUALIFIED WITNESSES WHO MUST BOTH BE PRESENT WHEN YOU SIGN OR ACKNOWLEDGE YOUR SIGNATURE. THE FOLLOWING PERSONS MAY NOT ACT AS WITNESSES: The person you have designated as your agent, health or residential care provider or one (1) of their employees, spouse, lawful heirs or beneficiaries named in your will or a deed, or creditors or persons who have a claim against you.

I hereby appoint _____ (name),
of _____ (address),
as my agent to make any and all health care decisions for me, except to the extent I state otherwise in this document. This durable power of attorney for health care shall take effect in the event I become unable to make my own health care decisions.

OPTIONAL - DESIGNATION OF ALTERNATE AGENT: If I revoke my agent's authority or if my agent is not willing, able, or reasonably available to make a health care decision for me, I designate as my first alternate agent

_____ (name of individual you choose as first alternate agent)
_____ (address)

STATEMENT OF DESIRES, SPECIAL PROVISIONS, AND LIMITATIONS REGARDING HEALTH CARE DECISIONS. **(Here you may include any specific desires or limitations you deem appropriate, such as when or what life-sustaining measures should be withheld, directions whether to continue or discontinue artificial nutrition and hydration, or instructions to refuse any specific types of treatment that are inconsistent with your religious beliefs or unacceptable to you for any other reason. Attach additional pages as necessary):**

THE SUBJECT OF LIFE-SUSTAINING TREATMENT IS OF PARTICULAR IMPORTANCE. **(For your convenience in dealing with that subject, some general statements concerning the withholding or removal of life-sustaining treatment are set forth below. If you agree with one of these statements, you may include the statement by initialing the space before the statement):**
[   ] If I suffer a condition from which there is no reasonable prospect of regaining my ability to think and act for myself, I want only care directed to my comfort and dignity and authorize my agent to decline all treatment which is primarily intended to prolong my life, including artificial nutrition and hydration.
[   ] If I suffer a condition from which there is no reasonable prospect of regaining the ability to think and act for myself, I want care directed to my comfort and dignity and also want artificial nutrition and hydration if needed, but authorize my agent to decline all other treatment which is primarily intended to prolong my life.
[   ] I want my life sustained by any reasonable medical measures, regardless of my condition.

I hereby acknowledge that this document contains a disclosure statement explaining the effect of this document. I have read and understand the information contained in the disclosure statement. The original of this document will be kept at:

_____ (address), and
the following person(s) and institution(s) will have signed copies (*list name[s] and address[es] of person[s] and attach additional pages if needed*):

Designation of Primary Physician

I designate the following physician as my primary physician: _____ (name)
_____ (address)
_____ (phone).

OPTIONAL- DESIGNATION OF ALTERNATE PRIMARY PHYSICIAN: If the physician I have designated above is not willing, able, or reasonably available to act as my primary physician, I designate the following physician as my primary physician:
_____ (name)
_____ (address)
_____ (phone).

Organ Donation

In the event of my death, I have placed my initials next to the following part(s) of my body that I wish donated for the purposes **that I have initialed below:**

[   ] any organs or parts **OR**

[ ] eyes	[ ] bone and connective tissue	[ ] skin
[ ] heart	[ ] kidney(s)	[ ] liver
[ ] lung(s)	[ ] pancreas	[ ] other _____

for the purposes of:

[   ] any purpose authorized by law **OR**

[ ] transplantation	[ ] research	[ ] therapy
[ ] medical education	[ ] other limitations _____	

Signature

I sign this Advance Health Care Directive, consisting of the following sections, **which I have initialed below and have elected to adopt:**

[   ] Living Will (Terminal Care Document)
[   ] Selection of Health Care Agent (Durable Power of Attorney for Health Care)
[   ] Designation of Primary Physician
[   ] Organ Donation

BY SIGNING HERE I INDICATE THAT I UNDERSTAND THE PURPOSE AND EFFECT OF THIS DOCUMENT. IF I AM IN OR IS BEING ADMITTED TO A HOSPITAL, NURSING HOME, OR RESIDENTIAL-CARE HOME, AN OMBUDSMAN, HOSPITAL REPRESENTATIVE, OR OTHER AUTHORIZED PERSON HAS PERSONALLY EXPLAINED THE DURABLE POWER OF ATTORNEY TO ME AND I UNDERSTAND ITS NATURE AND EFFECT

Signature _____   Date _____

City, County, and State of Residence _____

Notary Acknowledgment

State of _____
County of _____

On _____ , _____ came before me personally and, under oath, stated that he or she is the person described in the above document and he or she signed the above document in my presence. I declare under penalty of perjury that the person whose name is subscribed to this instrument appears to be of sound mind and under no duress, fraud, or undue influence.

_____
Notary Public
My commission expires _____

Witness Acknowledgment

The declarant is personally known to me and I believe him or her to be of sound mind and under no duress, fraud, or undue influence. I did not sign the declarant's signature above for or at the direction of the declarant and I am not appointed as the health care agent or attorney-in-fact herein. I am at least eighteen (18) years of age and I am not related to the declarant by blood, adoption, or marriage, entitled to any portion of the estate of the declarant according to the laws of intestate succession or under any will of declarant or codicil thereto, or directly financially responsible for declarant's medical care. I am not a health care provider of the declarant or an employee of the health facility in which the declarant is a patient.

Witness Signature _____ Date _____

Printed Name of Witness _____

Second Witness Signature _____ Date _____

Printed Name of Second Witness _____

Acceptance of Health Care Agent and Attorney-in-Fact for Health Care

I accept my appointment as Health Care Agent and Attorney-in-Fact for Health Care:

Signature of Agent _____ Date _____

Signature of Alternate _____ Date _____

Statement of Ombudsman, Hospital Representative, or Other Authorized Person

(To be signed only if the principal is in or is being admitted to a hospital, nursing home, or residential-care home.)

I declare that I have personally explained the nature and effect of this durable power of attorney to the principal and that the principal understands the same

(Sign below and insert date, printed name, and address):

Signature _____ Date _____

Printed Name _____

Address _____

Virginia Advance Health Care Directive

On this date of _____ , I, _____ , do hereby sign, execute, and adopt the following as my Advance Health Care Directive. I direct any and all persons or entities involved with my health care in any manner that these decisions are my wishes and were adopted without duress or force and of my own free will.

I have placed my initials next to the sections of this Directive that I have adopted:

[   ] Living Will
[   ] Appointment of Health Care Agent
[   ] Designation of Primary Physician
[   ] Organ Donation

Living Will

I, willfully and voluntarily make known my desire and do hereby declare: If at any time my attending physician should determine that I have a terminal condition where the application of life-prolonging procedures would serve only to artificially prolong the dying process, I direct that such procedures be withheld or withdrawn, and that I be permitted to die naturally with only the administration of medication or the performance of any medical procedure deemed necessary to provide me with comfort care or to alleviate pain.

I specifically direct that the following procedures or treatments be provided to me (*optional*):

In the absence of my ability to give directions regarding the use of such life-prolonging procedures, it is my intention that this advance directive shall be honored by my family and physician as the final expression of my legal right to refuse medical or surgical treatment and accept the consequences of such refusal.

Appointment of Health Care Agent

(Cross through if you do not want to appoint an agent to make health care decisions for you.)

I hereby appoint _____ (name),
of _____ (address),
as my agent to make health care decisions on my behalf as authorized in this document.

OPTIONAL - DESIGNATION OF ALTERNATE AGENT: If I revoke my agent's authority or if my agent is not willing, able, or reasonably available to make a health care decision for me, I designate as my alternate agent

_____ (name of individual you choose as alternate agent)
_____ (address)

I hereby grant to my agent, named above, full power and authority to make health care decisions on my behalf as described below whenever I have been determined to be incapable of making an informed decision about providing, withholding, or withdrawing medical treatment. The phrase "incapable of making an informed decision" means being unable to understand the nature, extent, and probable consequences of a proposed medical decision or unable to make a rational evaluation of the risks and benefits of a proposed medical decision as compared with the risks and benefits of alternatives to that decision, or unable to communicate such understanding in any way. My agent's authority hereunder is effective as long as I am incapable of making an informed decision.

The determination that I am incapable of making an informed decision shall be made by my attending physician and a second physician or licensed clinical psychologist after a personal examination of me and shall be certified in writing. Such certification shall be required before treatment is withheld or withdrawn, and before, or as soon as reasonably practicable after, treatment is provided, and every one-hundred-eighty (180) days thereafter while the treatment continues.

In exercising the power to make health care decisions on my behalf, my agent shall follow my desires and preferences as stated in this document or as otherwise known to my agent. My agent shall be guided by my medical diagnosis and prognosis and any information provided by my physicians as to the intrusiveness, pain, risks, and side effects associated with treatment or non-treatment. My agent shall not authorize a course of treatment which he or she knows, or upon reasonable inquiry ought to know, is contrary to my religious beliefs or my basic values, whether expressed orally or in writing. If my agent cannot determine what treatment choice I would have made on my own behalf, then my agent shall make a choice for me based upon what he or she believes to be in my best interests.

POWERS OF MY AGENT (optional) (Cross through any language you do not want and add any language you do want.)

The powers of my agent shall include the following: (1) To consent to, refuse, or withdraw consent to any type of medical care, treatment, surgical procedure, diagnostic procedure, medication, and the use of mechanical or other procedures that affect any bodily function, including, but not limited to, artificial respiration, artificially-administered nutrition and hydration, and cardiopulmonary resuscitation. This authorization specifically includes the power to consent to the administration of dosages of pain-relieving medication in excess of recommended dosages in an amount sufficient to relieve pain, even if such medication carries the risk of addiction or inadvertently hastens my death, (2) To request, receive, and review any information, verbal or written, regarding my physical or mental health, including but not limited to, medical and hospital records, and to consent to the disclosure of this information, (3) To employ and discharge my health care providers, (4) To authorize my admission to or discharge (including transfer to another facility) from any hospital, hospice, nursing home, adult home, or other medical care facility for services other than those for treatment of mental illness requiring admission procedures provided in Article 1 (§ 37.1-63 et seq.) of Chapter 2 of Title 37.1, and (5) To take any lawful actions that may be necessary to carry out these decisions, including the granting of releases of liability to medical providers.

Further, my agent shall not be liable for the costs of treatment pursuant to his or her authorization, based solely on that authorization. This advance directive shall not terminate in the event of my disability.

Designation of Primary Physician

I designate the following physician as my primary physician: _____ (name)
_____ (address)
_____ (phone).

OPTIONAL- DESIGNATION OF ALTERNATE PRIMARY PHYSICIAN: If the physician I have designated above is not willing, able, or reasonably available to act as my primary physician, I designate the following physician as my primary physician:

_____ (name)
_____ (address)
_____ (phone).

Organ Donation

In the event of my death, I have placed my initials next to the following part(s) of my body that I wish donated for the purposes **that I have initialed below:**

[   ] any organs or parts **OR**
[   ] eyes   [   ] bone and connective tissue   [   ] skin
[   ] heart   [   ] kidney(s)   [   ] liver
[   ] lung(s)   [   ] pancreas   [   ] other _____

for the purposes of:

[   ] any purpose authorized by law **OR**
[   ] transplantation   [   ] research   [   ] therapy
[   ] medical education   [   ] other limitations _____

Signature

I sign this Advance Health Care Directive, consisting of the following sections, **which I have initialed below and have elected to adopt:**
[   ] Living Will
[   ] Appointment of Health Care Agent
[   ] Designation of Primary Physician
[   ] Organ Donation

BY SIGNING HERE I INDICATE THAT I UNDERSTAND THE PURPOSE AND EFFECT OF THIS DOCUMENT.

Signature _____   Date _____

City, County, and State of Residence _____

Notary Acknowledgment

State of _____

County of _____

On _____ , _____ came before me personally
and, under oath, stated that he or she is the person described in the above document and he or she
signed the above document in my presence. I declare under penalty of perjury that the person whose
name is subscribed to this instrument appears to be of sound mind and under no duress, fraud, or
undue influence.

_____
Notary Public
My commission expires _____

Witness Acknowledgment

The declarant is personally known to me and I believe him or her to be of sound mind and under
no duress, fraud, or undue influence. I did not sign the declarant's signature above for or at the
direction of the declarant and I am not appointed as the health care agent or attorney-in-fact herein.
I am at least eighteen (18) years of age and I am not related to the declarant by blood, adoption,
or marriage, entitled to any portion of the estate of the declarant according to the laws of intestate
succession or under any will of declarant or codicil thereto, or directly financially responsible for
declarant's medical care. I am not a health care provider of the declarant or an employee of the
health facility in which the declarant is a patient.

Witness Signature _____ Date _____

Printed Name of Witness _____

Second Witness Signature _____ Date _____

Printed Name of Second Witness _____

Acceptance of Health Care Agent

I accept my appointment as Health Care Agent:

Signature _____ Date _____

I accept my appointment Alternate Health Care Agent:

Signature _____ Date _____

Washington Advance Health Care Directive

On this date of _____ , I, _____ , do hereby sign, execute, and adopt the following as my Advance Health Care Directive. I direct any and all persons or entities involved with my health care in any manner that these decisions are my wishes and were adopted without duress or force and of my own free will.

I have placed my initials next to the sections of this Directive that I have adopted:
[   ]   Living Will (Health Care Directive)
[   ]   Selection of Health Care Agent (Durable Power of Attorney for Health Care)
[   ]   Designation of Primary Physician
[   ]   Organ Donation

Living Will (Health Care Directive)

I, having the capacity to make health care decisions, willfully, and voluntarily make known my desire that my dying shall not be artificially-prolonged under the circumstances set forth below, and do hereby declare that:

If at any time I should be diagnosed in writing to be in a terminal condition by the attending physician, or in a permanent unconscious condition by two physicians, and where the application of life-sustaining treatment would serve only to artificially prolong the process of my dying, I direct that such treatment be withheld or withdrawn, and that I be permitted to die naturally. I understand by using this form that a terminal condition means an incurable and irreversible condition caused by injury, disease, or illness that would within reasonable medical judgment cause death within a reasonable period of time in accordance with accepted medical standards, and where the application of life-sustaining treatment would serve only to prolong the process of dying.

I further understand in using this form that a permanent unconscious condition means an incurable and irreversible condition in which I am medically assessed within reasonable medical judgment as having no reasonable probability of recovery from an irreversible coma or a persistent vegetative state.

In the absence of my ability to give directions regarding the use of such life-sustaining treatment, it is my intention that this directive shall be honored by my family and physician(s) as the final expression of my legal right to refuse medical or surgical treatment and I accept the consequences of such refusal. If another person is appointed to make these decisions for me, whether through a durable power of attorney or otherwise, I request that the person be guided by this directive and any other clear expressions of my desires.

If I am diagnosed to be in a terminal condition or in a permanent unconscious condition
(Initial one):
[   ]   I DO want to have artificially-provided nutrition and hydration.
[   ]   I do NOT want to have artificially-provided nutrition and hydration.

If I have been diagnosed as pregnant and that diagnosis is known to my physician, this directive shall have no force or effect during the course of my pregnancy. I understand the full import of this directive and I am emotionally and mentally capable to make the health care decisions contained in this directive. I understand that before I sign this directive, I can add to, delete from, or otherwise change the wording of this directive and that I may add to or delete from this directive at any time and that any changes shall be consistent with Washington state law or federal constitutional law to be legally valid. It is my wish that every part of this directive be fully implemented. If for any reason any part is held invalid it is my wish that the remainder of my directive be implemented.

Selection of Health Care Agent
(Durable Power of Attorney for Health Care)

I understand that my wishes as expressed in my living will may not cover all possible aspects of my care if I become incapacitated. Consequently, there may be a need for someone to accept or refuse medical intervention on my behalf, in consultation with my physician. Therefore, I, designate and appoint _____ (name), of _____ (address), as my attorney-in-fact for health care decisions.

OPTIONAL - DESIGNATION OF ALTERNATE ATTORNEY-IN-FACT: If I revoke my agent's authority or if my agent is not willing, able, or reasonably available to make a health care decision for me, I designate as my alternate attorney-in-fact:
_____ (name of individual you choose as alternate)
_____ (address)

This Power of Attorney shall take effect upon my incapacity to make my own health care decisions, as determined by my treating physician and one (1) other physician, and shall continue as long as the incapacity lasts or until I revoke it, whichever happens first.

The powers of my attorney-in-fact under this Power of Attorney are limited to making decisions about my health care on my behalf. These powers shall include the power to order the withholding or withdrawal of life-sustaining treatment if my attorney-in-fact believes, in his or her own judgment, that is what I would want if I could make the decision myself. The existence of this Durable Power of Attorney for Health Care shall have no effect upon the validity of any other Power of Attorney for other purposes that I have executed or may execute in the future.

In the event that a proceeding is initiated to appoint a guardian of my person under RCW 11.88, I nominate the person designated as my attorney-in-fact for health care decisions to serve as my guardian.

I make the following additional instructions regarding my care (list instructions if desired):

Designation of Primary Physician

I designate the following physician as my primary physician: _____ (name)
_____ (address)
_____ (phone).

OPTIONAL- DESIGNATION OF ALTERNATE PRIMARY PHYSICIAN: If the physician I have designated above is not willing, able, or reasonably available to act as my primary physician, I designate the following physician as my primary physician:

_____ (name)
_____ (address)
_____ (phone).

Organ Donation

In the event of my death, I have placed my initials next to the following part(s) of my body that I wish donated for the purposes **that I have initialed below:**

[   ] any organs or parts **OR**
[   ] eyes   [   ] bone and connective tissue   [   ] skin
[   ] heart   [   ] kidney(s)   [   ] liver
[   ] lung(s)   [   ] pancreas   [   ] other _____

for the purposes of:
[   ] any purpose authorized by law **OR**
[   ] transplantation   [   ] research   [   ] therapy
[   ] medical education   [   ] other limitations _____

Signature

I sign this Advance Health Care Directive, consisting of the following sections, **which I have initialed below and have elected to adopt:**

[   ] Living Will (Health Care Directive)
[   ] Selection of Health Care Agent (Durable Power of Attorney for Health Care)
[   ] Designation of Primary Physician
[   ] Organ Donation

BY SIGNING HERE I INDICATE THAT I UNDERSTAND THE PURPOSE AND EFFECT OF THIS DOCUMENT.

Signature _____   Date _____

City, County, and State of Residence _____

Notary Acknowledgment

State of _____

County of _____

On _____ , _____ came before me personally and, under oath, stated that he or she is the person described in the above document and he or she signed the above document in my presence. I declare under penalty of perjury that the person whose name is subscribed to this instrument appears to be of sound mind and under no duress, fraud, or undue influence.

_____

Notary Public

My commission expires _____

Witness Acknowledgment

The declarant is personally known to me and I believe him or her to be of sound mind and under no duress, fraud, or undue influence. I did not sign the declarant's signature above for or at the direction of the declarant and I am not appointed as the health care agent or attorney-in-fact herein. I am at least eighteen (18) years of age and I am not related to the declarant by blood, adoption, or marriage, entitled to any portion of the estate of the declarant according to the laws of intestate succession or under any will of declarant or codicil thereto, or directly financially responsible for declarant's medical care. I am not a health care provider of the declarant or an employee of the health facility in which the declarant is a patient.

Witness Signature _____ Date _____

Printed Name of Witness _____

Second Witness Signature _____ Date _____

Printed Name of Second Witness _____

Acceptance of Health Care Agent and Attorney-in-Fact for Health Care

I accept my appointment as Health Care Agent and Attorney-in-Fact for Health Care:

Signature of Agent _____ Date _____

Signature of Alternate _____ Date _____

West Virginia Advance Health Care Directive

On this date of _____ , I, _____ , do hereby sign, execute, and adopt the following as my Advance Health Care Directive. I direct any and all persons or entities involved with my health care in any manner that these decisions are my wishes and were adopted without duress or force and of my own free will.

I have placed my initials next to the sections of this Directive that I have adopted:

[   ] Living Will

[   ] Selection of Health Care Agent (Medical Power of Attorney)

[   ] Designation of Primary Physician

[   ] Organ Donation

Living Will

I, being of sound mind, willfully and voluntarily declare that I want my wishes to be respected if I am very sick and not able to communicate my wishes for myself. In the absence of my ability to give directions regarding the use of life-prolonging medical intervention, it is my desire that my dying shall not be prolonged under the following circumstances:

If I am very sick and not able to communicate my wishes for myself and I am certified by one (1) physician who has personally examined me to have a terminal condition or to be in a persistent vegetative state (that is, if I am unconscious and am neither aware of my environment nor able to interact with others), I direct that life-prolonging medical intervention that would serve solely to prolong the dying process or maintain me in a persistent vegetative state be withheld or withdrawn. I want to be allowed to die naturally and only be given medications or other medical procedures necessary to keep me comfortable. I want to receive as much medication as is necessary to alleviate my pain.

I give the following SPECIAL DIRECTIVES OR LIMITATIONS (**comments about tube feedings, breathing machines, cardiopulmonary resuscitation, and dialysis may be placed here. My failure to provide special directives or limitations does not mean that I want or refuse certain treatments**):

It is my intention that this living will be honored as the final expression of my legal right to refuse medical or surgical treatment and to accept the consequences resulting from such refusal. I understand the full import of this living will.

Selection of Health Care Agent (Medical Power of Attorney)

I, hereby appoint _____ (name),

of _____ (address),

as my representative to act on my behalf to give, withhold, or withdraw informed consent to health care decisions in the event that I am not able to do so myself.

OPTIONAL - DESIGNATION OF ALTERNATE AGENT: If I revoke my agent's authority or if my agent is not willing, able, or reasonably available to make a health care decision for me, I designate as my first alternate agent

_____ (name of individual you choose as first alternate agent)

_____ (address)

This appointment shall extend to, but not be limited to, health care decisions relating to medical treatment, surgical treatment, nursing care, medication, hospitalization, care and treatment in a nursing home or other facility, and home health care. The representative appointed by this document is specifically authorized to be granted access to my medical records and other health information and to act on my behalf to consent to, refuse, or withdraw any and all medical treatment, diagnostic procedures, or autopsy if my representative determines that I, if able to do so, would consent to, refuse, or withdraw such treatment or procedures. Such authority shall include, but not be limited to, decisions regarding the withholding or withdrawal of life-prolonging interventions.

I appoint this representative because I believe this person understands my wishes and values and will act to carry into effect the health care decisions that I would make if I were able to do so, and because I also believe that this person will act in my best interest when my wishes are unknown. It is my intent that my family, my physician, and all legal authorities be bound by the decisions that are made by the representative appointed by this document, and it is my intent that these decisions should not be the subject of review by any health care provider or administrative or judicial agency.

It is my intent that this document be legally binding and effective and that this document be taken as a formal statement of my desire concerning the method by which any health care decisions should be made on my behalf during any period when I am unable to make such decisions. In exercising the authority under this medical power of attorney, my representative shall act consistently with my special directives or limitations as stated below.

I am giving the following SPECIAL DIRECTIVES OR LIMITATIONS ON THIS POWER (**comments about tube feedings, breathing machines, cardiopulmonary resuscitation, and dialysis may be placed here. My failure to provide special directives or limitations does not mean that I want or refuse certain treatments**):

THIS MEDICAL POWER OF ATTORNEY SHALL BECOME EFFECTIVE ONLY UPON MY INCAPACITY TO GIVE, WITHHOLD, OR WITHDRAW INFORMED CONSENT TO MY OWN MEDICAL CARE.

Designation of Primary Physician

I designate the following physician as my primary physician: _____ (name)

_____ (address)

_____ (phone).

OPTIONAL- DESIGNATION OF ALTERNATE PRIMARY PHYSICIAN: If the physician I have designated above is not willing, able, or reasonably available to act as my primary physician, I designate the following physician as my primary physician:

_____ (name)

_____ (address)

_____ (phone).

Organ Donation

In the event of my death, I have placed my initials next to the following part(s) of my body that I wish donated for the purposes **that I have initialed below:**

[   ] any organs or parts **OR**

[   ] eyes   [   ] bone and connective tissue   [   ] skin

[   ] heart   [   ] kidney(s)   [   ] liver

[   ] lung(s)   [   ] pancreas   [   ] other _____

for the purposes of:

[   ] any purpose authorized by law **OR**

[   ] transplantation   [   ] research   [   ] therapy

[   ] medical education   [   ] other limitations _____

Signature

I sign this Advance Health Care Directive, consisting of the following sections, **which I have initialed below and have elected to adopt:**

[   ]   Living Will

[   ]   Selection of Health Care Agent (Medical Power of Attorney)

[   ]   Designation of Primary Physician

[   ]   Organ Donation

BY SIGNING HERE I INDICATE THAT I UNDERSTAND THE PURPOSE AND EFFECT OF THIS DOCUMENT.

Signature _____   Date _____

City, County, and State of Residence _____

Notary Acknowledgment

State of _____

County of _____

On _____ , _____ came before me personally and, under oath, stated that he or she is the person described in the above document and he or she signed the above document in my presence. I declare under penalty of perjury that the person whose name is subscribed to this instrument appears to be of sound mind and under no duress, fraud, or undue influence.

_____

Notary Public

My commission expires _____

Witness Acknowledgment

The declarant is personally known to me and I believe him or her to be of sound mind and under no duress, fraud, or undue influence. I did not sign the declarant's signature above for or at the direction of the declarant and I am not appointed as the health care agent or attorney-in-fact herein. I am at least eighteen (18) years of age and I am not related to the declarant by blood, adoption, or marriage, entitled to any portion of the estate of the declarant according to the laws of intestate succession or under any will of declarant or codicil thereto, or directly financially responsible for declarant's medical care. I am not a health care provider of the declarant or an employee of the health facility in which the declarant is a patient.

Witness Signature _____ Date _____

Printed Name of Witness _____

Second Witness Signature _____ Date _____

Printed Name of Second Witness _____

Acceptance of Health Care Agent and Attorney-in-Fact for Health Care

I accept my appointment as Health Care Agent and Attorney-in-Fact for Health Care

Signature _____ Date _____

I accept my appointment as Alternate Health Care Agent and Attorney-in-Fact for Health Care

Signature _____ Date _____

Wisconsin Advance Health Care Directive

On this date of _____ , I, _____ , do hereby sign, execute, and adopt the following as my Advance Health Care Directive. I direct any and all persons or entities involved with my health care in any manner that these decisions are my wishes and were adopted without duress or force and of my own free will.

I have placed my initials next to the sections of this Directive that I have adopted:

[   ] Living Will (Declaration to Physicians)
[   ] Selection of Health Care Agent (Power of Attorney for Health Care)
[   ] Designation of Primary Physician
[   ] Organ Donation

Living Will (Declaration to Physicians)

I, being of sound mind, voluntarily state my desire that my dying not be prolonged under the circumstances specified in this document. Under those circumstances, I direct that I be permitted to die naturally. If I am unable to give directions regarding the use of life-sustaining procedures or feeding tubes, I intend that my family and physician honor this document as the final expression of my legal right to refuse medical or surgical treatment

If I have a TERMINAL CONDITION, as determined by two (2) physicians who have personally examined me, I do not want my dying to be artificially-prolonged and I do not want life-sustaining procedures to be used. In addition, the following are my directions regarding the use of feeding tubes **(initial one):**

[   ] YES, I DO want feeding tubes used if I have a terminal condition.
[   ] NO, I do NOT want feeding tubes used if I have a terminal condition.
(If you have not initialed either box, feeding tubes will be used.)

If I am in a PERSISTENT VEGETATIVE STATE, as determined by two (2) physicians who have personally examined me, the following are my directions regarding the use of life-sustaining procedures **(initial one):**

[   ] YES, I DO want life-sustaining procedures used if I am in a persistent vegetative state.
[   ] NO, I do NOT want life-sustaining procedures used if I am in a persistent vegetative state.
(If you have not initialed either box, life-sustaining procedures will be used.)

If I am in a PERSISTENT VEGETATIVE STATE, as determined by two (2) physicians who have personally examined me, the following are my directions regarding the use of feeding tubes **(Initial one):**

[   ] YES, I DO want feeding tubes used if I am in a persistent vegetative state.
[   ] NO, I do NOT want feeding tubes used if I am in a persistent vegetative state.
(If you have not initialed either box, feeding tubes will be used.)

Selection of Health Care Agent (Power of Attorney for Health Care)

NOTICE TO PERSON MAKING THIS DOCUMENT: You have the right to make decisions about your health care. No health care may be given to you over your objection, and necessary health care may not be stopped or withheld if you object. Because your health care providers in some cases may not have had the opportunity to establish a long-term relationship with you, they are often unfamiliar with your beliefs and values and the details of your family relationships. This poses a problem if you become physically or mentally unable to make decisions about your health care. In order to avoid this problem, you may sign this legal document to specify the person whom you want to make health care decisions for you if you are unable to make those decisions personally. That person is known as your health care agent. You should take some time to discuss your thoughts and beliefs about medical treatment with the person whom you have specified. You may state in this document any types of health care that you do or do not desire and you may limit the authority of your health care agent. If your health care agent is unaware of your desires with respect to a particular health care decision, he or she is required to determine what would be in your best interests in making the decision. This is an important legal document. It gives your agent broad powers to make health care decisions for you. It revokes any prior power of attorney for health care that you may have made. If you wish to change your power of attorney for health care, you may revoke this document at any time by destroying it, directing another person to destroy it in your presence, signing a written and dated statement, or stating that it is revoked in the presence of two (2) witnesses. If you revoke, you should notify your agent, your health care providers, and any other person to whom you have given a copy. If your agent is your spouse and your marriage is annulled or you are divorced after signing this document, the document is invalid. You may also use this document to make or refuse to make an anatomical gift upon your death. If you use this document to make or refuse to make an anatomical gift, this document revokes any prior anatomical gift that you may have made. You may revoke or change any anatomical gift that you make by this document by crossing out the anatomical gifts provision in this document. Do not sign this document unless you clearly understand it. It is suggested that you keep the original of this document on file with your physician.

I, being of sound mind, intend by this document to create a power of attorney for health care. My executing this power of attorney for health care is voluntary. Despite the creation of this power of attorney for health care, I expect to be fully informed about and allowed to participate in any health care decision for me, to the extent that I am able. For the purposes of this document, "health care decision" means an informed decision to accept, maintain, discontinue, or refuse any care, treatment, service, or procedure to maintain, diagnose, or treat my physical or mental condition. In addition, I may, by this document, specify my wishes with respect to making an anatomical gift upon my death.

If I am no longer able to make health care decisions for myself, due to my incapacity, I hereby designate _____ (name), _____ (address), to be my health care agent for the purpose of making health care decisions on my behalf.

OPTIONAL - DESIGNATION OF ALTERNATE AGENT: If I revoke my agent's authority or if my agent is not willing, able, or reasonably available to make a health care decision for me, I designate as my alternate agent

_____ (name of individual you choose as alternate agent)

_____ (address)

The health care agent (or alternate) named above is not my health care provider, an employee of my health care provider, an employee of a health care facility in which I am a patient, or a spouse of any of those persons, unless he or she is also my relative. For purposes of this document, "incapacity" exists if two (2) physicians or a physician and a psychologist who have personally examined me sign a statement that specifically expresses their opinion that I have a condition that means that I am unable to receive and evaluate information effectively or to communicate decisions to such an extent that I lack the capacity to manage my health care decisions. A copy of that statement must be attached to this document.

Unless I have specified otherwise in this document, if I ever have incapacity I instruct my health care provider to obtain the health care decision of my health care agent, if I need treatment, for all of my health care and treatment. I have discussed my desires thoroughly with my health care agent and believe that he or she understands my philosophy regarding the health care decisions I would make if I were able. I desire that my wishes be carried out through the authority given to my health care agent under this document. If I am unable, due to my incapacity, to make a health care decision, my health care agent is instructed to make the health care decision for me, but my health care agent should try to discuss with me any specific proposed health care if I am able to communicate in any manner, including by blinking my eyes. If this communication cannot be made, my health care agent shall base his or her decision on any health care choices that I have expressed prior to the time of the decision. If I have not expressed a health care choice about the health care in question and communication cannot be made, my health care agent shall base his or her health care decision on what he or she believes to be in my best interest.

My health care agent may not admit or commit me on an inpatient basis to an institution for mental diseases, an intermediate care facility for the mentally retarded, a state treatment facility, or a treatment facility. My health care agent may not consent to experimental mental health research or psychosurgery, electroconvulsive treatment, or other drastic mental health treatment procedures for me.

My health care agent may admit me to a nursing home or community-based residential facility for short-term stays for recuperative care or respite care. If I have initialed "YES" to the following, my health care agent may admit me for a purpose other than recuperative care or respite care, but if I have initialed "NO" to the following, my health care agent may not so admit me **(initial one):**

(1) A nursing home: YES [   ] **OR**   NO [   ]
(2) A community-based residential facility: YES [   ] **OR**   NO [   ]

(If I have not initialed either "Yes" or "No" immediately above, my health care agent may only admit me for short-term stays for recuperative care or respite care.)

If I have initialed "YES" to the following, my health care agent may have a feeding tube withheld or withdrawn from me, unless my physician has advised that, in his or her professional judgment, this will cause me pain or will reduce my comfort. If I have initialed "NO" to the following, my health care agent may not have a feeding tube withheld or withdrawn from me. My health care agent may not have orally-ingested nutrition or hydration withheld or withdrawn from me unless provision of the nutrition or hydration is medically contraindicated **(initial one)**:

Withhold or withdraw a feeding tube: YES [   ] **OR**   NO [   ]

(If I have not initialed either "Yes" or "No" immediately above, my health care agent may not have a feeding tube withdrawn from me.)

If I have initialed "YES" to the following, my health care agent may make health care decisions for me even if my agent knows I am pregnant. If I have initialed "NO" to the following, my health care agent may not make health care decisions for me if my health care agent knows I am pregnant **(initial one):**

Health care decision if I am pregnant: YES [   ] **OR**   NO [   ]

(If I have not initialed either "Yes" or "No" immediately above, my health care agent may not make health care decisions for me if my health care agent knows I am pregnant.)

In exercising authority under this document, my health care agent shall act consistently with my following stated desires, if any, and is subject to any special provisions or limitations that I specify. The following are specific desires, provisions, or limitations that I wish to state **(insert desires, provisions, or limitations):**

Subject to any limitations in this document, my health care agent has the authority to do all of the following: (1) Request, review, and receive any information, oral or written, regarding my physical or mental health, including medical and hospital records, (2) Execute on my behalf any documents that may be required in order to obtain this information, and (3) Consent to the disclosure of this information.

Designation of Primary Physician

I designate the following physician as my primary physician: _____ (name)

_____ (address)

_____ (phone).

OPTIONAL- DESIGNATION OF ALTERNATE PRIMARY PHYSICIAN: If the physician I have designated above is not willing, able, or reasonably available to act as my primary physician, I designate the following physician as my primary physician:

_____ (name)

_____ (address)

_____ (phone).

Organ Donation

In the event of my death, I have placed my initials next to the following part(s) of my body that I wish donated for the purposes **that I have initialed below:**

[   ] any organs or parts **OR**

[   ] eyes   [   ] bone and connective tissue   [   ] skin

[   ] heart   [   ] kidney(s)   [   ] liver

[   ] lung(s)   [   ] pancreas   [   ] other _____

for the purposes of:

[   ] any purpose authorized by law **OR**

[   ] transplantation   [   ] research   [   ] therapy

[   ] medical education   [   ] other limitations _____

Signature

I sign this Advance Health Care Directive, consisting of the following sections, **which I have initialed below and have elected to adopt:**

[   ] Living Will (Declaration to Physicians)

[   ] Selection of Health Care Agent (Power of Attorney for Health Care)

[   ] Designation of Primary Physician

[   ] Organ Donation

BY SIGNING HERE I INDICATE THAT I UNDERSTAND THE PURPOSE AND EFFECT OF THIS DOCUMENT.

Signature _____   Date _____

City, County, and State of Residence _____

Notary Acknowledgment

State of _____

County of _____

On _____ , _____ came before me personally and, under oath, stated that he or she is the person described in the above document and he or she signed the above document in my presence. I declare under penalty of perjury that the person whose name is subscribed to this instrument appears to be of sound mind and under no duress, fraud, or undue influence.

_____
Notary Public
My commission expires _____

Witness Acknowledgment

The declarant is personally known to me and I believe him or her to be of sound mind and under no duress, fraud, or undue influence. I did not sign the declarant's signature above for or at the direction of the declarant and I am not appointed as the health care agent or attorney-in-fact herein. I am at least eighteen (18) years of age and I am not related to the declarant by blood, adoption, or marriage, entitled to any portion of the estate of the declarant according to the laws of intestate succession or under any will of declarant or codicil thereto, or directly financially responsible for declarant's medical care. I am not a health care provider of the declarant or an employee of the health facility in which the declarant is a patient.

Witness Signature _____ Date _____

Printed Name of Witness _____

Second Witness Signature _____ Date _____

Printed Name of Second Witness _____

Acceptance of Health Care Agent and Attorney-in-Fact for Health Care

I accept my appointment as Health Care Agent and Attorney-in-Fact for Health Care:

Signature _____ Date _____

Signature of Alternate _____ Date _____

Wyoming Advance Health Care Directive

On this date of _____ , I, _____ , do hereby sign, execute, and adopt the following as my Advance Health Care Directive. I direct any and all persons or entities involved with my health care in any manner that these decisions are my wishes and were adopted without duress or force and of my own free will.

I have placed my initials next to the sections of this Directive that I have adopted:

[   ] Living Will
[   ] Selection of Health Care Agent (Durable Power of Attorney for Health Care)
[   ] Designation of Primary Physician
[   ] Organ Donation

Living Will

I, being of sound mind, willfully and voluntarily make known my desire that my dying shall not be artificially prolonged under the circumstances set forth below, do hereby declare:

If at any time I should have an incurable injury, disease, or other illness certified to be a terminal condition by two (2) physicians who have personally examined me, one (1) of whom shall be my attending physician, and the physicians have determined that my death will occur whether or not life-sustaining procedures are utilized and where the application of life-sustaining procedures would serve only to artificially prolong the dying process, I direct that such procedures be withheld or withdrawn, and that I be permitted to die naturally with only the administration of medication or the performance of any medical procedure deemed necessary to provide me with comfort care.

In the absence of my ability to give directions regarding the use of life-sustaining procedures, it is my intention that this declaration shall be honored by my family and physician(s) and agent as the final expression of my legal right to refuse medical or surgical treatment and accept the consequences from this refusal. I understand the full import of this declaration and I am emotionally and mentally competent to make this declaration.

NOTICE: This document has significant medical, legal, and possible ethical implications and effects. Before you sign this document, you should become completely familiar with these implications and effects. The operation, effects, and implications of this document may be discussed with a physician, lawyer, and clergyman of your choice.

Selection of Health Care Agent (Durable Power of Attorney for Health Care)

I, hereby appoint _____ (name),
of _____ (address),
as my attorney-in-fact to consent to, reject, or withdraw consent for any medical care, treatment, service, or procedure.

OPTIONAL - DESIGNATION OF ALTERNATE AGENT: If I revoke my agent's authority or if my agent is not willing, able, or reasonably available to make a health care decision for me, I designate as my alternate agent

_____ (name of individual you choose as alternate agent)

_____ (address)

I authorize my attorney-in-fact to make any and all health care decisions for me, including decisions to withhold or withdraw any form of life-sustaining procedures. This power of attorney becomes effective when I can no longer make my own medical decisions and is not affected by my physical disability or incapacity. The determination of whether I can make my own medical decisions is to be made by my attorney-in-fact, or if he or she is unable, unwilling, or unavailable to act, by my successor attorney-in-fact, unless the attending physician determines that I have decisional capacity.

Designation of Primary Physician

I designate the following physician as my primary physician: _____ (name)

_____ (address)

_____ (phone).

OPTIONAL- DESIGNATION OF ALTERNATE PRIMARY PHYSICIAN: If the physician I have designated above is not willing, able, or reasonably available to act as my primary physician, I designate the following physician as my primary physician:

_____ (name)

_____ (address)

_____ (phone).

Organ Donation

In the event of my death, I have placed my initials next to the following part(s) of my body that I wish donated for the purposes **that I have initialed below:**

[   ] any organs or parts **OR**
[   ] eyes   [   ] bone and connective tissue   [   ] skin
[   ] heart   [   ] kidney(s)   [   ] liver
[   ] lung(s)   [   ] pancreas   [   ] other _____

for the purposes of:

[   ] any purpose authorized by law **OR**
[   ] transplantation   [   ] research   [   ] therapy
[   ] medical education   [   ] other limitations _____

Signature

I sign this Advance Health Care Directive, consisting of the following sections, **which I have initialed below and have elected to adopt:**

[   ] Living Will
[   ] Selection of Health Care Agent (Durable Power of Attorney for Health Care)
[   ] Designation of Primary Physician
[   ] Organ Donation

BY SIGNING HERE I INDICATE THAT I UNDERSTAND THE PURPOSE AND EFFECT OF THIS DOCUMENT.

Signature _____ Date _____

City, County, and State of Residence _____

Notary Acknowledgment

State of _____
County of _____

On _____ , _____ came before me personally and, under oath, stated that he or she is the person described in the above document and he or she signed the above document in my presence. I declare under penalty of perjury that the person whose name is subscribed to this instrument appears to be of sound mind and under no duress, fraud, or undue influence.

_____
Notary Public
My commission expires _____

Witness Acknowledgment

I declare under penalty of perjury under the laws of the State of Wyoming that the declarant is personally known to me and I believe him or her to be of sound mind and under no duress, fraud, or undue influence. I did not sign the declarant's signature above for or at the direction of the declarant and I am not appointed as the health care agent or attorney-in-fact herein. I am at least eighteen (18) years of age and I am not related to the declarant by blood, adoption, or marriage, entitled to any portion of the estate of the declarant according to the laws of intestate succession or under any will of declarant or codicil thereto, or directly financially responsible for declarant's medical care. I am not a health care provider of the declarant or an employee of the health facility in which the declarant is a patient.

Witness Signature _____ Date _____

Printed Name of Witness _____

Second Witness Signature _____ Date _____

Printed Name of Second Witness _____

Acceptance of Health Care Agent and Attorney-in-Fact for Health Care

I accept my appointment as Health Care Agent and Attorney-in-Fact for Health Care:

Signature _____ Date _____

I accept my appointment as Alternate Health Care Agent and Attorney-in-Fact for Health Care

Signature _____ Date _____

Appendix: State Laws Relating to Advance Health Care Directives

This Appendix contains a summary of the laws relating to advance health care directive issues for all states and the District of Columbia (Washington D.C.). It has been compiled directly from the most recently-available statutes and has been abridged for clarity and succinctness. It is recommended that you review the listing that pertains to your home state. As you review your state's particular laws, keep in mind that your advance health care directive documents are going to be interpreted under the laws of the state where you reside at the time of your hospitalization.

Every effort has been made to ensure that the information contained in this Appendix is as complete and up-to-date as possible. However, state laws are subject to constant change. While most laws relating to advance health care directives are relatively stable, it is advisable to check your particular state statutes to be certain there have been no major modifications since this book was prepared, especially for those legal points that are particularly important in your situation. To simplify this process as much as possible, the exact name of the statute and the chapter or section number of where the information can be found is noted after each section of information. Any of these official statute books should be available at any public library or on the internet. A librarian will be glad to assist you in locating the correct book and in finding the appropriate pages.

The correct terminology for each state is used in these listings. However, some states use certain language interchangeably. In those states, the most commonly-used language is stated. Although it has been simplified to some extent, you will find that the language in the Appendix is somewhat more complicated than the language used in the rest of this book. This is due to the fact that much of the language in the Appendix has been taken directly from the laws and statutes of each state, and most legislators are lawyers. We apologize for this. We feel, however, that, as a reference, the technical details of the laws should be provided. The state-by-state listings following in this Appendix contain the following information for each state:

State Website: This listing provides the internet website address of the location of the state's statutes. The addresses were current at the time of this book's publication; however, like most websites, the page addresses are subject to change. If an expired state webpage is not automatically redirected to a new site, laws can be searched at http://www.findlaw.com

State Law Description: This is the title where most of the relevant state laws on advance health care directives are contained.

Living Will Form: Under this listing, the exact location of a state's official Living Will Form is provided.

Other Directives: The existence and location of additional official state directives relating to advance health care and powers of attorney are indicated in this listing. Examples of such forms are Durable Power of Attorney for Health Care, Durable Power of Attorney for Financial Affairs, Anatomical Gift Act forms (organ donation forms), Designation of Primary Physician, and other related forms.

Living Will Effective: This listing indicates the requirements of state law regarding when a living will becomes effective. Most states require that two physicians must diagnose and document that a patient either has a terminal illness with no hope of recovery or is in a permanent state of unconsciousness, or some similar diagnosis.

Living Will Witness Requirements: Under this listing are noted the specific state requirements for witnesses to the signing of a living will and any related advance health care directives. In general, most states require that there are two witnesses, and that the witnesses be over eighteen, not related by blood or marriage to the declarant, not entitled to any part of the declarant's estate, and not financially responsible for the declarant's health care costs. Note that a few states require that, if the declarant is a patient in a nursing home or hospital, one of the witnesses be a patient advocate or patient ombudsman. In some states, the patient advocate or ombudsman is required to be a third witness, in addition to the other two required witnesses.

Alabama

State Website: www.legislature.state.al.us/CodeofAlabama/1975/coatoc.htm

State Law Reference: Code of Alabama.

Living Will Form: Living Will (Section 22-8A-4).

Other Directives: Durable Power of Attorney Act (Section 26-1-2). Anatomical Gift Act (Section 22-19-40).

Living Will Effective: Two (2) physicians, one being the attending physician, must diagnose and document in the medical records that you either have a terminal illness or injury or are in a permanent state of unconsciousness. (Section 22-8A-4).

Witness Requirements: Living will must be signed in the presence of two (2) or more witnesses at least nineteen (19) years of age. Witnesses cannot be related by blood, adoption, or marriage, entitled to any part of your estate, or be directly financially responsible for your health care. (Section 22-8A-4).

Alaska

State Website: www.legis.state.ak.us/folhome.htm

State Law Reference: Alaska Statutes.

Living Will Form: Advance Health Care Directive serves as Living Will. (Section 13.52.300).

Other Directives: Advance Health Care Directive contains Durable Power of Attorney for Health Care. (Section 13.52.300). Durable Power of Attorney (Sections 13.26.332 to 13.26.353). Anatomical Gift Act (Sections 13.52.170 to 13.52.280).

Living Will Effective: Effective when your primary physician determines that I am unable to make your own health care decisions. (Section 13.52.300).

Witness Requirements: Directive must be acknowledged by a notary or signed by two adult witnesses, neither of whom is a health care provider employed at the health care institution or facility where you are receiving care, an employee of your health care provider or health care facility where you are receiving care. Neither witness can be your appointed agent. At least one witness may not be related to you by blood, marriage, or adoption, or entitled to a portion of your estate upon your death under your will or codicil. (Section 13.52.300).

Arizona

State Website: www.azleg.state.az.us/

State Law Reference: Arizona Revised Statutes.

Living Will Form: Living Will (Sections 36-3261 and 36-3262).

Other Directives: Health Care Power of Attorney (Sections 36-3221 through 36-3224). Anatomical Gift Act (Sections 36-841 through 36-850). Durable Power of Attorney (Section 14-5501). Mental Health Care Power of Attorney (Sections 36-3281 through 36-3287). Prehospital Medical Care Directive (Section 36-3251).

Living Will Effective: No specific language is required, but the statute provides a Sample Living Will offering options when your condition is terminal, irreversible, or incurable. (Section 36-3251).

Witness Requirements: Sign in the presence of one or more witnesses or a notary public who affirms that he or she was present when you signed the Living Will and that you appeared to be of sound mind and free from duress at the time. A notary or witness cannot be your designated agent of be directly involved with the provision of health care to you at the time you sign the Living Will. If there is only one witness, he or she may not be related to you by blood, adoption, or marriage or entitled to any part of your estate under your will or state intestacy law. (Sections 36-3261 and 36-3221).

Arkansas

State Website: http://www.arkleg.state.ar.us/

State Law Reference: Arkansas Code.

Living Will Form: Declaration serves as Living Will (Section 20-17-202).

Other Directives: Declaration contains appointment of Health Care Proxy. (Section 20-17-202). Durable Power of Attorney for Health Care (Section 20-13-104). Anatomical Gift Act (Sections 20-17-601+). Durable Power of Attorney (Section 28-68-402).

Living Will Effective: Effective when you are determined by the attending physician and another physician, in consultation, either to be in a terminal condition and no longer able to make decisions regarding administration of life-sustaining treatment or to be permanently unconscious. (Section 20-17-203).

Witness Requirements: Sign in the presence of two (2) witnesses. No other restrictions apply. (Section 20-17-202).

California

State Website: www.leginfo.ca.gov/

State Law Reference: California Law.

Living Will Form: California Advance Health Care Directive serves as Living Will. (Probate Code, Section 4701).

Other Directives: California Advance Health Care Directive contains Power of Attorney for Health Care, Instructions for Health Care, Donation of Organs, and Appointment of Primary Physician (Probate Code, Section 4701). Uniform Anatomical Gift Act (Health and Safety Code, Sections 7150+). Durable Power of Attorney (Probate Code, Sections 4120+).

Living Will Effective: This Directive becomes effective in the event that you have an incurable and irreversible condition that will result in death within a relatively short time, become unconscious and, to a reasonable degree of medical certainty, will not regain consciousness, or the likely risks and burdens of treatment would outweigh the expected benefits. (Probate Code, Section 4701).

Witness Requirements: Sign in the presence of two adult witnesses or a notary public. A witness cannot be your health care provider or an employee of your health care provider, an operator or employee of a community care facility or residential care facility for the elderly, or the person you appoint as your agent. At least one witness cannot be related to you by blood, marriage, or adoption, or be entitled to any part of your estate under your will or state intestacy law. If you are in a skilled nursing facility, a third witness, who must be a patient advocate or ombudsman, is required. (Probate Code, Sections 4701, 4673, 4674, and 4675).

Colorado

State Website: www.leg.state.co.us/

State Law Reference: Colorado Revised Statutes.

Living Will Form: Colorado Declaration as to Medical or Surgical Treatment serves as Living Will (Section 15-18-104).

Other Directives: Durable Power of Attorney for Health Care (Section 15-14-506). Anatomical Gift Act (Section 12-34-101+). Durable Power of Attorney (Sections 15-14-501+, 15-1-1301+, and 15-14-601+). Certificate of Appointment of a Surrogate Decision-Maker for Health Care Benefits (Section 15-18.5-105).

Living Will Effective: Your attending physician plus one other physician must certify that you are in a terminal condition and life-sustaining procedures would only postpone death. The statute suggests that the Living Will require that this condition persist for seven days before the Living Will becomes effective. (Sections 15-18-103 and 15-18-104).

Witness Requirements: Sign in the presence of two (2) adult witnesses. A witness cannot be a physician, a person who has a claim against your estate upon your death, a person who knows or believes that he or she will inherit from your estate, or an employee of your attending physician or treating health care facility, or a patient of your treating health care facility. (Sections 15-18-105 and 15-18-106).

Connecticut

State Website: www.cga.state.ct.us/2001/pub/Titles.htm

State Law Reference: General Statutes of Connecticut.

Living Will Form: Connecticut Health Care Instructions serves as Living Will (Section 19a-575).

Other Directives: Connecticut Health Care Instructions also contain Appointment of Health Care Agent and Appointment of Attorney-In-Fact for Health Care Decisions. (Section 19a-575). Anatomical Gift Act (Section 19a-279+). Durable Power of Attorney (Section 45a-562).

Living Will Effective: When, in the opinion of your attending physician, you have an incurable or irreversible medical condition which, without the use of life support, will result in death in a relatively short period of time, or you are in a permanent coma or a persistent vegetative state. (Section 19a-575).

Witness Requirements: Sign in the presence of two (2) adult witnesses. Your appointed agent cannot be a witness. If you reside in a facility operated or licensed by the Department of Mental Health or Department of Mental Retardation, additional Witness Requirements must be met and you should consult an attorney. (Sections 19a-575, 19a-576).

Delaware

State Website: http://delcode.delaware.gov/index.shtml

State Law Reference: Delaware Code.

Living Will Form: Instructions for Health Care serves as Living Will (Section 16-2503).

Other Directives: Delaware Advance Directive contains Power of Attorney for Health Care and Instructions for Health Care (Section 16-2503). Anatomical Gift Act (Sections 16-2710+). Durable Power of Attorney (Sections 12-4901+).

Living Will Effective: Two (2) physicians determine in writing that you have a terminal condition and/or are in a permanent state of unconsciousness. (Section 16-2505).

Witness Requirements: Sign in the presence of two (2) adult witnesses. A witness cannot be a person who has claim against your estate upon your death, stands to inherit from your estate, be directly financially responsible for your health care, or be an owner, operator, or employee of a residential long-term health care institution in which you reside. If you are a patient in a nursing home, one of the witnesses must be a patient advocate or ombudsman. (Sections 16-2503 and 16-2505).

District of Columbia (Washington D.C.)

State Website: http://government.westlaw.com/linkedslice/default.asp?SP=DCC-1000

State Law Reference: District of Columbia Code.

Living Will Form: District of Columbia Declaration serves as Living Will (Section 7-622).

Other Directives: Durable Power of Attorney for Health Care (Section 21-2207). Anatomical Gift Act (Section 7-1521.04). Durable Power of Attorney (Section 21-2081).

Living Will Effective: Your attending physician plus one other physician must personally examine you and certify in writing that your death will occur whether or not life-sustaining procedures are used, and the procedures would only artificially prolong the dying process. (Sections 7-621 and 7-622).

Witness Requirements: Sign in the presence of two (2) adult witnesses. A witness cannot be your attending physician, an employee of your attending physician, or an employee of your health care provider. Witnesses also cannot be related by blood, marriage, or adoption; stand to inherit from your estate under your will or District intestacy law; be financially responsible for your health care; or be the person who signed the Declaration for you if you are unable to sign it yourself. (Section 7-622).

Florida

State Website: http://www.flsenate.gov/statutes/index.cfm

State Law Reference: Florida Statutes.

Living Will Form: Living Will (Section 765.303).

Other Directives: Designation of Health Care Surrogate (Section 765.203). Anatomical Gift Act (Sections 765.510+). Durable Power of Attorney (Section 709.08).

Living Will Effective: Two (2) physicians determine in writing that you have a terminal condition, an end-stage condition, and/or are in a persistent vegetative state. (Section 765.306).

Witness Requirements: Sign in the presence of two (2) adult witnesses. At least one (1) of your witnesses must not be related to you by marriage or blood. (Section 765.302).

Georgia

State Website: www.legis.state.ga.us

State Law Reference: Georgia Code.

Living Will Form: Georgia Living Will (Section 31-32-3).

Other Directives: Durable Power of Attorney For Health Care (Section 31-36-1). Georgia Anatomical Gift Act Section 44-5-140). Durable (Financial) Power of Attorney (Sections 10-6-140 through 10-6-142).

Living Will Effective: Two (2) physicians determine in writing that you have a terminal condition, coma, or persistent vegetative state. (Sections 31-32-2 and 31-32-8).

Witness Requirements: Sign in the presence of two (2) adult witnesses. A witness cannot be a person who has claim against your estate upon your death, stands to inherit from your estate, is directly financially responsible for your health care, is an owner, operator, or employee of a health care institution in which you are a patient, or your attending physician or the employee of your attending physician. Witnesses also cannot be related by blood or marriage.

Hawaii

State Website: http://www.capitol.hawaii.gov/
State Law Reference: Hawaii Revised Statutes.
Living Will Form: Instruction for Health Care serves as Living Will (Section 327E-3).
Other Directives: Hawaii Advanced Health Care Directive has Durable Power of Attorney for Health Care and Instructions for Health Care (Section 327E3). Anatomical Gift Act (Section 327-1). Durable Power of Attorney (Sections 551D-1 through 551D-7).
Living Will Effective: Unless the Instruction states otherwise, effective upon a determination that the principal lacks capacity, made by your primary physician. (Section 327E-3).
Witness Requirements: Sign in the presence of two (2) adult witnesses or a notary public. At least one (1) of your witnesses cannot be related to you by marriage or blood or entitled to any part of your estate under your will or state intestacy law. A witness cannot be the person you appoint as your agent, health care provider, or an employee of your health care provider. (Section 327E-3).

Idaho

State Website: http://www3.state.id.us/
State Law Reference: Idaho Statutes.
Living Will Form: Idaho Living Will and Durable Power of Attorney for Health Care (Section 39-4510).
Other Directives: Anatomical Gift Act (Section 39-3401+). Durable Power of Attorney (Section 15-5-501+).
Living Will Effective: Two (2) physicians determine that you are in a terminal condition, your death will result without using life-sustaining procedures, or you are in a persistent vegetative state. (Section 39-4510).
Witness Requirements: Although Idaho does not have any witness requirements, we suggest that you sign in the presence of two adult witnesses or a notary public, and we suggest that witnesses should

not be your appointed attorney-in-fact, your health care provider, or a person related to you by blood, marriage, or adoption.

Illinois

State Website: http://www.ilga.gov/
State Law Reference: Illinois Compiled Statutes.
Living Will Form: Illinois Declaration serves as Living Will (755 ILCS 35/3).
Other Directives: Durable Power of Attorney for Health Care (755 ILCS 45/4-1+). Anatomical Gift Act (755 ILCS 50). Durable Power of Attorney (755 ILCS 45/2-1+).
Living Will Effective: Effective when your attending physician personally examines you and verifies in writing that you have a terminal condition. (755 ILCS 35/2).
Witness Requirements: Sign in the presence of two (2) adult witnesses. Witnesses cannot be entitled to any part of your estate under your will or state intestacy laws, or directly financially responsible for your medical care. (755 ILCS 35/3).

Indiana

State Website: http://www.in.gov/legislative/ic/code/
State Law Reference: Indiana Code.
Living Will Form: Indiana Living Will Declaration (Section 16-36-4-10).
Other Directives: Durable Power of Attorney for Health Care Decisions and Appointment of Health Care Representative are contained within the Living Will document. (Section 16-36-4-10). Anatomical Gift Act (Section 29-2-16-1). Durable Power of Attorney (Section 29-3-5).
Living Will Effective: Your physician must certify in writing that you are in a terminal condition and your death would occur within a short period of time without the use of life-sustaining medical care. (Section 16-36-4-10).
Witness Requirements: Sign in the presence of two (2) adult witnesses. Witnesses cannot be entitled to any part of your estate under your will or state intestacy laws, related to you by blood or marriage, financially responsible for your medical care, or be the person who signed the Declaration on your behalf. (Section 16-36-4-8).

Iowa

State Website: http://www.legis.state.ia.us/

State Law Reference: Iowa Code.

Living Will Form: Iowa Declaration serves as Living Will (Section 144A.3).

Other Directives: Durable Power of Attorney for Health Care (Section 144B.2). Anatomical Gift Act (Section 142C). Durable Power of Attorney (Section 633B.1+).

Living Will Effective: Two (2) physicians must certify in writing that you are in a terminal condition or a state of permanent unconsciousness and your death would occur within a short period of time without the use of life-sustaining medical care. (Section 144A.5).

Witness Requirements: Sign in the presence of two (2) witnesses eighteen (18) years or older or a notary public. A witness cannot be your health care provider or an employee of your health care provider, or related to you by blood, marriage, or adoption. (Section 144A.3).

Kansas

State Website: http://www.kslegislature.org/

State Law Reference: Kansas Statutes.

Living Will Form: Kansas Declaration serves as Living Will (Section 65-28,103).

Other Directives: Durable Power of Attorney for Health Care (Section 58-629). Anatomical Gift Act (Section 65-3209+). Durable Power of Attorney (Section 58-629).

Living Will Effective: Two (2) physicians must certify in writing that you are in a terminal condition and your death would occur within a short period of time without the use of life-sustaining medical care. (Section 65-28,103).

Witness Requirements: Sign in the presence of two (2) witnesses eighteen (18) years or older or a notary public. Witnesses cannot be entitled to any part of your estate under your will or state intestacy laws, be financially responsible for your medical care, be related to you by blood or marriage, or be the person who signed the Declaration on your behalf. (Section 65-28,103).

Kentucky

State Website: http://lrc.ky.gov/

State Law Reference: Kentucky Revised Statutes.

Court with Probate Jurisdiction: District Court. (Section 24A.120).

Living Will Form: Living Will Directive (Section 311.625).

Other Directives: Anatomical Gift Act (Sections 311.165 through 311.235). Durable Power of Attorney (Section 386.093).

Living Will Effective: When you no longer have decisional capacity, have a terminal condition, or become permanently unconscious. (Section 311.625).

Witness Requirements: Sign in the presence of two (2) witnesses eighteen (18) years or older or a notary public. Witnesses cannot be your blood relatives; entitled to any portion of your estate under descent and distribution statutes; employees of a health care facility in which you are a patient, unless the employee is a notary public; your attending physician; or directly financially responsible for your health care. (Section 311.625).

Louisiana

State Website: http://www.legis.state.la.us/

State Law Reference: Louisiana Revised Statutes and Louisiana Civil Code.

Living Will Form: Louisiana Declaration serves as Living Will (Revised Statutes, Section 40:1299.58.3).

Other Directives: Anatomical Gift Act (Revised Statutes, Section 17:2354).

Living Will Effective: Your attending physician plus one other physician must personally examine you and certify in writing that your condition is terminal and irreversible (Revised Statutes, Section 40:1299.58.2).

Witness Requirements: Sign in the presence of two (2) adult witnesses. Witnesses cannot be entitled to any part of your estate or related by blood or marriage. (Revised Statutes, Sections 40:1299.58.2 and 40:1299.58.3).

Maine

State Website: http://janus.state.me.us/legis/statutes/

State Law Reference: Maine Revised Statutes.

Living Will Form: Instructions for Health Care serves as Living Will (Section 18A-5-804).

Other Directives: Durable Power of Attorney for Health Care (Section 18-5-506). Anatomical Gift Act (Section 22-2-710-2901+). Durable Power of Attorney (Section 18A-5-508).

Living Will Effective: The Living Will becomes effective when your primary physician determines that you are unable to make your own health-care decisions; alternatively, you can choose to make it effective immediately. (Section 18A-5-804).

Witness Requirements: Sign in the presence of two (2) adult witnesses. No other restrictions apply. (Section 18A-5-804).

Maryland

State Website: http://mlis.state.md.us/

State Law Reference: Maryland Code.

Living Will Form: Maryland Advance Directive: Planning for Future Health Care Decisions serves as Living Will (Health General, Section 5-603).

Other Directives: Selection of Health Care Agent is included in Maryland Advance Directive: Planning for Future Health Care Decisions (Health General, Section 5-603). Anatomical Gift Act (Estates & Trusts, Sections 4-501+). Durable Power of Attorney (Estates and Trusts, Section 13-601).

Living Will Effective: Effective when your attending physician and a second physician, both of whom shall have personally examined you, and one of whom shall have examined you within two hours of making the certification, certify in writing that you are incapable of making an informed decision regarding treatment. If you are unconscious or unable to communicate by any means, a second physician's certification is not necessary. Life-sustaining treatment cannot be withheld or withdrawn unless your attending physician and another physician certify that you are in a terminal or end-stage condition, or two physicians, one of whom is a neurologist, neurosurgeon, or specialist in the evaluation of cognitive functioning, certify that you are in a persistent vegetative state. (Health General, Section 5-606).

Witness Requirements: Sign in the presence of two (2) adult witnesses. The person you assign as your health care agent cannot be a witness. At least one (1) of your witnesses must be a person who is not entitled to any portion of your estate or otherwise financially benefit by reason of your death. (Health General, Section 5-603).

Massachusetts

State Website: http://www.mass.gov/legis/laws/mgl/

State Law Reference: General Laws of Massachusetts.

Living Will Form: No state statute governing the use of Living Wills. However, you have a constitutional right to state your wishes about medical care. A form is provided in this book.

Other Directives: Massachusetts Health Care Proxy. (Chapter 201D, Sections 1-17)

Living Will Effective: In the event that you develop an irreversible condition that prevents you from making your own medical decisions.

Witness Requirements: Because Massachusetts does not have a statute governing the use of Living Wills, there are no specific requirements to make your Living Will legally binding. We suggest that you sign in the presence of two (2) witnesses eighteen (18) years or older or a notary public. A witness should not be your health care provider or an employee of your health care provider. Witnesses should not be entitled to any part of your estate, financially responsible for your medical care, or related to you by blood or marriage.

Michigan

State Website: http://www.michiganlegislature.org/

State Law Reference: Michigan Compiled Laws.

Living Will Form: No state statute governing the use of Living Wills. However, you have a constitutional right to state your wishes about medical care. A form is provided in this book.

Other Directives: Michigan Designation of Patient Advocate for Health Care (Sections 700.5506+); Uniform Anatomical Gift Act (Sections 333.10101+); Durable Power of Attorney (Sections 700.5501+).

Living Will Effective: In the event that you develop

an irreversible condition that prevents you from making your own medical decisions.

Witness Requirements: Because Michigan does not have a statute governing the use of Living Wills, there are no specific requirements to make your Living Will legally binding. We suggest that you sign in the presence of two (2) witnesses eighteen (18) years or older or a notary public. A witness should not be your health care provider or an employee of your health care provider. Witnesses should not be entitled to any part of your estate, be financially responsible for your medical care, or be related to you by blood or marriage.

Minnesota

State Website: http://www.revisor.leg.state.mn.us/stats/

State Law Reference: Minnesota Statutes.

Living Will Form: Health Care Living Will (Section 145B.04).

Other Directives: Appointment of Health Care Agent is included in Living Will (Section 145B.04). Anatomical Gift Act (Sections 525.9211+). Durable Power of Attorney (Section 523.07).

Living Will Effective: Effective if you are in a terminal condition (defined as an incurable or irreversible condition for which the administration of medical treatment will serve only to prolong the dying process) and become unable to participate in decisions regarding your health care. (Sections 145B.02 and 145B.04).

Witness Requirements: Sign in the presence of two (2) witnesses eighteen (18) years or older or a notary public. Neither of the witnesses can be entitled to any part of your estate under your will or state intestacy law. Neither of the witnesses nor the notary may be named as a proxy. (Section 145B.03).

Mississippi

State Website: http://www.mscode.com/

State Law Reference: Mississippi Code.

Living Will Form: Instructions for Health Care contained in Advance Health Care Directive serves as Living Will (Section 41-41-209).

Other Directives: Advance Health Care Directive

contains Power of Attorney for Health Care and Instructions for Health Care (Section 41-41-209). Advance Health Care Directive contains Certificate of Authorization for Organ Donation (Section 41-41-209); see also Anatomical Gift Act (Sections 41-39-31+). Durable Power of Attorney (Sections 87-3-105/ 41-41-163).

Living Will Effective: No separate statute, but statutory Instructions for Health Care form allows you to specify that you do not want your life to be prolonged if you: 1) have an incurable and irreversible condition that will result in death within a relatively short time; 2) become unconscious and, to a reasonable degree of medical certainty, will not regain consciousness; or 3) the likely risks and burdens of treatment would outweigh the expected benefits. (Section 41-41-209).

Witness Requirements: Sign in the presence of two (2) witnesses eighteen (18) years or older or a notary public. A witness cannot be the person whom you appointed as your agent, health care provider, or an employee of your health care provider or facility. At least one (1) witness cannot be related to you by blood, marriage, or adoption, or entitled to any part of your estate under your will or state intestacy law.

Missouri

State Website: http://www.moga.state.mo.us/STATUTES/STATUTES.HTM#T

State Law Reference: Missouri Revised Statutes.

Living Will Form: Missouri Declaration serves as Living Will (Section 459.015).

Other Directives: Power of Attorney for Health Care (Section 404.822). Uniform Anatomical Gift Act (Sections 194.210+). Durable Power of Attorney (Section 404.705).

Living Will Effective: Effective when your condition is determined to be terminal and you are not able to make treatment decisions. Such determinations shall be recorded in your medical record. (Section 459.025).

Witness Requirements: Sign in the presence of two (2) adult witnesses. If you have someone sign the Declaration on your behalf, that person cannot serve as a witness. (Section 459.015).

Montana

State Website: http://data.opi.state.mt.us/bills/mca_toc/index.htm

State Law Reference: Montana Code Annotated.

Living Will Form: Montana Declaration serves as Living Will (Section 50-9-103).

Other Directives: Appointment of Health Care Agent is included in Declaration (Section 50-9-103). Uniform Anatomical Gift Act (Section 72-17-101+). Durable Power of Attorney (Section 72-5-501).

Living Will Effective: Effective when you are determined by the attending physician or attending advanced practice registered nurse to be in a terminal condition and no longer able to make decisions regarding administration of life-sustaining treatment. (Section 50-9-105).

Witness Requirements: Sign in the presence of two (2) adult witnesses. No other restrictions apply. Do not use your appointed health care agent as one of your witnesses. (Section 50-9-103).

Nebraska

State Website: http://www.unicam.state.ne.us/web/public/home

State Law Reference: Nebraska Revised Statutes.

Living Will Form: Nebraska Declaration serves as Living Will (Section 20-404).

Other Directives: Power of Attorney for Health Care (Section 30-3408). Anatomical Gift Act (Section 71-4804). Durable Power of Attorney (Section 30-2665).

Living Will Effective: Effective when your attending physician determines that you are in a terminal condition or a persistent vegetative state, and that you are unable to make decisions regarding administration of life-sustaining treatment; attending physician must notify a reasonably available family member or guardian, if any, of his or her diagnosis and of the intent to invoke your declaration. (Section 20-405).

Witness Requirements: Sign in the presence of two (2) adult witnesses or a notary public. Witnesses cannot be employees of your life insurance or health insurance provider and at least one (1) witness must not be an administrator or employee of your treating health care provider. (Section 20-404).

Nevada

State Website: http://www.leg.state.nv.us/NRS/

State Law Reference: Nevada Revised Statutes.

Living Will Form: Nevada Declaration serves as Living Will (Section 449.610).

Other Directives: Durable Power of Attorney for Health Care Decisions (Section 449.830). Uniform Anatomical Gift Act (Sections 451.500+).

Living Will Effective: Effective when your attending physician determines you are in a terminal condition and no longer able to make decisions regarding administration of life-sustaining treatment. (Section 449.617).

Witness Requirements: Sign in the presence of two (2) adult witnesses. No other restrictions apply. (Section 449.610).

New Hampshire

State Website: http://gencourt.state.nh.us/rsa/html/indexes/default.html

State Law Reference: New Hampshire Revised Statutes.

Living Will Form: New Hampshire Declaration serves as Living Will (Section 137-H:3).

Other Directives: Durable Power of Attorney for Health Care (Chapter 137-J). Uniform Anatomical Gift Act (Chapter 291-A).

Living Will Effective: Two (2) physicians must certify in writing that you are in a terminal condition and your death would occur within a short period of time without the use of life-sustaining medical care. (Section 137-H:3).

Witness Requirements: Sign in the presence of two (2) witnesses eighteen (18) years or older and a notary public. A witness cannot be your spouse or heir, your doctor or a person acting under direction or control of your doctor, or a person who has a claim against your estate. If you are a resident of a health care facility or a patient in a hospital, one of your witnesses may be your doctor or an employee of your health care provider, but the other cannot. (Sections 137-H:3 and 137-H:4).

New Jersey

State Website: http:/www.njleg.state.nj.us

State Law Reference: New Jersey Permanent Statutes.

Living Will Form: New Jersey Instruction Directive serves as Living Will (Section 26:2H-55).

Other Directives: Appointment of a Health Care Representative (Section 26:2H-58). Anatomical Gift Act (Section 26:6-57+). Durable Power of Attorney (Section 3B:13A-10).

Living Will Effective: Effective when your attending physician and one (1) other physician confirm in writing that you are unable to make health care decisions. (Sections 26:2H-59 and 26:2H-60).

Witness Requirements: Sign in the presence of two (2) witnesses eighteen (18) years or older or a notary public. A witness cannot be the person whom you appointed as your agent. (Section 26:2H-56).

New Mexico

State Website: http://www.legis.state.nm.us/

State Law Reference: New Mexico Statutes.

Living Will Form: Optional Advance Health Care Directive (Section 24-7A-4).

Other Directives: Power of Attorney for Health Care (Section 247A4). Anatomical Gift Act (Sections 24-6A-1+). Durable Power of Attorney (Sections 45-5-501+).

Living Will Effective: Effective if you are unable to make or communicate health care decisions, and 1) you have an incurable and irreversible condition that will result in death within a relatively short time; or 2) if you become unconscious and, to a reasonable degree of medical certainty, will not regain consciousness; or 3) the likely risks and burdens of treatment would outweigh the expected benefits. (Section 24-7A-4).

Witness Requirements: The law recommends but does not require that you sign in the presence of two (2) witnesses eighteen (18) years or older. We recommend that you comply with this suggestion or sign in the presence of a notary public. A witness should not be the person whom you appointed as your agent. (Section 24-7A-4).

New York

State Website: http://assembly.state.ny.us/leg/

State Law Reference: New York Consolidated Laws.

Living Will Form: Order Not To Resuscitate acts as Living Will. (Public Health, Sections 2960+).

Other Directives: Health Care Agent and Proxy (Public Health, Sections 2980+). Anatomical Gift Act (Public Health, Sections 4300+). Durable Power of Attorney (General Obligations, Sections 5-1501+).

Living Will Effective: Effective when your attending physician and another physician determine that you are terminally ill or permanently unconscious, that resuscitation would be medically futile, or that resuscitation would impose an extraordinary burden on you in light of the patient's medical condition and the expected outcome of resuscitation. (Public Health, Section 2965).

Witness Requirements: You must sign in the presence of two (2) adult witnesses. You can also give an Order Not To Resuscitate orally, during hospitalization, in the presence of two adult witnesses, if one of those witnesses is a physician affiliated with your hospital. (Public Health, Section 2964).

North Carolina

State Website: http://www.ncga.state.nc.us/

State Law Reference: North Carolina General Statutes.

Living Will Form: Declaration of a Desire for a Natural Death serves as Living Will (Section 90-321).

Other Directives: Health Care Power of Attorney (Sections 32A- 15+). Anatomical Gift Act (Sections 130A-402+). Durable Power of Attorney (Section 32A-8+).

Living Will Effective: Your attending physician plus one other physician must determine that your condition is terminal and incurable or a persistent vegetative state. (Section 90-321).

Witness Requirements: Sign in the presence of two (2) adult witnesses and a notary public. A witness cannot be a person who has a claim against your estate, stands to inherit from your estate under your will or state intestacy law, be your attending physician, an employee of the attending physician, or an employee of a health care institution in which you are a patient. Witnesses also cannot be related by blood or marriage. (Section 90-321).

North Dakota

State Website: http://www.legis.nd.gov/
information/statutes/cent-code.html

State Law Reference: North Dakota Century Code.

Living Will Form: Health Care Directive serves as Living Will (Section 23-06.5-17).

Other Directives: Appointment of Health Care Agent is contained in Health Care Directive. (Section 23-06.5-17). Anatomical Gift Act (Sections 23-06.6-01+). Durable Power of Attorney (Section 30.1-30).

Living Will Effective: Effective when you lack capacity to make health care decisions, as certified in writing by your attending physician. (Section 23-06.5-17).

Witness Requirements: Sign in the presence of two (2) adult witnesses or a notary public. Neither a witness nor a notary can be your health care agent or alternate agent; your spouse or a person related to you by blood, marriage, or adoption; or a person who has a claim against your estate upon your death or stands to inherit from your estate. At least one witness must not be a health care or long-term care provider providing you with direct care, or an employee of such a provider. A notary may be such an employee. (Section 23-06.5-17).

Ohio

State Website: http://codes.ohio.gov/

State Law Reference: Ohio Revised Code.

Living Will Form: Living Will Declaration. (Section 2133.02 is not a statutory form, but it provides suggestions for phrasing the Declaration, cross-referencing to Sections 2133.01+, the Modified Uniform Rights of the Terminally Ill Act.).

Other Directives: Power of Attorney for Health Care (Sections 1337.11+). Anatomical Gift Act (Sections 2108.01+). Durable Power of Attorney (Section 1337.09). Anatomical Gift Form (Section 2133.07).

Living Will Effective: Effective when your attending physician and one other physician examine you and determine that you are in a terminal condition or permanently unconscious state, whichever is addressed in the Declaration, and the attending physician determines that you no longer are able to make

informed decisions regarding the administration of life-sustaining treatment. Other statutory requirements apply; please consult statute for details. (Section 2133.03).

Witness Requirements: Sign in front of two (2) witnesses eighteen (18) years or older or a notary public. Witnesses cannot be related to you by blood, marriage, or adoption, be your attending physician, or be the administrator of a nursing home in which you are receiving treatment. (Section 2133.02).

Oklahoma

State Website: http://www.lsb.state.ok.us/

State Law Reference: Oklahoma Statutes.

Living Will Form: Living Will is Part 1 of Advance Directive for Health Care (Section 63-3101.4).

Other Directives: Appointment of Health Care Proxy is Part 2 of Advance Directive for Health Care (Section 63-3101.4). Anatomical Gifts are part 3 of Advance Directive for Health Care (Section 63-3101.4); see also Uniform Anatomical Gift Act (Sections 63-2201+). Durable Power of Attorney (Sections 15-1001+).

Living Will Effective: Effective when given to the attending physician and you are no longer able to make decisions regarding administration of life-sustaining treatment. (Section 63-3101.5). The attending physician and another physician must examine you and make this determination. (Section 63-3101.3).

Witness Requirements: Sign in the presence of two (2) adult witnesses. A witness cannot be any person who would inherit from you under your will or state intestacy law. (Section 63-3101.4).

Oregon

State Website: http://www.leg.state.or.us/ors/

State Law Reference: Oregon Revised Statutes.

Living Will Form: Health Care Instructions contained in Advance Directive serves as Living Will (Section 127.531).

Other Directives: Appointment of Health Care Representative is contained in Advance Directive (Section 127.531). Anatomical Gift Act (Sections 97.950+). Durable Power of Attorney (Section 127.005).

Living Will Effective: No separate statute, but

Health Care Instructions statutory form provides you with the opportunity to state your wishes if your doctor and another knowledgeable doctor confirm that you are: 1) close to death; 2) permanently unconscious; 3) in an advanced progressive illness; or 4) in extraordinary suffering.

Witness Requirements: Sign in the presence of two (2) adult witnesses. A witness cannot be your attorney-in-fact for health care or an alternative agent or your attending physician. At least one (1) of your witnesses cannot be related to you by blood, marriage, or adoption, entitled to any portion of your estate under your will or state intestacy law, or be an owner, operator, or employee of your treating health care facility. If you are a patient in a long-term care facility, one witness must be an individual designated by the facility and having any qualifications that may be specified by the Department of Human Services. (Section 127.515).

Pennsylvania

State Website: http://members.aol.com/StatutesPA/Index.html

State Law Reference: Pennsylvania Code.

Living Will Form: Declaration serves as Living Will. (Section 20-5404).

Other Directives: Anatomical Gift Act (Section 20-8613).

Living Will Effective: The Declaration becomes effective when your physician receives a copy of it and determines that you are incompetent and in a terminal condition or a state of permanent unconsciousness.

Witness Requirements: Sign in the presence of two (2) adult witnesses. If you have someone sign the Declaration on your behalf, that person cannot serve as a witness.

Rhode Island

State Website: http://www.rilin.state.ri.us/Statutes/Statutes.html

State Law Reference: Rhode Island General Laws.

Living Will Form: Declaration serves as Living Will (Section 23-4.11-3).

Other Directives: Health Care Power of Attorney (Sections 23-4.10+). Uniform Anatomical Gift Act (Sections 23-18.6+). Short Form Power of Attorney Act (Sections 18-16-1+).

Living Will Effective: Effective when the declaration is communicated to the attending physician; you are determined by the attending physician to be in a terminal condition; and you are unable to make treatment decisions. (Section 23-4.11-3).

Witness Requirements: Sign in the presence of two (2) adult witnesses. Witnesses cannot be related to you by blood, marriage, or adoption. (Section 23-4.11-3).

South Carolina

State Website: http://www.scstatehouse.net/

State Law Reference: South Carolina Code of Laws.

Living Will Form: Declaration of a Desire for a Natural Death serves as Living Will (Section 44-77-50).

Other Directives: Health Care Power of Attorney (Section 62-5-504). Uniform Anatomical Gift Act (Sections 44-43-310+). Durable Power of Attorney (Section 62-5-501).

Living Will Effective: Effective when two physicians, one of whom is your attending physician and both of whom have personally examined you, certify your condition as terminal or in a state of permanent unconsciousness. (Section 44-77-30).

Witness Requirements: Sign in the presence of two (2) adult witnesses and a notary public. A witness cannot be a beneficiary of your life insurance policy, your health care provider, or an employee of your health care provider. Witnesses cannot be related to you by blood, marriage, or adoption, be entitled to any part of your estate under your will or state intestacy law, have a claim against or your estate, or be directly financially responsible for your health care. In addition, at least one (1) witness must not be an employee of a health facility in which you are a patient. If you are a resident in a hospital or nursing facility, one of the witnesses must also be an ombudsman designated by the State Ombudsman, Office of the Governor. (Section 44-77-40).

South Dakota

State Website: http://legis.state.sd.us/statutes/
State Law Reference: South Dakota Codified Laws.
Living Will Form: Living Will Declaration (Section 34-12D-3).
Other Directives: Power of Attorney for Health Care (Sections 34-12C and 59-7-2.1). Anatomical Gift Act (Sections 34-26-20 through 34-26-47). Durable Power of Attorney (Section 43-30S-5-19).
Living Will Effective: Declaration is effective when you are determined by your attending physician and one other physician to be in a terminal condition and no longer able to make decisions regarding administration of life-sustaining treatment. (Section 34-12D-5).
Witness Requirements: Sign in the presence of two (2) witnesses eighteen (18) years or older or a notary public. (Section 34-12D-2). Although South Dakota does not have any restrictions on who can be a witness, we suggest that you not use your appointed attorney-in-fact or your health care provider.

Tennessee

State Website: http://www.michie.com
State Law Reference: Tennessee Code.
Living Will Form: Living Will (Section 32-11-105).
Other Directives: Durable Power of Attorney for Health Care (Section 34-6-201+). Anatomical Gift Act (Section 68-30-101+). Durable Power of Attorney (Section 34-6-101+).
Living Will Effective: The Living Will becomes effective when your death will result without using life-sustaining procedures. (Section 32-11-105).
Witness Requirements: Sign in the presence of two (2) adult witnesses and a notary public. A witness cannot be a person who has a claim against your estate upon your death; stands to inherit from your estate; is your doctor or an employee of your doctor; or is an owner, operator, or employee of a health care institution in which you are a patient. Witnesses also cannot be related by blood or marriage. (Sections 32-11-104 and 32-11-105).

Texas

State Website: www.capitol.state.tx.us
State Law Reference: Texas Statutes and Codes.
Living Will Form: Directive to Physicians and Family or Surrogate serves as Living Will (Health and Safety Code, Section 166.033).
Other Directives: Out-of-Hospital Do Not Resuscitate Order (Health and Safety Code, Sections 166.081 through 166.102). Medical Power of Attorney (Health and Safety Code, Sections 166.151 through 166.166). Texas Anatomical Gift Act (Health and Safety Code, Chapter 692). Durable Power of Attorney (Probate Code, Sections 481+).
Living Will Effective: The Directive becomes effective when your attending physicians certifies in writing that you are in a terminal or irreversible condition. (Health and Safety Code, Section 166.031).
Witness Requirements: At least one (1) witness cannot be designated to make treatment decisions for you, related to you by blood or marriage, entitled to any part of your estate under your will or state intestacy laws, or be your doctor or an employee of your doctor. A witness cannot be an employee of a health care facility in which you are a patient; an officer, director, partner, or a business office employee of the health care facility or any part of any parent organization of the health care facility; or have a claim against your estate after you die. (Health and Safety Code, Section 166.003).

Utah

State Website: http://www.le.state.ut.us/
State Law Reference: Utah Code.
Living Will Form: Directive to Physicians and Providers of Medical Services serves as Living Will until 1/1/08. (Section 75-2-1104). After 1/1/08, Utah Advance Health Care directive serves as Living Will. (Section 75-2a-117).
Other Directives: Special Power of Attorney for Health Care (Section 75-2-1106) (effective until 1/1/08). Revised Uniform Anatomical Gift Act (Section 26-28-101+). Durable Power of Attorney (Section 75-5-501).
Living Will Effective: Effective 1/1/08, when you lose your health care decision-making capacity. (Sections 75-2a-103 and 75-2a-109).

Witness Requirements: Effective 1/1/08, sign in the presence of two (2) witnesses eighteen (18) years or older. A witness cannot be entitled to any part of your estate, financially responsible for your medical care, related to you by blood or marriage, a health care provider who is providing care to you, or an administrator at a health care facility at which you are receiving care. (Section 75-2a-117).

Vermont

State Website: http://www.leg.state.vt.us/statutes/statutes2.htm

State Law Reference: Vermont Statutes Annotated.

Living Will Form: No form; Title 18, Chapter 231 governs.

Other Directives: Anatomical Gift Act (Sections 18-109-5238+). Durable Power of Attorney (Section 14-123-3508).

Living Will Effective: Effective when clinician determines, after speaking with an interested individual if one is reasonably available, that principal lacks capacity, and makes specific findings regarding cause, nature, and projected duration of principal's lack of capacity; has made reasonable efforts to notify principal of this determination; and has made reasonable efforts to notify principal's agent or guardian of same. Can also become effective under other specified statutory provisions; please see the statute for details. (Section 18-231-9706).

Witness Requirements: Sign in the presence of two (2) witnesses eighteen (18) years or older. A witness cannot be your agent, your spouse's agent, your reciprocal beneficiary, parent, adult sibling, adult child, or adult grandchild. (Section 18-231-9703).

Virginia

State Website: http://leg1.state.va.us/

State Law Reference: Code of Virginia.

Living Will Form: Advance Medical Directive serves as Living Will (Section 54.1-2984).

Other Directives: Anatomical Gift Act (Section 32.1-290).

Living Will Effective: This directive becomes effective in the event that you develop a terminal condition or can no longer make your own medical decisions. (Section 54.1-2984).

Witness Requirements: Sign in the presence of two (2) witnesses eighteen (18) years or older. Witnesses can be related by blood or marriage, or can be employees of health care facilities or physicians' offices, acting in good faith. (Sections 54.1-2982, 54.1-2983).

Washington

State Website: http://www.leg.wa.gov/

State Law Reference: Revised Code of Washington.

Living Will Form: Health Care Directive serves as Living Will (Section 70.122.030).

Other Directives: Power of Attorney (Section 11.94.010+). Anatomical Gift Act (Section 68.50.520+).

Living Will Effective: Effective when your attending physician personally examines you and diagnoses in writing that you have a terminal condition, or when two physicians, one of whom is your attending physician and both of whom have personally examined you, diagnose in writing that you are in a permanent unconscious condition in accordance with accepted medical standards. (Section 70.122.020).

Witness Requirements: Sign in the presence of two (2) witnesses eighteen (18) years or older. A witness cannot be entitled to any part of your estate under your will or state intestacy laws, related by blood or marriage, be your attending physician, an employee of the attending physician or a health facility in which you are a patient, or any person who has a claim against your estate. (Section 70.122.030).

West Virginia

State Website: http://www.legis.state.wv.us/

State Law Reference: West Virginia Code.

Living Will Form: Living Will, (Section 16-30-4).

Other Directives: Medical Power of Attorney (Section 16304). Anatomical Gift Act (Section 16-19-2). Durable Power of Attorney (Sections 39-4-1 through 39-4-7).

Living Will Effective: Your physician must certify in writing that you are in a terminal condition or a persistent vegetative state. (Section 16-30-4).

Witness Requirements: Sign in the presence of two (2) adult witnesses and a notary public. A witness cannot be a person who stands to inherit from your estate, be directly financially responsible for your health care, be your attending physician, or be your health care representative or successor if you have a medical power of attorney. A witness cannot be related by blood or marriage or be the person who signed the document on your behalf. (Section 16-30-4).

Wisconsin

State Website: http://www.legis.state.wi.us/
State Law Reference: Wisconsin Statutes.
Living Will Form: Declaration to Physicians serves as Living Will (Section 154.03).
Other Directives: Power of Attorney for Health Care (Section 155.05). Anatomical Gift Act (Section 157.06). Durable Power of Attorney (Section 243.07).
Living Will Effective: This directive becomes effective in the event that your attending physician and one other physician certifies you have developed a terminal condition or are in a permanent vegetative state.
Witness Requirements: Sign in the presence of two (2) adult witnesses. A witness cannot be a person who stands to inherit from your estate, be directly financially responsible for your health care, be your attending physician, or be an employee of your health care provider or an inpatient health care facility in which you are a patient, unless the employee is a chaplain or social worker. A witness also cannot be related by blood, adoption, or marriage.

Wyoming

State Website: http://legisweb.state.wy.us/
State Law Reference: Wyoming Statutes.
Living Will Form: Advance Health Care Directive (Section 35-22-405). The statute is scheduled to be repealed on 6/30/09. Thereafter, an advance health care directive may be in any form not inconsistent with the act.
Other Directives: Anatomical Gift Act (Section 35-5-101+). Durable Power of Attorney (Section 3-5-101).
Living Will Effective: The Declaration becomes effective when your supervising health care provider determines that you lack the capacity to make your own health care decisions.
Witness Requirements: Sign in the presence of two (2) witnesses eighteen (18) years or older or a notary public. Witnesses cannot be your treating health care provider or an employee of your health care provider; the attorney-in-fact identified in the directive; or an operator or employee of your community care or residential care facility. (Section 35-22-403).

Notes

Notes

Notes

Notes

Notes

Notes

Nova Publishing Company
Small Business and Consumer Legal Books and Software

Law Made Simple Series

Advance Health Care Directives	ISBN 13: 978-1-892949-23-3	Book w/CD	$24.95
Estate Planning Simplified	ISBN 1-892949-10-5	Book w/CD	$34.95
Living Trusts Simplified	ISBN 0-935755-51-9	Book w/CD	$28.95
Living Wills Simplified	ISBN 0-935755-50-0	Book w/CD	$28.95
Personal Bankruptcy Simplified (4th Edition)	ISBN 1-892949-34-2	Book w/CD	$29.95
Personal Legal Forms Simplified (3rd Edition)	ISBN 0-935755-97-7	Book w/CD	$28.95
Powers of Attorney Simplified	ISBN 13: 978-1-892949-40-0	Book w/CD	$24.95

Small Business Made Simple Series

Corporation: Small Business Start-up Kit (2nd Edition)	ISBN 1-892949-06-7	Book w/CD	$29.95
Employer Legal Forms	ISBN 13: 978-1-892949-26-4	Book w/CD	$24.95
Landlord Legal Forms	ISBN 13: 978-1-892949-24-0	Book w/CD	$24.95
Limited Liability Company: Start-up Kit (2nd Ed.)	ISBN 13: 978-1-892949-37-0	Book w/CD	$29.95
Partnership: Start-up Kit (2nd Edition)	ISBN 1-892949-07-5	Book w/CD	$29.95
Real Estate Forms Simplified	ISBN 0-935755-09-1	Book w/CD	$29.95
S-Corporation: Small Business Start-up Kit (2nd Edition)	ISBN 1-892949-05-9	Book w/CD	$29.95
Small Business Accounting Simplified (4th Edition)	ISBN 1-892949-17-2	Book only	$24.95
Small Business Bookkeeping System Simplified	ISBN 0-935755-74-8	Book only	$14.95
Small Business Legal Forms Simplified (4th Edition)	ISBN 0-935755-98-5	Book w/CD	$29.95
Small Business Payroll System Simplified	ISBN 0-935755-55-1	Book only	$14.95
Sole Proprietorship: Start-up Kit (2nd Edition)	ISBN 1-892949-08-3	Book w/CD	$29.95

Legal Self-Help Series

Divorce Yourself: The National Divorce Kit (6th Edition)	ISBN 1-892949-12-1	Book w/CD	$39.95
Incorporate Now!: The National Corporation Kit (4th Ed.)	ISBN 1-892949-00-8	Book w/CD	$29.95
Prepare Your Own Will: The National Will Kit (6th Edition)	ISBN 1-892949-15-6	Book w/CD	$29.95

National Legal Kits

Simplified Divorce Kit (2nd Edition)	ISBN 1-892949-20-2	Book only	$19.95
Simplified Family Legal Forms Kit	ISBN 1-892949-18-0	Book only	$18.95
Simplified Incorporation Kit	ISBN 13: 978-1-892949-33-2	Book w/CD	$19.95
Simplified Limited Liability Company Kit	ISBN 1-892949-32-6	Book w/CD	$19.95
Simplified Living Will Kit	ISBN 1-892949-22-9	Book only	$15.95
Simplified S-Corporation Kit	ISBN 1-892949-31-8	Book w/CD	$19.95
Simplified Will Kit (3rd Edition)	ISBN 1-892949-21-0	Book w/CD	$19.95

Ordering Information

Distributed by:
National Book Network
4501 Forbes Blvd. Suite 200
Lanham MD 20706

Shipping: $4.50 for first & $.75 for additional
Phone orders with Visa/MC: (800) 462-6420
Fax orders with Visa/MC: (800) 338-4550
Internet: www.novapublishing.com
Free shipping on all internet orders